PRAISE FOR *THE EXTRAORDINARY LIFE OF EDWIN BARUCH WINANS*

The Extraordinary Life of Edwin Baruch Winans: From the Stampede for Gold in California to the Capitol of Michigan provides an insightful study of the full life of Gov. Winans. All too often, gubernatorial biographies focus so intently on the politician that they neglect the person.

Happily, Valerie Winans takes excellenat care to round out of the life of this often-overlooked chief executive.

A hard-working farmer, brave prospector, successful banker, and conscientious public official, Winans wasn't afraid to upset the status quo for the sake of principled leadership. Now readers can journey with Winans to the gold fields of California, meet his supportive wife, and survey his Livingston County farm fields. Those hungry for political details will learn how Winans spoke for peace during wartime, supported controversial currency reforms, and guaranteed Michigan voters the secret ballot.

Next time I stand in front of the Governor's official portrait, I know I'll find myself musing over the remarkable life of Edwin Winans, as related in this interesting retelling of his rags-to-riches story. *The Extraordinary Life of Edwin Baruch Winans* is an engaging, evocatively written addition to Michigan's gubernatorial biography cannon.

Valerie Marvin, Michigan State Capitol Historian and Curator

Valerie Winans has written a wonderful biography of the life and times of Edwin Baruch Winans, Michigan's 22nd Governor. Using a wide range of primary sources, she has creatively weaved together Winans' journey from a gold rusher, successful businessman, and farmer to legislator and governor within the context of the dynamic era of nineteenthcentury America. This work reveals an important state leader whose character and contributions deserve better recognition and serve as a model of honest hard-working leadership today.

Stephen Siciliano, President, Traverse Area Historical Society

Valerie Winans is a storyteller and researcher who found adventure, history, and love of America in her own family. The story of Edwin Baruch Winans, untold until now, fills a historical gap between national and state events in the 1800's which gives a deeper understanding of the growth of America. It's an exciting read about the man of the people, an adventurer, an overcomer and farmer whose extraordinary life begins on the overland trail to the gold rush to the Governor of Michigan and the Congress of the United States. This story belongs in school libraries and on bookshelves across America.

—-Charlene Anne Lutes, Ph.D., Author, Writer, Journalist, Instructor

What a fascinating true story. One travels west with Edwin B. Winans, immersed in the gold rush era's many trials and tribulations, and then back east as he followed his passionate career path. It is a captivating journey of determination, loss, luck, love, and ultimate success in Michigan politics. I highly recommend this book if you enjoy history spiced with mystery and difference – success made possible only by hard work, true grit, and visionary leadership.

Peg Jonkhoff, Co-Author *Perry Hannah's Gifts Then and Now*

The Extraordinary Life of Edwin Baruch Winans

From the Stampede for Gold in California to the Capitol of Michigan

Valerie Winans

A Writer for Readers of All Ages

PUBLICATION
CONSULTANTS
We Believe In The Power Of Authors

8370 Eleusis Drive, Anchorage, Alaska 99502-4630
books@publicationconsultants.com—www.publicationconsultants.com

Soft Cover ISBN Number: 978-1-63747-405-1
Hard Cover ISBN Number: 978-1-63747-413-6
eBook ISBN Number: 978-1-63747-406-8

Library of Congress Number: 2024911463

Manufactured in the United States of America

This book is dedicated to
David Winans

Other books by Valerie Winans

Alaska's Savage River
Road Trip with Remington Beagle
A Hero's Journey

ACKNOWLEDGMENTS

The whole thing started with the walking stick. Some family members referred to it as the governor's cane, but Dave always corrected them, "It's not a cane; it's a walking stick. Discussions on the walking stick did not happen frequently. It was rarely mentioned. When I first married into the family, I learned there was a walking stick that had been passed from generation to generation, but it was a long time before I saw it. The stick lived in the hall closet at my in-law's house. I thought it must be some old thing the family buried in the closet and unwilling to throw away. I was wrong. Edwin's walking stick is a treasure, a piece of history wrapped in gold, quartz, and redwood.

Who was the man who owned this stick? Answers varied, but most agreed he was an ancestor, maybe a grandfather, who was also governor of Michigan. That was the extent of our knowledge for decades. Without any factual information, made-up stories were in good supply. Then along came Ancestry.com. Several of us liked to do searches to see what we could find, but my daughter, Lisa, was the one who seriously delved into the Winans family. She had an old copy of the Winans' family history, which helped to verify the information on Ancestry.com. She had a good time sleuthing through the familial connections and the records available on the site. She learned that Edwin was not our grandfather but our uncle. Each fun new fact encouraged us to learn more, but most of the information was only stored in a faulty, unreliable place – our brains.

Then Dave and I went to Alaska to work as campground hosts in Denali National Park and Preserve. We fell in love with Alaska and couldn't get enough information about our campground. I read everything I could get my hands on about Savage River Campground, but I could find only a paragraph here and there. I had to write the book myself. Writing is one thing, and publishing is another. I serendipitously found the perfect publisher for my book. Publication Consultants, Anchorage, Alaska, owned by Evan and Lois Swensen, who guided my nascent publishing journey until my book, *Alaska's Savage River: Inside Denali National Park and Preserve*, was in my hands as an accomplishment I never expected to see. But this is not the end of the story. Evan began to ask questions about a second book. My response was, "What? No. Well, maybe."

I am an author; I have a published book. If I wrote another book, what would it be about? I thought writing a book about the governor would be awesome, but then I thought there wouldn't be enough information to fill a book. The research involved would take too much time. That idea was shelved, and I moved on to write *Road Trip with Remington Beagle: Michigan to Alaska and Back,* and then, *A Hero's Journey: Life Lessons from A Dog and His Friends.* As I researched and wrote these books, I continued to gather information about the governor. His story intrigued me. I knew I had to write it.

The research was years long because I would gather information and file it away, get busy with life, find some more tidbits, and tuck them in a safe spot. I often did not get back to the research until something triggered me. When I finally started to write the book, I had the contents page in my mind. I knew the puzzle – I just didn't have all the pieces. I started with the Overland Trail because I thought that was the most interesting – it would capture the reader's attention. Edwin didn't leave us a journal, so I read books about walking to California in 1850 for a month or so. The story progressed from trail to gold rush and on to days in Rough and Ready before heading back home to Michigan. I researched these and then wrote about them, but with each new topic, Edwin began to emerge, and I realized how much I admired Uncle Ed. When he started in politics, there were newspaper stories. As he got famous, there were anecdotes in some articles that gave us insight. Census records provide a wealth of information. One piece of information guides you to the next nugget and that one leads you to the next. Down the rabbit hole you go without any assurance of another nugget at the bottom. Obsession means waking up hours later without any realization of how much time has elapsed. Research is engrossing and so much fun.

But the best part of writing a book is the people you connect with along the way. Since I couldn't tell the story about Edwin Winans without including the place he loved the most, Hamburg, Michigan, it was one of the first places I contacted for information on Edwin. I talked to Suzanne Hines, the dedicated curator and protector of history at the Hamburg Historical Society. Suzanne Hines and Pat Majher connected me to Hamburg's history through people and places, for which I am most grateful.

The aid provided by staff at the Library of Michigan and the State of Michigan Archives was essential. The speeches made by the governor, correspondence saved from the 1951 fire, the help in figuring out how the microfilm readers work, and how to locate old, and I mean really old newspaper articles were treasures not obtainable without their service.

Research on Edwin Winans's life also took me to The Howell Library, where we serendipitously found some precious gems about Elizabeth Galloway Winans. The staff there is exceptionally helpful, and the building is a delight. The original Carnegie Library's expansion is aesthetically pleasing and functional—a rare occurrence.

Giving your time and talent to help a friend, especially when it is hours reading a manuscript and then commenting, is to be applauded. I am pleased and appreciative to my colleagues, Peg Jonkhoff, Charlene Lutes, Valerie Marvin, and Stephen Siciliano, for their interest and contribution to this project. Valerie Marvin, Michigan State Capitol Historian and Curator, was also a gracious hostess on a tour of the Capitol and shared little-known and hard-to-find documentation. She is a true state treasure.

My family spent years hearing about the book, listening to my commiserations, and encouraging me. My husband, David, is the inspiration for this book. Next are my daughters, who brought their talents to this endeavor, each as time allowed in their busy schedules. Two of my daughters are retired allowing them some time to travel and help with research. We took some book research trips together, made many discoveries, and solidified our relationships. All together the value of those trips was priceless.

Lisa is the researcher extraordinaire. She dug in like a little ferret for newspaper stories, census records, gravesites, and family history. Her research took us step by step into new arenas of thought and provided tidbits of information we never expected. Wendy is the caregiver and cares for her grandmother, which is like a second full-time job so that I could spend time writing without worry. Natalie is the pragmatic organizer, travel planner, security detail, micro-fiche reader, and overall support daughter who reads, re-reads, and edits. Kym is my business manager, running businesses of her own and with a million things to do, but she finds the time to read over chapters and has a talent for identifying what needs to be fixed. Lastly, Marcia encouraged me long-distance through many telephone conversations. The book would not exist without their help and emotional support.

I am stuck in Technology 101 and may never pass the course. Therefore, I can't do much without my technical support person, Kevin Winans. He tutors me, advises me, and even makes house calls. His patience is infinite, and his services, as is his love, are invaluable.

I have no presumption that I accomplished this project alone. I am grateful to all these people for their help, and taking the advice of Bishop Barron, I prayed daily for inspiration with full knowledge that "it is God who acts, and if we give ourselves to his creative power, he will make us into something far better than we ever could."

CONTENTS

The Extraordinary Life of Edwin Baruch Winans

PREFACE

The more I learned about Edwin Winans, the more regard I had for him. I turned into a one-woman Edwin Winans fan club. Since I am devoted to telling his story, I think everyone will be captivated by the narrative, but realistically, why would someone whose surname is not Winans want to read the book? I will tell you. It is an opportunity to go with Edwin on adventures walking the Overland Trail to California during the gold rush, returning to Michigan via the Isthmus of Panama, and then back to Rough and Ready, California, with a new bride. Stay with him as he returns to Michigan with so much gold his wife sews it into her dress, and he has to guard it with a gun. Consider if you can support his Civil War positions as a member of the state legislature. Follow him to Washington, D.C., when he was in Congress and connect with events in the 1880s. It's also a love story and a tale of success in both business and government; in the end, you will like him and be glad you have met him.

The challenge in writing his story is the lack of extant documents. He left Michigan in 1850 and traveled the Overland Trail to California, but other than a paragraph or two in newspapers after he made a name for himself, there is no diary, no letters home, and no biography to help describe the trip. Come with me as I trek through my research on the Overland Trail, embellished with the stories of others who made that journey. I have inserted two initiatives called "A Place In Time" and "Notes" into the narrative. A Place in Time is meant to connect you to concurrent events, and my opinion or thoughts are injected via Notes. However, it is up to the reader to go beyond the author's opinion and engage the narrative with thoughts of their own. As Edwin's story continues, the newspaper articles, speeches, and official records when Edwin was a public figure are helpful; all these combined give us a picture of who he was.

Edwin Winans stood out in life and death as an exceptional man. As people began to reminisce about the presidency of Theodore Roosevelt, some in Michigan compared his appearance, actions, and personality with their favorite Michigan governor, Edwin B. Winans. People began to honor Edwin Winans, saying he was the Teddy Roosevelt of Michigan. The comparison of these men gives insight into who they were. The men were similar in height and weight; they wore mustaches and wireframe glasses but had more in common than semblance.

Both men attributed hard work to their success in anything they did. Peers recognized them for their courage, honesty, compassion, and generosity. Their sameness, however, runs deeper - the two men had similar experiences and philosophies.

Edwin walked west seeking his fortune and learned tremendous lessons in human nature, self-sufficiency, and integrity. The lawless West of the 1850s made him a witness of dishonesty and betrayal and great courage and honesty. He learned not only to function in the lawless West but also to flourish due to his persistence and high moral values. He came forward as a leader in the West and found leadership came naturally to him for the rest of his life.

Theodore went west as well. He went to learn, and the West was a magnificent school. T.R. (a rare person recognized only by initials) often referred to his time in the West and the people he met there. They differed from those he knew and worked with in New York City. He recognized their learning by experience and valued what he gleaned from them. He had to earn their respect through hard work and determination; Theodore valued their regard. The lessons he learned translated into how he worked with people in government, leading soldiers up San Juan Hill or as President of the United States.

Employed in various jobs in government, both men learned from the bottom up how the government operation worked or didn't work. Edwin and Theodore operated within the spoils system but worked for civil service reform, which did not happen during either of their administrations.

They were both blinded in one eye because of accidents. Theodore was punched in the eye by a boxing trainer, and Edwin lost an eye straining to move a massive boulder by himself.

They both had women they adored - Theodore's first wife died, and Edwin's first love turned him down. Then, after heartbreak, they both had successful, lifelong relationships with remarkable women, which was providential.

During his presidency, Roosevelt reduced the national debt by $90 million, and Winans reduced expenditures at the state level. They both recognized that the government does not spend any money it hasn't taken from a hard-working citizen.

Roosevelt acknowledged many kinds of success but believed that a household of children "makes all other forms of success and achievement lose their importance by comparison." Winans agreed with that philosophy. He had two sons but brought others into his home and helped shape their lives.

These great leaders were laser-focused on who they were serving. Roosevelt said it, and Winans lived it. "It is a gratification to me to have owed my election …to the folk who worked hard on the farm, in the shop, or on the railroad, or who owned little stores, little businesses which they managed themselves. I would literally, not figuratively, rather cut off my right hand than forfeit by any improper act of mine the trust and regard of these people."

They were very much alike, but there were also some striking differences. Theodore Roosevelt was born into a wealthy family with every advantage money could buy. Edwin Winans was born into a family that struggled for existence. Theodore had the best education - he graduated Phi Beta Kappa from Harvard. Edwin graduated with a degree from Albion College. Roosevelt did not want to be seen as an aristocrat, and Winans wished to leave a legacy of culture and refinement from his beginnings in a one-room log cabin. His prestigious walking stick, gold watch, and respectable carriage spoke of the success for which he was pleased to be known.

Theodore Roosevelt was a prolific writer. We know his life in detail through biographies, autobiographies, letters, and speeches. Not so with

Edwin Winans. We have a handful of speeches and some newspaper articles. We have bits and pieces to paint a picture of a monumental man who left the state better than he found it.

Why should you read Edwin Winans' story? For the same reason, you should read about Theodore Roosevelt or other consequential leaders - whether or not you can find their faces on a mountain. Theodore and Edwin both loved America and the representative democratic experiment it represents. They were dedicated to its continuance and knew a delicate balance kept it strong. They leave us lessons in what we acknowledge as important: respect, honesty, compassion, hard work, kindness, gratitude, cooperation, and generosity. They instill the importance of virtue in our personal lives and want us to realize that we must insist on those virtues in our politicians. More importantly, they leave us their legacy of governance as an example to secure our way of life for future generations.

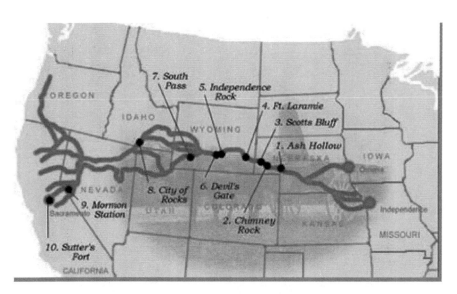

The Overland Trail was not a single track, but many that took people west to California during the gold rush. The route began at various jumping-off points along the Missouri River and followed on both sides of the Platte River to the Rocky Mountains.

THE OVERLAND TRAIL

Cold nights prevail in Michigan during the month of March, but daylight hours bring warm sunshine, inspiring the restless soul. As they trekked along, the cool, fresh air made them want to pause and take a deep breath occasionally, but it was a long way to California, and they needed to put miles behind them.

The gold strike at Sutter's Mill in Coloma, California, inspired thousands to go west for treasure, but it was foolish to leave without a plan. There were essays, newspaper articles, and guidebooks about traveling on the overland trail to California and what that journey entailed. Thousands had emigrated in 1843 to Oregon and California - so many it was called the Great Migration. Letters they sent back to loved ones described the sacrifices they endured on the way, along with descriptions of the trails they traveled. Some immigrants had returned to share their stories in newspapers and by word of mouth.

It was 1850, and 24-year-old Edwin Winans remembered and felt the lasting effects of the 1837 recession. He lived with his widowed mother, and it was, without a doubt, hard to make ends meet in rural Michigan at the time. Edwin had a degree from Albion College and taught school, but school teaching didn't pay much. He wanted to complete his education at the University of Michigan and get a law degree, but that meant a cost not easily obtainable in the 1840s economy. Gold-rich California would be his answer.

Edwin Winans, with two friends, four horses, and a wagon loaded with supplies, traveled westward in search of riches. They chose the Overland Trail because it was the least expensive way to the goldfields. Others came from all over the world to California seeking fame and

19

fortune; they came in ships from Europe, Asia, and Australia. Some gold seekers along the east coast of the United States traveled by ship around Cape Horn and north along the coast of South America to California. This was the slowest route reported to take 160 days. Some took ships from New York City or New Orleans to Chagres, Panama. Then they went by boat up the Chagres River to Gorgona. The Central American journey then took them to Panama City from Gorgona on foot and by mules. There, they awaited the first available ship going north to California. The trip across the isthmus was grueling in 1850, but shorter in duration than either the trip around Cape Horn or the overland trails.[1]

The first milestone in an overland trip west was a hub or jumping-off point, depending on whether the choice was for the northern or southern route. Those who had served in the Mexican War were likely to choose the southern route, but most from Michigan chose the trails along the northern route known as the Mormon or Oregon Trail. There were numerous ways by trail and river to reach a jumping-off point. From Hamburg, Michigan, it made sense to follow the Chicago Road, which ran from Detroit, Michigan, to Chicago, Illinois. The Chicago Road developed from a native trail, and it was not much more than a trail in 1850, but the route was grassy and hilly, just like the terrain at home. Once they reached Chicago, they would continue west toward Kanesville, later known as Council Bluffs, Iowa, or maybe they would take a route toward Old Fort Kearny, later established as Nebraska City. These were the two most northern starting points for those migrating west, whether their destination was California or Oregon.[2]

The three argonauts considered which of the four main jumping-off points or possibly several smaller ones they should choose along the Missouri River. It seems unlikely Michiganders would travel farther south than they had to before hooking up with the trails west. The choice of either Kanesville or Old Fort Kearny over St. Joseph, Fort Leavenworth, Kansas City, or Independence took them closer to the northern Platte River Road and the start of the prairie.

In 1850, Kanesville, Iowa, a community in a hollow between two bluffs and across the river from Omaha, Nebraska, offered sanctuary to thousands of immigrants of the Mormon faith. It was a temporary winter headquarters for them, but they built houses and put in crops for their comfort and provision and to support the saints coming after them on their way to Salt Lake City.

During the 1849 gold rush, George Jewett described Kanesville as "a scrubby town of 80 to 100 log cabins three miles from the river in a deep hollow."[3] The principal function of the town was trading and ferrying for the many people passing through. George Belshaw said, "It was only a little burg between two high bluffs, but it was crammed to capacity with emigrant teams and wagons, while the river bottom was one vast camp."[4]

There were three ferry points near the town. There was an upper, middle, and lower ferry. The Upper Ferry consisted of a "flatboat big enough for two wagons"[5] and pulled from east to west with ropes. The stock had to swim. The Lower Ferry, also called Sarpy's, was located at a bend in the river called Trader's Point, eight miles from Kanesville. It was cheap but risky, described as a "fur boat calked with buffalo tallow."[6] The middle ferry was three miles from Kanesville. A steamboat ferry there could move "eleven wagons and 100 head of cattle"[7] on each crossing.

Another choice for men from Michigan was to cross the Missouri River at Old Fort Kearny, Nebraska, later founded as Nebraska City. Like Kanesville/Council Bluffs, this crossing put the travelers north from the other main crossings and farther west. The army put the first Fort Kearny 1/2 mile from the Missouri River. The thinking was that this was where they would be of best use to immigrants, but the fort was later moved 180 miles west to a more suitable location. However, a Fort Kearny ferry was still in operation at the original site and in much demand in 1850.

Rev. Henry T. Davis describes the scene: "Here we crossed the Big Muddy in an old, dilapidated ferry boat. We pitched our tent on the western slope of "Kearney [sic] Hill," Table Creek winds along the foot of Kearney Hill. Just across this creek, and a few hundred yards to the northwest stood Old Fort Kearney. The garrison there consisted of a blockhouse, made of logs, white port-holes for cannon and muskets, and two rows of barracks."[8] Simon Doyle said of the old fort, "Ft. Kerny [sic] that once was, is beautifully situated on a fine slope of prairies as beautiful as ever laid out of doors, a half mile from the river. It is only a small Blockhouse with soldiers' quarters."[9]

Note: Reading the descriptions left by some of the actors in this drama makes me long for some written accounts from Edwin Winans. It is unknown where he crossed and what he saw. We are left to the stories of others to set the scene for us. Thousands of Americans contracted gold fever and left everything to go on a quest for treasure. Crossing the Missouri put the seekers outside the United States and into Indian Territory. It was a milestone in the journey, and the invaders were excited in anticipation of conquest.

Once collected on the prairie, the people began to gather in groups. Some people joined groups before arriving at a jumping-off point. It was preferable in many ways to travel in a group. There was safety in numbers, to be sure, and if they could get a guide to lead them, the guides usually charged per wagon and wanted a large group to make the trip worthwhile. Also, they were crossing Indian Territory, and it was less likely natives would attack a large group. As a group, the immigrants could circle the wagons to protect animals, goods, and persons.

Another reason to organize was to be sure all agreed with the rules of the road. There was no government where they went, so they had to govern themselves. Groups came together, elected officers, and agreed to rules of conduct. Some went so far as to write constitutions, elect officials, and judges. No matter how organized the groups were, not all remained the cohesive group they started out as. Once the reality of trail life began, there were as many different reasons for the breakup of groups as differences in people.

It would have been helpful to be in a group for fording rivers. The rivers raged with runoff in the spring, which could be very treacherous. Many people lost all their belongings and even their lives while fording rivers. Immigrants in the wagon trains helped each other, rafting the wagons and swimming with the livestock across streams.

There is no evidence Edwin and his cohorts joined such a group. Travel was slower with a large group. For example, although groups could help rafting and fording, getting everyone in a large wagon train across a swollen stream could take days. Individuals or small groups did not have to wait for a whole wagon train - they could move on as soon as they were across the river. But if the Michigan men didn't sign on to one of the wagon trains, it would make sense that they at least traveled close to groups and connected with groups along the way.

In 1849, Alonzo Delano described wagon train traffic: "There were probably twenty thousand people on the road west of the Missouri, and our train did not travel for an hour without seeing many others and hundreds of men. For days, we would travel in company with other trains, which would stop to rest when we would pass them, and then perhaps we would lay up, and they pass us. Sometimes, we would meet again after many days, and others, perhaps, never. As near as we could ascertain, there were about a thousand wagons before us, and probably four or five thousand behind us."[10]

Journals of overland travelers often note how many miles traveled in a day. They could measure miles traveled because some wagons were equipped with odometers. The crude mechanics consisted of wooden gears mounted on the wagon wheels. The collection and preservation of this information shows how farsighted the immigrants were to leave a record for those who followed them. Some followed in wagons, and later by stagecoach, then by train. Some followed vicariously in the written accounts left by these intrepid crusaders.[11]

Folks from Michigan think they have witnessed rugged weather but camping on the prairie proved quite different from farming back home. Some said they had never experienced such horrific rainstorms. Some journal accounts of thunderstorms sound more like tornadoes. Torrents of spring rain left the travelers wet to the core and all their belongings wet as well. The argonauts did not feel so adventurous when they woke up in soggy bedding with rain coming down in buckets and the fire they used to cook their supper underwater. It meant uncooked jerky meat and hardtack for breakfast. In the continuing rainstorm, they had no choice but to hook up horses and travel in wet clothes and boots. The prairie taught some lessons about misery and survival. Edwin and his friends were farm boys; they were practical problem solvers. After the first experience, as they moved across the prairie, they would have looked for a place on high ground to put their tents, and then they dug a trench around the tents to allow water to flow away instead of through their shelter. Walking the trail in wet clothes and boots was disagreeable, but hot and dry could also be challenging.

Hiking the prairie when it was hot and dry meant everything was covered in dust. Grit in your boots was even worse than walking in wet ones. Grit in their eyes and mouths was worse, but through their suffering, the travelers had to be vigilant, watching for snakes. Rattlesnakes - lots of rattlesnakes. Many migrants kept a record of the snakes they encountered each day, and some days the numbers were in double digits. The snakes presented a danger, it's true, and some overlanders were injured. Some journals recorded the death of horses due to rattlesnake bites as well.

The men moved along well-worn trails from campsite to campsite, following the sun as it set in the west. The routes generally followed rivers, but there was no single path. Wagon ruts spread over more than half a mile in places; some were on one side of a river, and some on the other. Wagons stopped for the night depending on where they could find water and grass for their livestock. Immigrants in large numbers had been moving west and leaving ruts for others to follow for years, but the 1843 "Great Migration" numbers were small compared to 1849 and after.

Drinking water came from rivers or streams - wherever they could find it. Some travelers dipped water from the middle of the stream, and others felt if they dug down a few feet and reached water, it was better because of its filter through the sand. Many of them suffered and succumbed to cholera because no one knew, at the time, that bacteria in water caused cholera. Some victims recovered, and some recovered only to suffer a later relapse. Others died shortly after coming down with symptoms of nausea and diarrhea. Most people heading west were men during the early gold rush years, but both men and women became widows and widowers on the trail hundreds of miles from family and friends to help and console. It was enough to return some of them to their families in the States.

The dead were buried in shallow graves along the roadside because the bereaved did not have time to pause very long to dig a traditional deep burial hole. While mourning their loss, they knew they were racing to get beyond the mountains in their path before snow blocked their travel. Grave markers consisted of piles of stones or maybe a wooden cross. Wooden ones were subject to destruction over time, leaving graves unmarked. There could be a row of graves marking where numerous people from the same caravan died from drinking water from the same stream.

We have no idea who was traveling with Edwin Winans. The two men who went with him remain nameless. We know that one of the men died along the trail - it likely could have been from cholera.

Note: *It must have been heartbreaking to bury your friend trailside and move on. Edwin did not leave a record for us of this man's name or where he was buried. Edwin and his remaining companion must have grieved their friend, but they had no choice - they moved on - driven to continue west toward their future, but the death of their friend certainly made them wonder about their own mortality. At the outset of their journey their focus was wealth and glory, but now that golden dream was tarnished.*

Following the trail left by others, Ft. Kearny was another milestone destination for the voyagers; it meant provisions and protection from natives. They found a store, a blacksmith shop, a post office, and a hospital. Several trails converged there, and thousands of people passed there on any given day in the 1850s. There were improvements from the prior year, and the gold seekers could partake at "eating houses, where they feasted on such delicacies as cheese, fresh butter, and milk."[12]

The voyagers could send mail back home or pick up mail at places like Fort Kearny, but communication opportunities came in various forms. Members of groups traveling east would sometimes agree to post letters. Roadside graffiti was also used to share information with other travelers. Immigrants of one wagon train sometimes knew travelers in another train, and they would leave messages regarding where they found water, a danger, or maybe a change of route.

It could be a note on paper attached to a stick, a message painted on a rock, or carved into a tree.

A Place in Time: *News was available at the fort, even if there were no newspapers. The travelers were undoubtedly curious about national and worldwide events since they left Michigan in March. Abolition had been a*

25

topic for some time, and some states had threatened to secede from the union. News at Fort Kearny would have included the debate in Congress called the Compromise of 1850. Congress was looking for a solution, even though temporary, to calm the heated emotions around the slavery issue.

Fear of natives was prevalent among the travelers, but the record shows most encounters were peaceful in the early years of migration. The natives were interested in trading with people in wagon trains for fishhooks, clothing, or rifles. The immigrants enjoyed the help when crossing rivers, using them as guides, and traded with them in some places for food. The frequent complaint from pioneers was not attack but the theft of goods and livestock by Indians.

L. Dow Stephens, in *Life Sketches of a Jayhawker of '49,* relates his first contact with natives on the prairie. "Our first experience with the Indians came with our first camp across the river. Our campfires were going nicely, and supper was started when we heard gunshots, volley after volley. In a few minutes, from over the ridge came two to three hundred Pawnee Indians, riding at full run straight for our camp. It was a few minutes work for us to get our rifles in readiness, but the Indians put up a white flag, and they were allowed to enter the camp. It seemed that a party of the Sioux tribe had given them battle, the two being at war, and the Pawnees had rushed to our camp expecting protection, but we ordered them off, telling them we wished no trouble with the Sioux as we had to travel their country, and wanted no enemies. We took the precaution to organize our body with regular military style Colonels and Captains. For a while we were very vigilant. Our picket guards were stationed three hundred yards from camp and had to lie down to see any approaching object, but firing was strictly prohibited unless you thought an enemy approached."[13]

From Ft. Kearny, the wagon trains followed the Platte River, running shallow and wide across what we now know as the state of Nebraska. The bed of the Platte was composed of quicksand constantly changing with the current movement, adding to the difficulty in crossing. James Evans, described the Platte River in his *Journal of a Trip to California.* "From the sand hills, it had the appearance of a great inland sea. It looked wider than the Mississippi and showed to a much better advantage, there being no timber on the banks to check the scope of the human eye. My first impression on beholding the Platte River was that it looked so wide and muddy, and rolled along within three feet of the top of the bank with such majesty - that it was unusually swollen and perfectly impassable. Judge my surprise when I learned that it was only three or four feet deep. The water is exceedingly muddy, or I should say sandy. What adds greatly to the singular appearance of this river, is the water so filled with glittering particles of Micah or Isinglass that its shining waves look to be rich with floating gold. The plains are so low and level that if the Platte River could rise five feet it would cover the country at least ten miles wide!"[14]

The Platte River Valley was a place that attracted bison or buffalo. The gigantic herds of buffalo were dangerous to the wagon trains because they would stampede at the slightest provocation. Overlanders lit fires around the parameters of their camps to keep the buffalo from running through campsites. Herds of buffalo could be found in and out of the river. The migrants killed buffalo for the fresh meat, for which they were thankful. But after learning the knack of hunting buffalo, they killed many more than they could eat just for the sport. They also were known to kill a buffalo for the tongue and marrow bones and leave the rest. There were times when there were buffalo as far as the eye could see to the horizon, and so no thought was given to the possibility of extinction or how their actions affected the ecology.

As the voyagers followed the Platte westward, the next milestone was more than 300 miles away at the foot of the Rocky Mountains - Fort Laramie. Some wagon trains followed the river's south bank and eventually descended into a beautiful hollow. Immigrants wrote in their journals of the steep decline into the valley below. Once they reached the valley, they were impressed with the clear water and access to firewood.

"With their breath catching in their throats, they dropped with locked wheels down the Ash Hollow slope to the river's northern arm. As they plodded on, the valley rim to the south grew higher its slopes eroded into fantastic shapes - the domes of Courthouse Rock, the high thin stem of Chimney Rock, the colorful battlements of Scotts Bluff. Anticipation rose again. Fort Laramie, its adobe walls and honeycomb of rooms built around a central plaza was near now. They could rest, wash clothes, repack wagons, buy a few supplies, treat the sore feet of the oxen, and celebrate with a dance."[15]

Travel on the north side of the Platte River was sometimes called the Mormon Road, but during the gold rush, the prospectors going to California outnumbered the Mormons traveling to Salt Lake City. The wagons traveling the north side of the Platte River valley, as they neared Ft. Laramie, could see for miles the rock formation called Courthouse Rock, albeit from a different angle than those from the south side of the river. The block-shaped formation was an imposing landmark for migrants on the Platte River Road to view.

Alonzo Delano describes this natural feature: "The atmosphere in this region is of remarkable clearness, for which cause we were unable to estimate distances with any precision. Court-house Rock appeared only about two miles off when in reality, it was ten or twelve... It stood upon a little ridge above the bottom - was of a circular form, with an elevation on the top much like a flattened dome, and at the distance at which we stood, it resembled a huge building. It was really about two hundred feet high, although from the road it appeared only about fifty. Near it, on the east end, was another blunt pointed rock, not quite as high, which was not particularly remarkable, but which is embraced in the same view. Both of these stand isolate on the plain, although a few miles west are bare bluff ridges of the same kind of rock - a soft sand and clay, intermixed with lime, easily cut with a knife - all probably of volcanic origin; and this is the general character of the rock in this region."[16]

At the Courthouse Rock site, Chimney Rock was visible. "Chimney Rock, rising almost 350 feet above the sagebrush plain of the North Platte valley, is a pointed sandstone column resting on a conical base. In their diaries and letters home, the pioneers made this landmark as recognizable to Americans as Niagara Falls."[17] Some thought it looked like an inverted funnel, and many drew sketches as they traveled in sight of it for 4 or 5 days.

Another day of travel exposed Scott's Bluff to the travelers. "...an informed minority of travelers thought more impressive than Chimney Rock. The bluff yellow clay and soft sand rock, washed and broken into fantastic shapes by wind, rain and storm, presented the appearance of an immense city of towers and crenellations."[18]

Note: Edwin and his friends were sure to see these three famous landmarks because the overland trail took adventurers along the Platte River either on the north or the south side with a view of these unique natural phenomena. Some travelers from the north side of the Platte forded the river for a closer experience. It must have been a serendipitous delight to see these rare natural rock formations after walking mile after grueling mile for days across the monotonous prairie and plain.

Even though the travelers enjoyed seeing natural wonders, they were more than ready to see something reminiscent of civilization - Fort Laramie. The 1850s adventurers found, at the confluence of the Platte River and the Laramie River, a fort, but a fort not surrounded by walls. The location made this trading post a military fort in 1849, and it was a significant military influence for decades. From Fort Laramie, Laramie Peak was sure to be seen by the men from Michigan as it is the tallest mountain in the range. Snow-covered all year, it is over 10,000 feet in height and dominates the horizon. The view of Laramie Peak was a teaser of what was to come as they moved westward.

A Place in Time: *Those who stopped at Fort Laramie after July 9, 1850, would have learned of the death of President Zachary Taylor. President Taylor, like many of those traveling the overland trail, died of cholera. Zachary Taylor opposed the Compromise of 1850, but his successor, Millard Fillmore, did not. Did the death of Zachary Taylor change history - or postpone the inevitable?*

The next challenge was crossing the Rocky Mountains. Many left wagons behind or burned them for campfires due to anticipation of the rugged trail ahead. Some rebuilt their wagons into carts that were smaller and easier to pull. This meant most left belongings along the trail - things that no longer were valued if they had to be carried in a backpack or took up room in a small cart.

Independence Rock rose into view along the Sweetwater River trail through South Pass and provided entertainment to travelers. It was named Independence Rock because earlier trekkers stopped there on the way west to celebrate Independence Day and carve their names or messages on the soft rock. Many voyagers stopped to add their names or messages for posterity. It was like a giant bulletin board and as a bonus could be easily climbed. The view from the top made it worth the climb and provided a change from the rigors of the trail.

Travelers soon came to another distinction of the trail called Devil's Gate. James Abbey describes it as "a remarkable fissure in the Rocky Mountain wall. ... the Sweet Water River passes between perpendicular rocks four hundred feet high. The fissure is about fifty feet in breadth, and the height of the walls from the top to the bottom is upwards of four hundred and fifty feet."[19] They must have felt as though they had seen a lifetime of remarkable things by the time the gold seekers got through the pass to the west side of the Rocky Mountains, but there were more wonders to come.

The trail through the Rockies took overlanders up a steep incline to a flat open stretch of land. There was no indication as they traveled through the South Pass that they were crossing the continental divide where rivers begin to flow west. The breathtaking view from South Pass encompasses the mountains of Wind River and Bear with Fremont's Peak to the north. From South Pass, travelers had to choose a trail to Oregon Territory or California. But it did not matter which route the overlanders took; the trail was much more difficult from here than any they had yet traveled.

Note: Edwin and companion chose one of the routes to California. We don't have any details on their route to the goldfields, but we do know that they suffered much before they got to California. They were hungry and parched. They were forced to leave the wagon and then the horses. To complicate matters, Edwin's companion was ill and needed his help. He must have often thought about the wisdom of leaving the comfort of home to walk thousands of miles and risk death for the possibility, not the assurance of some gold, but the commitment had been made and they were now closer to the goldfields than they were to home. They had no choice, they had to move toward civilization for food and water. The stampeders had come far and were so close to a life of promise and hope - and they trudged on.

South Pass is where the California and Oregon trails converge. Trails split off in many directions, forcing the immigrants to choose from several of options. From South Pass, some headed to Fort Bridger and then to Salt Lake City or Fort Hall. Wayfarers coming from the south used the Cherokee Trail to Fort Bridger. The choices were, at best, confusing and, at worst, an enigma.

Every group migrating west searched for the best way to the coast, or after 1848, the goldfields. Some promoted specific routes through the Sierra Nevada Mountains, usually for financial gain. On the Sublette Cutoff, the immigrants turned toward Fort Hall before going to Fort Bridger. Another cutoff called the Hudspeth eliminated Fort Hall. From Fort Hall travelers could follow the Snake River and then go southwest from there to follow the Humboldt River[20] to its sink into the earth, and then west across the desert to California.

Travel along the Humboldt was good until the river disappeared at the Humboldt sink. After the sink, they had to traverse the desert and the Sierra Nevada Mountains before reaching their destination. In 1844, Elisha Stephens searched for a route after reaching the sink. His group met up with a Paiute Indian whom they called "Truckee." The Indian had them follow a river, now called the Truckee, to a pass over the Sierra Nevada. After a journey on an arduous trail, the Stephens Party made it to Sutter's Fort. There were various choices of trails through the Sierras, and many followed the Humboldt River to its sink and then trails diverted to specific destinations.

Those who chose the Salt Lake City route did it for various reasons. Once in Salt Lake, they had three options to choose from to get them to California: the Hastings Cutoff, the Spanish Trail, or Hensley's Cutoff.[21]

The trail from Fort Bridger to Salt Lake City through mountainous territory was difficult, with many rivers to be forded and costly ferry crossings. Once at Salt Lake City, the voyagers could trade with or buy what they needed from the inhabitants. Some chose to stay in that growing community for a while - some stayed all winter before moving on.

The Hastings Cutoff was named for Lansford Hastings, who traveled west and then wrote an immigrant guide sold in the east. He could be found along the trail in 1846, convincing travelers to take a shortcut to California. The Donner party took his cutoff, and disaster resulted. Many factors comprised success or failure in whatever route was taken.

One factor was the season - the Donners traveled late and got caught in snow in the Sierra Nevada Mountains. Another factor is that groups traveling the trails improved them, making it easier for those coming behind them.

The Spanish Trail took them to southern California and north to the goldfields. Hensley's took another route around the Great Salt Lake to the Humboldt River.

Another alternative was to take a new branch of the California Trail north of the Great Salt Lake and south of the Oregon Trail straight west to the headwaters of the Humboldt River - follow the river to its sink, desert, and Sierra Nevada before reaching the end of the rainbow. This route went past Soda Springs in the Bear River valley; the springs are full of carbonic acid gas. Alonzo Delano says they are "equal to any soda water in the world, and though good without any additional concomitants, with lemon-syrup, or sugar, they are delicious. Also, there is a spring on the right bank, near the Soda Springs, through which columns of gas are discharged with a loud noise, resembling the ejection of steam from a boiler, and is, in consequence, called Steamboat Spring."[22]

Note: *These are only some possibilities for Edwin to reach his destination in 1850. The U.S. Army had been pursuing routes to the Pacific for years, and immigrants always looked for a shortcut to Oregon and California. By the time Edwin and his friends immigrated, routes were more established than when the Donners took the Hastings Cutoff, but the men were travel weary. They had to spend time looking for food and were hungry most of the time. Water was crucial, of course, and when they found it was not always palatable. The two remaining friends suffered much but toughed it out and journeyed on.*

Journals from that time and place tell a story of grueling walks through mountains and deserts on this last leg of the trip. James Abbey relates, "The desert through which we are passing is strewed with dead cattle, mules, and horses. I counted in a distance of fifteen miles three hundred fifty dead horses, two hundred eighty oxen, and one hundred twenty mules; and hundreds of others are left behind being unable to keep up. Such is traveling through the desert. These dead animals, decaying on the road, keep the air scented all the way through. ...Vast amounts of valuable property have been abandoned and thrown away in this desert - leather trunks, clothing, wagons, etc. ...The cause of so many wagons being abandoned, is to endeavor to save the animals and reach the end of the journey as soon as possible by packing through; the loss of personal goods is a matter of small importance comparatively."[23]

Trouble with natives was not prevalent in the 1850s, especially along the Platte River Road. But journaling immigrants tell of problems with those they called Digger Indians on the other side of the Rockies. They were Paiute or Shoshone, and the slang digger was used for any natives in the area. The habits of these natives led to the uncomplimentary name given to them by immigrants because they lived in grass huts and appeared dirty looking. Their diet consisted of gathered acorns and other nuts, ground into a paste. The natives made the paste into a pudding or baked it into cakes.

The overlanders report instances where natives riddled their stock with arrows so the migrants would leave them behind. The wounded animals were then easy prey for the natives and provided a feast for the tribe. Some of the wagon trains soon figured out the methodology of the attacks on the stock. Instead of leaving the animals for the Indians, they butchered them and either ate the meat or made jerky.

The indigenous people felt the wagon trains owed them for trekking through their territory. The immigrants and the natives did not have any understanding of each other's cultures. They certainly had no common trust. The immigrants thought the natives were thieves, and the natives thought the immigrants were trespassers. The overlanders were running out of supplies and worn out from months of hard travel. The immigrants wanted to put the threat of the natives in the past and move to their goal of wealth in the goldfields.

The overland trail was indeed a grueling experience. Franklin Langworthy shares his feelings when, he saw California for the first time after cresting a mountain in the Sierra Nevada. "We now come to a break in the wall like a gateway; through this we pass, and in an instant the New World of California bursts at once upon our impatient sight. The view is so vast and of such surpassing grandeur, that the mind is bewildered and lost amidst the boundless expanse, like attempting to grasp

eternity or infinite space by the aid of our feeble powers. The interme-
diate space consists of the great valley of the Sacramento and Joachin
River embosoming the Bay of San Francisco which penetrates far into
the plain, sending out numerous arms in all directions. Immediately in
front, we have a more distinct view of the great western slope of the
Sierra Nevada. This slope consists of a great number of ridges or chains
of mountains, running a westerly course in zigzag lines, starting from
the main ridge on which we now stand, and gradually diminishing in
height until they terminate at the eastern limit of the broad plain of the
Sacramento."[24] They knew now that they would succeed. The prize was
within their grasp - they could see it.

Note: *Edwin Winans began the journey with two friends, four horses,
and a wagon of supplies. By the time he got to California, he had no horses
or wagon, and one friend was dead. Forced to abandon the supply wagon
and horses, the two remaining Michiganders walked the last miles to the
goldfields. Edwin's last companion died shortly after reaching their destination. The death of this second companion must have been brutal for Edwin
to endure. This was the man who left Michigan with him, full of excitement
and anticipation of wealth and good fortune. This man walked across a
continent with Edwin for months, suffering with him heat and cold, hunger
and thirst, loss of horses, and even the death of their companion. His goal
of reaching the goldfields left Edwin worn out physically and mentally, but
he was driven by purpose. Now was not the time to falter but to stand firm.
Time to grieve was not a luxury Edwin could afford. He had to get to work.*

In 1850, Kanesville, Iowa, later called Council Bluffs,
was the winter stopping place for Mormon settlers heading west.
Many stampeders for gold used Kanesville as a stop before
leaving the U.S. and entering Indian Territory.

Old Fort Kearny, Nebraska, was located near the mouth of Table Creek.
It was a military post for protecting travelers. The post was moved from
its original site closer to the Platte River in 1847.

Court House and Jail Rocks were landmarks for emigrants on the Overland Trail. The massive clay and sandstone rock formations are the first of several landmarks along the trail. Early travelers west gave the rocks their names as they passed them on their way west.

Chimney Rock is a rock formation south of the Oregon, California, and Mormon Trails in Nebraska. Early travelers made many drawings of the rock, which has been reduced in height by erosion.

Independence Rock is a massive granite rock approximately 130 feet high and 1,900 feet long in the high plateau region of Wyoming. Many travelers carved their names on the rock. Although Edwin Winans passed the rock on his way to the goldfields, we cannot find any affirmation that his name is or was on the rock.

THE GOLD RUSH

Note: Although his overland journey had physically challenged him, Edwin Winans was twenty-four years old and in the prime of his life in July of 1850. The quintessential picture of a miner was a flannel shirt, corduroys, and solid leather boots. Edwin would have looked good in the outfit because his 5' 11" frame and broad shoulders radiated the capable, solid miner. But he was, I'm sure, still in the clothes he walked west in and less concerned about the clothing suitable for mining than he was about finding the gold.

In January 1848, James Marshall saw something shiny in the tail-race of the sawmill he had built for John Sutter in Coloma. On closer inspection, he found several pieces of what he thought might be gold but was unsure. The laborers at the mill laughed at him and then scrutinized the pieces. The consensus was gold, and the laborers were no longer laughing as they searched for more of the shiny metal in the American River. The loose pieces of gold Marshall and the mill workers found were placer gold. [1]

Placer gold is not always in full view for easy picking like it was for James Marshall. Early miners used shallow pans to separate the gold from the dirt. Would-be miners removed shovels of soil from a likely spot, added water, and swirled the mixture in a pan, allowing the heavier gold to sink to the bottom. They repeated the process of dipping and swirling the slurry in the pan and washed away lighter material each time. The anticipation of reward at the bottom of the pan kept the gold miners washing pan after pan - a nugget might be in the next shovel of dirt. A miner needed only a bucket, a shovel, a pan, and just as important was water.

Fortune seekers who had been mining for some time learned that often gold could be found where it had come to rest in an alluvial plain. The miners panned for gold along the banks of rivers and then dammed the rivers to look for gold in the beds of the rivers. They knew if they moved boulders at the riverside, there was a chance there would be gold held in place there for millennia by the weight of the rock. A knife was one of the early tools the miners used to mine gold. A knife could reach into fine crevices and pick the gold from its hiding spot.

Frank Marryat describes a mining scene in his memoir *Mountains and Molehills*. "On the banks was a village of canvas that the winter rains had bleached to perfection, and round it, the miners were at work at every point. Many were waist-deep in the water to construct a race and dam to turn the river's course; others were entrenched in holes, like gravediggers, working down to the bedrock. Some were on the brink of the stream washing out prospects from tin pans or wooden "batteas," and others worked in company with the long-tom, by means of water-sluices artfully conveyed from the river. Many were coyoteing in subterranean holes, from which from time to time their heads popped out like those of squirrels, to take a look at the world, and a few with drills, dissatisfied with nature's work, were preparing to remove large rocks with gunpowder." [2]

Gold mining was hard work. Locating a good place to mine was often a complex decision. Finding gold was not enough; in 1850, consideration had to be made for separating the gold from the earth and then getting the gold to market.

March 30, 1851: "It is astonishing how many people are coming to California. The hills are crowded with miners and prospectors, and we hear good reports everywhere. It's a queer sort of life we lead; backbreaking work all day; doing our own cooking and washing; no amusements, except a friendly game of euchre and an occasional trip to town."[3]

Chauncey Canfield, *The Diary of a Forty-Niner.*

Edwin started his search for gold with a shovel and a pan. When he wasn't washing dirt to find gold, he was involved with domestic duties. Edwin probably first lived in a canvas tent. A tent was portable and functional until Edwin decided to stay in one place for a while. A log cabin would have been a step up from a floor-less canvas covering. Miners either cut down the trees and built their own houses or bought one from another miner who was moving on, or they would take an abandoned place and make it their own. Edwin undoubtedly cooked his meals, most likely over a wood fire. He would have cut and stacked wood for a fire, hunted game for supper, and washed his clothes.

Supplies were hard to get miles from any city; some miners used Soapwort to wash their clothes. It grows wild in California - its root looks like an onion, and it works as well as commercially manufactured soap. Time to look for soap plants, cut wood, hunt for supper, or build a log cabin was at a minimum, though, because his priority was finding gold. [4]

Seeking better methods for separating the gold from gravel and dirt, miners devised a solution called a cradle. It's a "wooden box or a hollowed-out log, two sides and one end of which are closed...a sieve, usually made of a plate of sheet iron or a piece of rawhide perforated with holes about half an inch in diameter, is rested upon the sides. Some "bars" or "rifflers," which are little pieces of board from one to two inches in height, are nailed to the bottom and extend laterally across it." [5]

There are rockers like a baby's cradle on the bottom and a handle to rock it. The cradle took several men to operate, one to shovel in the dirt, while a second man poured water over the dirt and another to rock the cradle. During the process, the gold is caught in the rifflers. This method could wash far more gold-rich dirt in a day than the individual panning method.

Another invention was called the long-tom. "It consisted of three planks nine to twelve feet long, nailed together, one of which served as a bottom for this sort of a boat; one of the ends was cut in an elongated bevel, and a sheet-iron plaque pierced with fairly big holes was nailed on this bevel. This boat was set at a slope so that the iron sheet was horizontal. They threw the dirt to be washed on the open end, which was cut square, then threw water on this upper part of the boat. Water was brought to the long tom, either by a bucket, a canal, or hose. The long tom was supported from below by a sort of square wooden box with a flange all around and inclined the same direction as the boat." [6]

Better than the cradle or the long-tom was the sluice - a trough from 100 to 1000 feet long with a descent of one foot in twenty. The water rushes through, catching the gold in riffles or cleats at the bottom. The man with the rocker or cradle might wash one cubic yard in a day, with the tom maybe twice that much, with the sluice 4 yards. [7]

April 25, 1852: "It is a pity we did not know enough two years ago to wash the ground through sluices instead of rocking it. We thought when the Long Tom came in that it would never be improved upon. Now one rarely sees either rocker or tom except in dry gulches and ravines where water is scarce." [8]

Chauncey Canfield, *The Diary of a Forty-Niner*

Miners worked hard to extract the gold, then went to town and lost it all at a casino. The men getting rich were the ones running the casinos. Others provided goods and services to the miners and turned huge profits into wealth. Temporary towns had temporary shops. Entrepreneurs set up their goods in tents, and the miners paid with gold dust measured on a scale. The shop owners knew the miners did not want to go far from the claim they were working, so they brought the goods to the customer. The cost of convenience was high, and the profit made by the sellers of goods was considerable.

December 22, 1850: "Sacramento is the liveliest place I ever saw. There are over 5,000 people living there, mostly in tents and not more than a dozen wooden houses. Hundreds of people from San Francisco are coming up the river every day, and the bank is piled up with all sorts of goods and provisions for the mines. About every tent is a gambling house, and it made my head swim to see the money flying around." [9]

Chauncey Canfield, *The Diary of a Forty-Niner*

Edwin arrived at the goldfields of California in July of 1850, when mining had been underway for nearly two years. The easy gold had already been mined. Prospecting in 1850 was often like looking for a pot of gold by chasing after a leprechaun. After hearing of a hot new spot, prospectors raced to the end of a rainbow only to find that the leprechaun had arrived first, and the gold was gone or possibly had never been there. We know Edwin mined for gold and did it the hard way with a shovel, pickaxe, and pan. He started prospecting in Placerville, California and mined along the North Yuba River. Edwin must have not only done well at placer mining but was careful to keep the gold he found because he soon had enough funds to buy stock in the Randolph Hill Mining Company and bought into the Rough and Ready Ditch Co.

The documents referring to the celebrated Randolph Hill Mining Company state the primary metal mined at the Randolph Company in Nevada County was gold, and the secondary, silver, copper, and lead. In less than two years, Randolph Mine took out over $400,000 clear of all expenses, done by ground sluicing, before the hydraulic pipe came into use." [10]

February 29, 1852: "I rode over to Rough and Ready Tuesday and found a lively camp. The diggings have been rich all around it, and they have found on the ridge, near Randolph Flat, claims that have paid big. A peculiarity is the number of rich pockets that have been struck. A miner named Axtell uncovered one two weeks ago, from which he has taken out $14,000, and there have been any number that yielded from $500 to $5,000." [11]

Chauncey Canfield, *The Diary of a Forty-Niner*

From July 1850 until 1858, Edwin Winans settled in and near Rough and Ready, Nevada County, California. The township lies in the foothills with rolling knolls and gentle slopes. There are "springs of excellent water, and it is generally fairly timbered."[12] The weather in the foothills of the Sierra Nevada mountains was not too hot in the summer, and not too cold in the winter, the soil was good for growing crops, and fruit trees flourished there. The circumstances that brought Edwin to Rough and Ready proved to be profitable and as a bonus he was sure to enjoy his surroundings.

The town was named Rough and Ready in 1849 by a group of ex-soldiers who had served under General Zachary Taylor. Zachary Taylor got the nickname, "Old Rough and Ready," and the people who had served under Taylor in the military kept the name Rough and Ready for their company when the war ended. They were on a mission for gold with their leader Captain Townsend. When their company discovered gold, they decided to stay and prospect so they built some cabins, called the community Rough and Ready, and it stuck.

Word soon got out there was gold at Rough and Ready, and miners came in droves for their share. There was no law for miles, and as the town grew some kind of government was a necessity. The occupants of the town came together and appointed a committee, and their powers were almost absolute - there was no appeal. The committee did a good job until the following fall when an election was held for Justice of the Peace and Constable.[13]

The townspeople were rough, ready, and angry over what they considered a lack of justice and the passage of a new mining tax. "They voted in 1850 to secede from the union and form the Great Republic of Rough and Ready." [14] The Republic lasted less than three months when the townspeople started thinking about the Fourth of July and how much fun they had at that celebration every year. Then they realized they were no longer a part of the United States, and Independence Day for them was not July 4. The more they thought about it, the more depressed they became over no reason to celebrate. They soon got together and voted to rejoin the union - just in time to celebrate the Fourth of July. This all took place before California achieved statehood on September 9, 1850.

In the fall of 1850, the townspeople lived in clapboard houses and some in tents. The town even had a "ten-pin saloon" with a 90-foot alley. There was sufficient population to support the bowling alley, as shown by records of an election held in October of 1850, which "polled a little less than 1,000 votes."[15]

February 23, 1851: "There is another town down the ridge called Rough and Ready, and it's as lively as Nevada. They hung a man there last week for stealing. It's a queer thing how well we get along without any courts or law. Over in Nevada, the miners have elected an alcalde, but his decisions are not binding, only as they are accepted by the people. Most of the cases are mining disputes, and a miners' jury decides these...Stealing is punished by whipping and banishment.

We find that the gold streaks run into the banks and under the hills and in some places, as at Rough and Ready, on the tops of the ridges, and instead of being played out, there are more and richer diggings discovered every day. I would not be surprised if it took three or four years before it will all be worked out."[16]

Chauncey Canfield, *The Diary of a Forty-Niner*

Miners found gold in the banks of rivers, in the rivers themselves, and where rivers had previously flowed. Gold was in the dry diggings, but miners needed water to separate the gold from surrounding dirt and rocks. Some tried tossing the gold-bearing dirt in the air and letting the wind blow away the lighter material, but that method was inefficient. The miners needed water.

The ditch system of bringing water to miners worked for the miners who were glad to pay for water, and the ditch companies were happy to make their money from selling water without the speculation involved in mining gold. Between 1850 and 1858, six thousand miles of mining canals were made in California. "Where the surface of the ground furnished the proper grade, a ditch was dug in the earth; and, where it did not, flumes were built of wood, sustained in the air by a framework that sometimes rose to a height of three hundred feet in crossing deep ravines, and extending for miles at an elevation of 100-200 feet."[17]

October 20, 1850: "Anderson says it will be a good idea to extend our ditch and sell the water to the miners who might want to use it, but I don't see what right we have got to it more than anybody else. Anyway, he has put a notice at the head of the ditch claiming all the water it will hold, and as there is no law in the case, he says he will make a law out of the precedent."[18]

Chauncey Canfield, *The Diary of a Forty-Niner*

Ditch systems did not originate with gold miners. The natural climate in California varies enormously from north to south. Runoff from snow in the mountains is critical to providing water needs in the summer months. Before the Spanish arrived in the area, native tribes dug irrigation canals to ensure the growth of seasonal crops.

Water rights were critical to the success of both miners and farmers. The controversy turned into court cases. The law concerning water rights was two-fold. English common law gave the landowners bordering the waterways the exclusive and nontransferable rights to that water. In the northern part of the state, where water is abundant, those laws make a lot of sense, but in the south, a concept of appropriation is the doctrine. Appropriation comes from Spanish law. It allows the first users of the water to divert it. The first user system works for mining and farming in dry southern counties. "This dual water rights system has endured."[19]

As gold became harder to find, miners banded together to form companies. Even if miners found a good vein of gold, they required help to extract that gold or get water to dry diggings. It was difficult, if not impossible, to find laborers, so miners and ditch diggers formed companies and then worked to benefit those companies.

Miners needed lumber almost as much as water. The sawmill industry thrived in Rough and Ready because timber was plentiful. There was a need for lumber to build houses and for the miles of sluice boxes, ditches, flumes, and timbering the mines in Nevada County.

In the 1850s, the Rough and Ready Ditch traveled from Deer Creek 16 miles to the mining areas of Rough and Ready, Nevada County, California. A man named Moore initiated digging the ditch, completed one mile, and then quit. Brothers Alfred Lorenzo Williams and Benjamin Williams took over from Moore and completed the ditch to Rough and Ready. The brothers came from Michigan, where they had been successful in the fur trading business, and founded their own town, Owosso. They invested in several businesses in Michigan, including the Amboy Lansing and Traverse Bay railroads. Portions of the Rough and Ready canal are still in use today for irrigation."[20]

Selling water to miners was a hazardous occupation. Miners were tough guys. It took strength and stamina to get to the goldfields, and digging, panning, rocking, or sluicing were also not easy tasks. Miners undoubtedly had muscles - and attitude. They were paying for water to wash the dirt away, which cut their profit. They wanted every drop they felt entitled to. On the other hand, the ditch companies had to protect their water service. Every mile of The Rough and Ready Ditch had to be patrolled and protected.

As part owner of the Rough and Ready Ditch Company, Edwin was the man persuading miners to follow the rules. He patrolled the Rough and Ready Ditch for two years with only one serious confrontation. There was an argument after Edwin shut off the water to one of the miners. The miner challenged Edwin to fight or give up the water. Edwin felt he had to fight the guy because other miners were present, and he had to set an example. This was not a gentlemen's boxing match. Miners fought as they did in the old west - punching, gouging, kicking, and biting. During the fight, his opponent chewed the end of the middle finger of Edwin's right hand and left him with a deformed finger and fingernail for the rest of his life. We don't know how the other guy ended up physically, but he did it without water because Edwin won the fight. [21]

Fighting for water rights in the field and the courts was necessary for the company. In 1853, Edwin Winans and ten other men under the name Rough and Ready Water Co. sued another company for diverting the water of Squirrel Creek, to which their company held the rights. The Rough and Ready Water Co. won their case. The court issued a cease and desist order. [22]

Note: *As Edwin walked along the ditch at night, I muse that he looked up at the stars and thought about how small he was in the universe. Did he feel a special connection with his maker? He was miles from home - essentially alone in the wilderness. He wondered what his family and friends in Hamburg, Michigan were doing. The friends who started the journey with him were dead. Why was he spared? Did God have a higher purpose for him?*

Placer gold was where Edwin made his money. First, he used a shovel, a pick, and a pan to get enough gold to invest. Then he bought into the Randolph Hill Mine Co. and the Rough and Ready Ditch Company who were in the business of mining or serving those who were mining placer gold. Finally, he bought gold from the miners and sold it to the United States Mint. These endeavors were all profitable for Edwin, but near Rough and Ready, California hard rock mining was also done. Veins of gold were found in quartz rock. The gold veined quartz was mined and then the rocks were crushed to separate the gold from the quartz. There were also some stamping mills nearby, but hard rock mining was never very profitable in the area.

A Place in Time: While Edwin was busy protecting his company's water rights, other things were happening in the world. The news was slowly coming to out-of-the-way places like Rough and Ready. People along the East Coast talked about a new novel, "Uncle Tom's Cabin," by Harriet Beecher Stowe. Issues concerning slavery were dividing the nation.

Britain and France declared war on Russia, Florence Nightingale went to the Crimean War, and many needed nursing due to the Charge of the Light Brigade.[23]

Note: Edwin's financial situation improved in two short years from his beginnings in the goldfields. He likely lived in his own house, either a log cabin or a clapboard house, or maybe he lived at the Rough and Ready Hotel.

In 1853, the town of Rough and Ready consisted of clapboard houses, canvas tent dwellings, a hotel, a church, seven saloons, a Masonic Lodge, an Odd Fellows Lodge, stores, and a blacksmith shop. On June 28, 1853, a candle left too close to a canvas wall reportedly started a fire that burned most of the town. Neighboring communities helped to rebuild the town, so it was done quickly. The new Rough and Ready was better than ever, with widened streets and a more organized village. The businesses decided to locate closer together, and the buildings were bigger and better than before. They also included a school and had Miss Franklin as a teacher.[24]

Whether it was his gnarled finger or dissatisfaction with his job, Edwin decided to change his life. His next endeavor was getting into the banking business. He and a partner opened a bank in Rough and Ready. They bought gold from the miners and sold it to the mint.

Note: Success gave Edwin time to ponder; his thoughts often took him back to where he had come from. He wondered how his family was and what was happening with his friends, the Galloways. He was attracted to Sarah Galloway and hoped that now that he had established himself in business, she would consent to marry him. A trip back home was in order.

Panning for Gold is a classic portrayal of a California stampeder
who dipped and swirled until the dirt washed away and left gold.

In 1848, James Marshall found some nuggets of gold at
Sutter's Mill on the American River. Before long, the
stampede was on, and thousands rushed west in search of fortune.

Miners were in a rush to separate gold from dirt.
The panning method took too long. They invented a
rocking mechanism called a cradle or rocker, then the long tom,
and fially the sluice. The sluice was four times faster than the rocker.

THE ISTHMUS OF PANAMA

Note: In March of 1850, when Edwin traveled to the California gold-fields on the overland trail, he could have taken a ship south around the Cape of Good Hope and then north beyond the South American and Central American coasts to San Francisco. He could have gone by ship from a port in North America to Chagres, the only Atlantic Ocean port in Panama. After crossing the isthmus to the Pacific Ocean, travel to San Francisco from Panama by boat took about three weeks. The Isthmus of Panama route was the shortest in terms of time but was more costly than going overland, as Edwin and his companions chose to do. Edwin was raised on a farm and knew about horses, farm wagons, and living off the land, so he chose the mode of travel he knew the best and the least expensive. However, considering a return trip, he undoubtedly decided on the shortest route; fortunately, it was something he could now afford.

There had been an interest in expediting travel from the Atlantic to the Pacific for many years. England and France had expressed interest in a serviceable road across the isthmus, but the jungle climate, the mountainous terrain, the reptiles, insects, and resultant malaria were prohibitive. The cost of road building was budgeted in the millions, so nothing had been done. Therefore, travel across the isthmus in 1850 was much the same as it had been for as long as anyone could remember. [1]

In March of 1850, when Edwin traveled west, the trip across the isthmus was grueling, although of a shorter duration than other routes. In his book *Gold Rush: Three Years in California*, John David Borthwick described his journey across the isthmus. Borthwick and Edwin shared the same destination and traveled simultaneously, both men on a quest for gold. The journeys they chose were both arduous. [2]

51

Borthwick was from Edinburgh, Scotland, and experienced in sea travel. He traveled first to Canada in 1845 and then to New York City. Talk of gold was prevalent in New York City after President Polk mentioned the excellent prospects for finding gold in the West. Borthwick's plan to get to the goldfields as quickly as possible meant choosing the route through the Isthmus of Panama.[3]

To get passage on a ship to Chagres, Panama, a traveler had to queue up for hours the day before the tickets went on sale. The overloaded ship he sailed on from New York to Chagres no longer had sleeping cabins. All passengers had to deal with the same harsh conditions. The captain had difficulty finding a crew, so he hired two men with no experience as stewards to reduce the cost of their passage. The weather was rough, and most passengers, including the cooks, were seasick. Borthwick and those well enough to eat had to scrounge for their meals after the galley was destroyed in a storm. The sail was not pleasant, but their landing was worse. The bay was too shallow for ships to dock at Chagres, so passengers had to take small boats from the ship to land. They arrived in Chagres in a rainstorm, and by the time they got to shore with their baggage, they were as wet as if they had swum from ship to shore.[4]

From Chagres, Borthwick got a spot in an open boat, called bongoes by the natives, for travel upstream as far as the river would take them. The trip up the Chagres River against the current, in the jungle with either rain soaking them or the hot sun beating down on them, was at the least unpleasant. It took them a day and a night to reach the first stopping place. Late arrival there meant they had no supper and were happy to have breakfast before they started their journey to the second stop. The second stop was also overcrowded with gold rushers. The natives who lived along the river and provided services to travelers had not previously heard of the gold rush and were unprepared for the onslaught of travelers. The emigrants got their supper piecemeal on this second stop and spent the night under a roof with open sides, but Borthwick was grateful to have a place to sleep and be out of the rain. The third stop was Dos Hermanos, where their supper was boiled rice and coffee. Sixty or seventy travelers huddled in small, covered spaces without a place to lie down. After another day on the river, they arrived in Gorgona. The Gorgona Hotel, a large canvas dwelling, served a delightful dinner of plantains, eggs, ham, and beans. They did have the luxury of a cot, although the cots were crammed together with barely enough room to walk between them. They could have chosen to get off the river here and travel by road to Panama City, but Cruces was only seven more miles by river, and the road from Cruces to Panama City was supposed to be a much better road than the one from Gorgona to Panama City. In Cruces, they found a repeat of the canvas hotel.

Borthwick put his baggage on a mule and walked 25 miles from Cruces to Panama City. Trudging through water and mud up to his knees to Halfway House, he found a miserable little tent twelve-foot square. There was food available, but only two plates and two forks, so the travelers took turns using them to eat their beans and rice. The next day, they found the road much improved because the country was more open, and about noon, they arrived at Panama City. "The town is built on a small peninsula and is protected on the two sides facing the sea by batteries and on the land side by a high wall or moat. A large portion of the town lies outside of this."[5]

After reaching the milestone of Panama City, the travelers endurance continued to be tested. Two to three thousand emigrants lived in Panama City, waiting for passage on a ship to San Francisco. One of those waiting was Daniel Horn. In letters home, he describes: "Panama is an old Spanish town at the head of the bay of the same name; it is on a narrow tongue of land surrounded by water on three sides and has five or six thousand inhabitants. A high stone wall surrounds part of the city. The better class resides within the wall, where all business is transacted. The harbor is very poor, and vessels must anchor from one to two miles off and discharge their freight in small boats and canoes."[6]

He spent a dime for the privilege of sleeping in a broken chair outside the city wall on his first night there. After perusing the available places to stay in the city, he found most of them miserable places with no beds, lousy food, and costly. Fortunately, he found a room to rent in the best part of town. He ate at restaurants, bought food from local shops, or found it growing wild. There were lemon trees, coconut, plantain, and pineapples, among many other tropical fruits available for picking. He fished as well to supplement his diet.[7]

Daniel Horn was unsure when the ship he had booked passage on would reach Panama. The booking agent told him he might have to wait ten or fifteen days for his ship to arrive. There were thousands of immigrants in Panama City waiting for passage to California. Many had been waiting for weeks for the ship they had booked passage on to arrive. Some sold their tickets at a loss and bought tickets at an exorbitant price on a boat currently available in Panama Bay. Speculators bought tickets when the price was low and sold them for a profit of one or two hundred percent. This put the price of tickets out of the reach of most of those waiting for passage.[8]

While waiting for his ship, the Sarah Sands, Daniel took the opportunity to see and experience as much as possible. He paid a local altar boy to give him a tour of one of the cathedrals. Daniel counted at least 25 priests and was impressed with the silver there. He witnessed a Corpus Christi celebration. "All the priests were there in full dress, I saw the consecration of the wafer, which was carried through the church and city in procession. It was held up on high by an old priest who walked under a silk canopy covered with gold, which was held up by six gentlemen who, I suppose, were the grandees of the city. As they passed, all the spectators took off their hats, and some got devoutly on their knees until they passed. They paid the same homage to the wafer as should be paid to the Savior, as it is their doctrine that after consecration, it is His real body. All the time of the ceremony all the bells of the city, and they are legion, were ringing and cannon firing." [9]

There were many small shops in town, run mainly by women, but the prices were very high. Mules or boats brought imported goods into the city, increasing the cost. Not impressed with the local culture, Daniel stated: "It is the most miserable country on this hemisphere; the people are indolent, sloven; nothing showing prosperity or comfort and scarcely any of the conveniences of civilization." Men, women, and children all smoked cigars, and they all drank wine or liquors.[10]

The scenery was another matter. Mountains surrounded the city. "The tops are covered with dense, black clouds under which the deep green sides, more beautiful by the contrast, look like a splendid carpet richly ornamented. I look out on the bay, which is a most beautiful sheet of water, barren rocks rising abruptly from the water, or beautiful green islands covered to the tops with tropical fruits and vegetation."[11] Daniel loved to walk the beach and breathe the fresh air away from the stench of the city.

More people were living in Panama in 1850 than the town could support. Living conditions were less than sanitary, and there was much sickness. People died in their quest for gold before ever reaching the goldfields. Daniel witnessed some funerals while waiting for his ship to come in. As two funeral processions traversed the way to the graveyard, Daniel followed. The casket of one fell apart on being lowered into the grave, which was only about two feet deep. "Oh! How hard it seemed to die and be buried in a foreign land," said Daniel.[12]

Daniel Horn spent eight weeks, not ten or fifteen days, in Panama before selling his ticket on the Sarah Sands for one on the Columbus to speed up his travel to the goldfields. Daniel heard of an American company building a railroad across the isthmus but did not think it would ever come to much.[13]

Jonathan Borthwick and Daniel Horn depict travel across the Isthmus of Panama in 1850. While they were suffering depravities in the jungle, Edwin and his companions were suffering in the deserts of the West. However, by the time Edwin decided to return to Michigan for a visit in 1855, travel via the Isthmus of Panama had considerably changed.

In 1848, the Congress of the United States approved contracts for two steamship lines. One route was from New York or New Orleans to Chagres. The other route was from Panama to California or Oregon. The purpose was for mail delivery from one side of the continent to the other. Mr. William Aspinwall owned the line on the Pacific side, but he could not make shipping from Panama north along the West Coast profitable. Aspinwall, however, had a design in mind for the future. He wanted to build a railroad across the isthmus. The plan was to build the railroad in increments as time and labor would allow.[14]

The 1849 influx of migrants crossing the isthmus to get to the gold made the prospect of a railroad viable. Investors were willing to speculate on future earnings and made funds available. The Atlantic terminus was at Limon Bay, also called Navy Bay, and on the Pacific side, it was Panama City, but knowing the route and having the money to proceed in no way ensured success.[15]

The company owners knew the local people were not used to hard work and didn't believe they would comprise a reliable workforce. They recruited workers in Europe, Asia, South America, and the Caribbean. The project managers had to continually hire more workers due to jungle sickness, death, and desertion. After the track was down on the first thirteen miles, the route took them out of the swamp and onto the solid higher ground, making the work more manageable.

An event occurring in November 1851 drastically changed the prospects of the railroad. Chagres did not have a deep-water port; ships were forced to anchor in the bay, and passengers had to be shuttled to shore. Two steamships had arrived, and the weather was so bad some lost their lives trying to get from ship to shore. The weather forced the ships to take refuge in Navy Bay. The ships could dock there, and as passengers debarked, they learned of the railroad right there at Navy Bay with tracks available as far as Gatun. If they could get to Gatun, they could go up the Chagres River from there as usual. There were no passenger cars, but the immigrants were happy to ride to Gatun in working railroad cars. News of the ease and safety of traveling by rail from Navy Bay to Gatun was enticing to prospectors, and soon, all ships were docking at Navy Bay, and passengers were taking the train for the first part of the journey. The railroad became the chosen mode of transportation as far as it progressed. It soon passed Gatun and was at Barbacoas. The value of the railroad stock increased exponentially, and soon, the Atlantic terminus was renamed Aspinwall after one of the originators of the railroad. [16]

The railroad still had difficulty keeping workers who could work in the jungle environment. The company hired a thousand Chinese, and within months, there were barely 200 left due to disease and suicide. Some workers persevered through the death of coworkers and illness, and they reached the summit ridge by January 1854, just eleven miles from Panama City.[17]

The railroad struggled through the jungle toward their goal of Panama Bay. After the bridge was constructed at Barbacoas, it was swept away when the Chagres River rose forty feet in one night. The Chagres was not the only river to cross on their path to the Pacific. The railroad had to build more bridges. They crossed the Obispo and the Rio Grande (of Panama) before they reached the Pacific Ocean at Playa Prieta, a northern suburb of Panama City, in 1855.[18]

Even after reaching the Pacific terminus, the railroad was far from being done. They built additional sidings at each end of the road, a blacksmith shop, a long pier at the Panama terminus, and increased services to the public. It changed the time required for crossing the isthmus from days to hours.

The trip by ship from New York to Aspinwall (Navy Bay) and Panama to San Francisco also was smoother due to improvements in steamships in terms of convenience and time spent in travel.[19]

Note: Edwin's financial status had improved - he could afford the cost, and time was of the essence on this trip. He intended to return home, entice Sarah to marry him, and return to his business in California. Edwin's trip in 1855 to return to Michigan for a visit was very different from that taken by Borthwick or Horn.

To reach his own Panama experience, the first leg of Edwin's journey meant traveling west from Rough and Ready to Sacramento, California. About two miles south of Sacramento was Sutter's Fort, where in 1849, John Sutter had a thriving agricultural operation. As a part of an expansion plan, he needed lumber and sent James Marshall to build a sawmill at Coloma. The building of the mill precipitated the discovery of gold in the American River and changed the history of the United States.

The Sacramento River was a thoroughfare from Sacramento to San Francisco. The harbor at San Francisco enticed ships in the Pacific to use its beautiful natural harbor. The vessels in San Francisco's harbor brought people from around the world and returned them from where they came. Boarding a steamship at Sacramento was the quickest way to San Francisco and the Pacific and a ship to points beyond.

At the beginning of the gold rush, Sacramento consisted of a few slapped-together buildings and tents. The town was on a floodplain, and when it wasn't wiped out by a flood, it was burned down or plagued by cholera. Due to its location, the town grew, built levees, and established a fire company. The Sacramento Edwin visited in 1855 was a bustling, economically prosperous community and already the capital city of California.

San Francisco was a small community of about 200 residents before the discovery of gold a couple of miles south of Sacramento at Coloma. When the first emigrants arrived by ship and rushed as fast as possible to the goldfields, the town's residents went with them. The sailors left the vessels empty in the bay to join the quest for gold. As more arrivals paused in San Francisco to ask for directions or look for supplies, some people stopped and stayed to become suppliers of services and materials.

Soon, restaurants, hotels, shops, and warehouses were springing up all over town. "Everyone was either rich or expected soon to be so. Opportunity awaited every man at every corner. A story was told about a newcomer offering a small boy fifty cents to carry his valise to the hotel. The urchin looked with contempt at the coin, fished out two fifty-cent pieces, and handed them to the owner of the valise, saying, "Here's a dollar; carry it yourself."[20]

The city was built on a narrow strip of land between the bay and the hills. When fires destroyed the town, sand from the hills was used to extend the town into the bay and, at the same time, provide building sites not as steep, lessening the chance that the fires would jump from building to building. "This left many of the old ships, that a year ago were beached as storehouses, in a curious position; for the filled-up space that surrounds them has been built on for some distance, and new streets run between them and the sea so that the old ships become perched in the middle of a street."[21]

The storehouse ships were an odyssey, and so were the banks. "At the corner of a street is Burgoyne's Bank…crowded and full of tobacco smoke. Instead of the chinking of money, you hear a succession of thumps on the counter as the large leather bags of gold dust come down on it. Some clerks are weighing dust, some are extracting the black sand with a magnet, and others are packing it in bags and boxes. Large blocks of quartz lie about the room in all of which are rich veins of gold." [22]

The people, anxious to rebuild, put up canvas tents and slipshod buildings. After several fires, they built more substantial structures and established a fire service. As the town grew, so did the crime. The crime problem proved much more challenging to solve than the fire problem. Many saloons, casinos, and bordellos were ready to take a man's money, and no one was there to regulate the industries or punish the criminals. The conditions were ripe for corruption and graft. "Politicians voted themselves salaries of six-thousand dollars apiece as alderman."[23] The people representing law and order could be bought, adding insult to injury.

The criminal element was prevalent and included lawyers and judges. Murderers got off without punishment because their name was spelled wrong on the indictment. When citizens were pushed to the limit by the rampant crime, they decided to take matters into their own hands and formed the Vigilance Committee. Vigilantes held trials, convicted criminals, and imposed death penalties. Victims of crime began to get justice even if it was not under a legal system. The action of the Vigilance Committee "brought about a complete reform in the administration of justice."[24]

Note: *When Edwin traveled through San Francisco in 1855, the situation concerning lawlessness had much improved. Edwin was in San Francisco for one reason - to board a ship to Panama. He had no intention of staying long enough to be a witness to or a victim of any lawlessness.*

A Place in Time: *Deprived of news concerning the rest of the country, Edwin may not have been fully aware of the degree of opposing stands about slavery outside California. Unrest and division in the country over slavery had not improved - it was only getting worse. Franklin Pierce was elected president because he was considered a moderate, but his moderate views only flamed the fires of dissension.[25]*

Edwin most likely traveled by steamship from San Francisco to a port near Panama City. The SS Golden State made that trip from 1851 to 1862. The first-class passage was $250, the second class was $175, and steerage was $100. He then traveled from near Panama City on the Pacific coast to Aspinwall on the Atlantic coast, which took about 5 hours by train and cost $25.00 one way. "The railroad charged $6.00 to walk across the isthmus on the roadbed." Edwin traveled by steamship from Aspinwall to New York, possibly on the SS Cherokee or the SS Crescent City. Then, he went overland to Hamburg, Michigan.[26]

Note: *Edwin's anticipation of reuniting with friends and family was filled with joy for him because he could return with pride as a successful banker. He must have been excited thinking about the prospect of seeing his mother, his sister, and the friends he left behind - especially Sarah Galloway.*

There could not have been much correspondence with friends and family when Edwin was in the West. The journey from Rough and Ready, California, to Hamburg, Michigan, was filled with thoughts of a cheerful reunion, but instead, upon arrival, he learned the situation at home was different from the one he anticipated. First, he learned of the death of his mother. She died July 1, 1852, while Edwin was making his fortune in the goldfields of California. Instead of a joyful reunion, Edwin visited the graves of his parents in the Sprout Cemetery near Pinckney, Michigan. The poem at the bottom of Eliza Winans' headstone offers insight into the young Edwin.

When thou wurt with me, Mother,
Here on this dreary earth,
Though I did love thee dearly,
Yet I knew not half thy worth.

E. B. Winans

Edwin had returned home with high hopes but was then heartbroken by the news of his mother's death. Seeking the comfort of friends, he re-connected with people he knew best. The Galloways owned a farm near the village, and Edwin enjoyed their company. He was especially attracted to Sarah Galloway and thought about her when he lived and worked in Rough and Ready, California, where there were few women. Edwin imagined returning to Michigan, marrying Sarah, and then returning with Sarah to where he had been successful in the gold business.

When he accumulated wealth and status in Nevada County, California, he knew it was time to turn his dream into action.

Edwin thought highly of all the Galloway family but possibly had the most respect for the patriarch, George Galloway. George was an early settler of the village and was well thought of by his neighbors. He was known for his excellent judgment, and the people of Hamburg were beneficiaries of his hospitality. Edwin liked and respected him but learned, unfortunately, that George Galloway had also died in his absence the year before Edwin's return to Hamburg. George died in the prime of his life. While on a business trip to New York, he contracted cholera and died suddenly. The loss of a beloved parent was something Edwin shared with the Galloways.

Edwin didn't waste any time getting to the Galloway farm to see Sarah again and ask for her hand in marriage. Still, Sarah surprised Edwin by telling him she had no desire to go to a wild place like California, and besides, she had found a suitor while Edwin was gone, and she liked him very much. Sarah suggested that Edwin ask her sister Elizabeth if she would marry him and go off into the wilderness. Edwin was heartbroken by Sarah's rejection but then considered her suggestion.

Edwin surely courted Elizabeth, but not for long. Edwin did not have time to waste - the pragmatic Edwin had a successful business waiting for his return to California. Fortunately, Elizabeth soon said, "Yes," and they were married on September 4, 1855.

Note: *The Galloway family attended St. Stephens Episcopal Church in Hamburg, but Elizabeth and Edwin may not have been married there. The rector at St. Stephens in 1855 was Algernon Hollister, and the couple was married by Wm. M. Henne, Minister of the Gospel, and witnessed by Elizabeth's brother and mother, Stephen and Susan Galloway.*

Elizabeth Galloway Winans soon found herself on the way to Rough and Ready, California - a huge adventure for a young bride in 1855. There must have been some anxiety not knowing exactly what obstacles she would face, but she obviously had trust in Edwin, and together, they forged ahead.

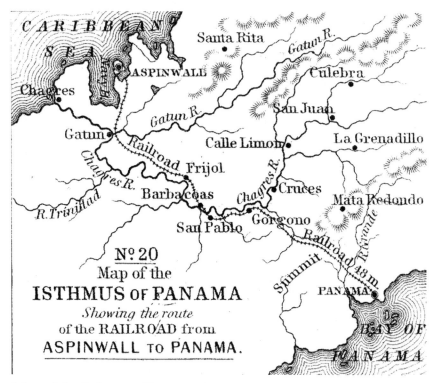

Map of the Isthmus of Panama showing the railroad from Aspinwall to Panama.

Small open boats called bongos carried people upstream from Chagres on the Atlantic Ocean as far as the river would take them to Gorgona or Cruces. Then, they walked the rest of the way to Panama City on the Pacific Ocean prior to the completion of the railroad.

During the gold rush, sailors left ships at the docks to mine for gold. At the same time, they leveled the hills of the city to reduce fires and spread dirt at the waterfront. Eventually, ships were surrounded by land.

The S.S. California was a steamship that shuttled people and goods between San Francisco and Panama City.

The marker for Eliza Winans, Edwin's mother, is
in the Sprout Cemetery near Pinckney, Michigan.

Edwin's poem at the bottom of his mother's gravestone.

Edwin and Elizabeth Winans were members of St. Stephens Church in Hamburg, Michigan. St. Stephens is the oldest operating church in the state.

Rough and Ready

Edwin had just traveled from California through the Isthmus of Panama to Michigan. He knew the reverse trip was the easiest way for them to reach California because a railroad across the continental United States was not complete. After sailing from New York to Panama, the railroad trip from Aspinwall to Panama City contributed to the relative ease of the travel across the Isthmus. Steamship travel had also improved, making their trip from Panama to California comfortable. The Sacramento River was usually an uneventful thoroughfare from San Francisco to Sacramento. The most challenging part of the journey for Edwin and Elizabeth was the last leg from Sacramento to Rough and Ready.

The newly married couple took the Telegraph Road from Sacramento to their home in Rough and Ready, most likely by horse and buggy or wagon. When Captain Townsend's company, The Rough and Ready Company, discovered gold, they "struck out through the woods on a beeline for Sacramento to procure provisions and made the first wagon tracks that became the Telegraph Road." [1] A toll company maintained a portion of the Telegraph Road leading to Rough and Ready from Sacramento. There was a steep grade where the Toll House was. Rain or snow sometimes produced so much mud it made the road impassible. "Maud Taylor Calvert told many stories of freighting and toll activities on the Rough and Ready grade. Her home was just at the top of the grade where she had an excellent view. A relay station stable was where toll road workers added horses to the freight wagons for the hill haul. After a storm, everyone in town fell to with shovels to go along and fill chuck holes that endangered the wagons. Maud remembered seeing as many as 24 horses used to make the haul." [2]

Mud hill or not the couple traveled with a load of supplies. Edwin was aware of the limitations of goods in the small town where he was taking his bride and was sure to be returning with needed provisions - some were hard to get at the little store in Rough and Ready, and of course, things cost more there. Also, Elizabeth would not have traveled across the continent unprepared to be a homemaker. She undoubtedly brought clothing and personal items as well.

Edwin had planned to return to Michigan for some time and bring back a bride. He would not have brought Elizabeth to California without a suitable place to live. The town of Rough and Ready had made improvements, and by 1855, it bragged about having the finest buildings in the mountains. The fire of 1853 burned most of the town, leaving only some buildings on the outskirts, but the town's businesspeople quickly rebuilt their businesses, bigger and better.[3] "There were buildings on each side of an oak lined street which ended at a ridge. At the end, and considerably elevated, stood an imposing church, complete with steeple and a broad flight of steps. It was dubbed Piety Hill." [4]

The culture of Rough and Ready in 1855 was struggling toward refinement. There was even talk that Rough and Ready would be the county seat. There were about 300 houses then, and many were clapboard - the town could nearly be called civilized. There was a sabbath school and a public school. "One church was headed by a hell-roaring preacher, James Dunleavy."[5] Dunleavy was sent to Oregon as a missionary but relocated to Rough and Ready in January 1850. He was not just a preacher - he owned the first whiskey shop in the settlement. Dunleavy also owned what was called a ten-pin saloon. E. W. Roberts, in his *Historical Sketch of Rough and Ready Township*, reported his attendance at the dedication of the bowling alley and that he rolled the first game on the 90-foot alley.[6]

As soon as preacher Dunleavy got enough money together, he sent for his wife, who waited in San Francisco. "Mrs. Dunleavy was the first woman to arrive in camp, and excitement stirred the crowd into meeting her at the stage and deluging her with gifts including 21 ounces of gold dust." [7]

Note: Be assured there was no crowd to meet Elizabeth and Edwin when they rolled into town. Edwin had tried to paint a rosy picture for Elizabeth because he genuinely wanted her to be happy there. Elizabeth was taking it all in as they rode into town. She couldn't help but like the tree-lined streets and the beautiful church at the top of the hill. Elizabeth was as committed to making a home in Rough and Ready as Edwin was. She was anxious to meet new friends and set up her first house. Edwin could see potential for continued success in Rough and Ready, and no such opportunities were readily available for them in Michigan.

The Women of Rough and Ready

By the time Elizabeth arrived in Rough and Ready, several enterprising young women were there to welcome her. One of those was Mary Downey, who owned the Downey House. She had arrived in Rough and Ready in 1850 and built the hotel. Her husband died on the way to the gold fields at Fort Laramie and left her to raise twelve children. Building and running a profitable hotel was the solution. The Downey House had an excellent reputation for providing the best food in the mountains.[8]

Another possible acquaintance and female friend was Mrs. Riddle. She and her husband were miners who worked in the area and called Rough and Ready home from 1850 to 1860. [9]

Julia Single was a very young girl when Elizabeth met her. Julia arrived from Boston in 1856 at the age of 10. The Single family owned a carpenter shop, and right next to the carpenter shop was the blacksmith, John Fippin. John and Julia eventually married.[10]

The early years in Rough and Ready were indeed rough and ready, but those years brought many fine people to the town. The Buffington sisters, the women of the Grant family, and, of course, the Downey girls were some of the women Elizabeth Winans undoubtedly knew.[11]

The entertainment business lured Jenny Moore to Rough and Ready. She arrived to amuse the population as part of a circus. It was rumored that she brought Lotta Crabtree to Rough and Ready. Lotta, who started her career dancing and singing at Flippin's Blacksmith Shop at the age of seven, became a world-famous actress.[12] Crabtree grew up in California. She met Lola Montez, who taught her how to dance, at a mining camp in Grass Valley. Miners applauded Lotta's abilities which encouraged her to enhance her dancing and singing skills. She was soon a popular entertainer in both the United States and abroad. "For thirty-five years, Lotta was the perennial little pet of the Western theater, and when she retired at forty-four, she still wore her red curls. When Lotta died in 1924, she left behind a four-million-dollar fortune that went to charity."[13]

A Place in Time: *In 1854, in Jackson, Michigan, the Republican Party was formed by individuals who opposed slavery and the Kansas-Nebraska Act. A virtual civil war happened in Kansas between pro and anti-slavery forces.*[14]

Slavery was a hot topic in the United States in the years leading up to the Civil War, and although California came into the union as a free state, there was no enforcement of the law. Colonel William English brought fifty or more enslaved people to Rough and Ready to provide workers for a mine in the Randolph Flat owned by him and two associates - Able and Porter. One of the slaves with the colonel was Caroline Allen. She "came around the horn in a sailing ship in the late 1850s." The Colonel was killed in a robbery. After his death, the people he had enslaved gradually drifted away from Rough and Ready. Caroline stayed long enough to make a reputation for herself. She liked to drink at the saloon in the hotel because she got her drinks for free. On one of her trips to the saloon, she tied her pony to the hitching rail at the blacksmith shop across the street from the hotel. It was a wet day early in 1851 when she shoved a cottonwood switch into the ground near the hitching post. The switch rooted and grew into a giant tree. It later became known as the Slave Girl Tree.[16]

The Men of Rough and Ready

One of John Fippin's relatives, Asa Fippin, was a well-known character in Rough and Ready. One day, He was looking for the family cow and noticed an unusual rock. When he picked it up, he noticed it was heavy for its size. It assayed at over $1200 - a lot of money then. Asa is credited with another story about Reverend Dunleavy. "The Reverend had just completed prayers over a fresh grave, and when he lifted his eyes, all the mourners were out staking claims. They had found nuggets in the newly dug earth." [17] Asa said, "It was a different kind of life in Rough and Ready in the early days. One day a mortally injured miner was brought into the saloon and made as comfortable as possible on the pool table, then the good old boys took bets on when he would die."[18]

Although Rough and Ready was not a hub of culture, it was "the hub of transportation into the northern mines and had a climate ideal for growing food for the hordes of miners."[19] The climate was delightful. It was mild in both summer and winter. It didn't get too hot in the summer, and there was always a pleasant breeze from the south in the middle of the day. There were no extreme temperature changes in the winter or wet season. There was occasional snow, but it rarely stayed on the ground for more than a day. The rich soil produced fruit trees such as apples, peaches, plums, cherries, nectarines, figs, almonds, oranges, and pomegranates.[20] Both Edwin and Elizabeth grew up on farms. It stretches the imagination to think they did not grow some of their food when the cost of fresh fruits and vegetables were prohibitive. The location and the climate made it easy to grow your own. Even if Edwin and Elizabeth only had a garden for their own needs, they shared what they grew with friends and probably bartered what they grew for other goods and services.

Whether working as a farmer or a banker, Edwin was a leader wherever he went. He only remained a prospector and miner as long as it took him to accumulate enough wealth to buy into some successful endeavors, such as the Rough and Ready Ditch Company and the Randolph Hill Mine. Those endeavors were as successful as his prospecting and mining, leading him to open a bank where he continued building on his wealth.

The Searls Library in Nevada City, California, reports that E.B. Winans was the Rough and Ready delegate to the Democratic County Convention in 1856. More locally, he was secretary in a meeting at Rough and Ready called to close businesses on the Sabbath Day after

71

June 7, 1856. In 1856, Edwin operated the Pacific Express on Main Street in Rough and Ready, where he provided not only banking services but facilitated shipments of specie and bullion as well as mail services.[21] Edwin Winans was fully involved in his community's business. He took a leadership role and stepped in wherever he was called. He is also listed as operating the Post Office in Rough and Ready.[22]

In 1848, the mail was delivered by James Birch, who came by mule from Sacramento. By 1850, Mr. Birch was driving an express wagon, or sometimes a stage for Bowers Brothers Express Line, regularly over his route. By 1851, Wells Fargo began running freight, mail, and passengers. Though there were many express companies, they were eventually almost all part of the Wells Fargo system.[23]

Days in Rough and Ready were good ones for Elizabeth and Edwin. The Winans had status in the community - revered as the banker and his wife. The people of Rough and Ready took care of each other - it was a small community, and the townspeople there were friends, and some were more than friends they were like family. There was often excitement in the town when someone made good on their claim. There were gatherings with food and fun activities, and even though Rough and Ready was far from any big city, there was sometimes top-notch entertainment in town, such as the singing and dancing of Lotta Crabtree.

Note: *Edwin also came home with another treasure - a prestigious walking stick made of redwood and topped with a gold setting holding a quartz nugget with a veining of gold. There is no extant evidence to establish Edwin obtained the walking stick in California, but using Occam's Razor principle it is the simplest explanation. The materials are obviously from the area in which he lived, the gold quartz mined in the Rough and Ready neighborhood, and the redwood from nearby forests. There was also a stamping mill near Rough and Ready where they crushed quartz to remove the gold. A handsome piece of quartz veined with gold was as highly valued then as it is now. It's easy to visualize him walking the streets of Rough and Ready as the town's banker using the extraordinary walking aid and status symbol.*

Their journey home with baby George and all their gold was the reverse of the one that brought them from Michigan to the Wild West.

It took them first from Rough and Ready by wagon to Sacramento. From Sacramento by steamship downriver to San Francisco, where they boarded an ocean vessel for travel to Panama. They may have had an overnight in San Francisco or Panama City depending on when they arrived and the transport schedules. By the time the Winans made this trip accommodations were more improved than they had been in 1855. Once on the train in Panama, it was only hours, not days, to Aspinwall on the other side of the Isthmus. Another steamship from there went to New York City. They were relieved once they arrived in New York because they could deposit their money in a bank for safekeeping. From New York City, the Winans could have gone by train part of the distance to Hamburg and the remaining probably by coach. Their friends and family easily knew of their imminent arrival via telegraph message. The family in Hamburg couldn't wait to see baby George; Edwin and Elizabeth, at the same time, were anticipating a happy reunion with family.

Note: *Edwin thought about what he would do to support his family after they got back to Michigan. He knew how to farm, and he had enough money to buy a farm, but would farming be enough for him after being the town banker, and a respected leader in his community?*

Old Rough and Ready Hotel. Edwin would have been
familiar with the hotel as it operated when he lived there.

Fippin's Blacksmith Shop and the Slave Girl Tree.
The building of Fippin's still exists in Rough and Ready. The story
about how the tree originated is still told, but the tree itself is gone.

The town of Rough and Ready in 1857.

HAMBURG

At their homecoming, Edwin, Elizabeth, and George settled in with the Galloways at their farm on Pleasant Lake while they made plans for their future. Before many decisions were made Fred Galloway and George Royce talked Edwin into helping them in what they hoped would be a profitable business venture. They planned to ship a load of merchandise to St. Joseph, Missouri. The cohort then planned to travel to meet their inventory in St. Joseph; their tactics included the purchase of wagons and teams to transport the merchandise to the silver and gold fields in Idaho. They knew the goods were in demand there, and they would not have any difficulty selling the merchandise, wagons, and teams at a profit and then returning richer to Michigan. Edwin's experience traveling the overland trail and living in the West made him a valuable partner in their endeavor. They persuaded him to go, and Edwin was soon back on the road to the West.

Their trip from Hamburg to St. Joseph was uneventful. They bought wagons and teams of oxen, loaded their merchandise, and started their journey across Nebraska and Wyoming to their destination of Idaho. Everything went according to plan, and they moved along the trail with only some minor annoyance from the natives. The extra oxbows carried on the back of the wagons were items much desired by Native Americans living along the trail. The oxbows were made of hickory and were great for making bows for shooting. The natives would take any opportunity to steal an oxbow, so the entrepreneurs had to guard them. One day Edwin came across a native about to run off with an oxbow and was able to retrieve the oxbow only after a sustained wrestling match with him.[1]

The trio sold their goods, wagons, and oxen in Idaho and started back home via stagecoach. Although stagecoach travel was better than driving a wagon pulled by oxen, it was still dangerous because the Wild West was full of bandits and some hostile natives. All three of the men were armed. Edwin carried a loaded shotgun. He loaded it with buckshot and reportedly said, "The man that gets that will get _____." [2] They did not encounter robbers or hostile natives, but the stagecoach hit a rough spot in the road and overturned. Edwin was thrown off the stagecoach, his gun discharged, and gave him what he had planned for an outlaw. He was seriously wounded in his right breast and arm. They were far from any medical help. It took them five days to reach Salt Lake City, where he received medical treatment. Only after spending a few weeks in Salt Lake City was he well enough to return home.

When Edwin returned to Hamburg, Michigan, he had to spend some additional time recovering fully from his injury. Recovery gave him time to search for some farmland. Edwin purchased 106 acres in 1859, and the assumption may be made that is where Edwin and Elizabeth lived until they bought the Galloway farm and built their house on Pleasant Lake - later named Winans Lake. In March of 1866, Edwin purchased the 400-acre Galloway farm from his brother-in-law, Stephen Galloway. The bill of sale, recorded by the State of Michigan, shows Edwin paid $6,900 for the farm. Elizabeth must have been delighted with purchasing the home and land where she grew up. Edwin and Elizabeth knew the farming business well and had the hardiness to make a success out of it.

Farming in 1866 meant hard manual labor. Edwin plowed the earth with a horse-drawn steel plow, an improvement over a wooden plow but still a labor-intensive activity. The farming industry was continually changing at the time with each invention. The straddle-row cultivator, patented in 1856, was a significant time and labor-saving device. It meant a farmer could cultivate on either side of a row of plants to eliminate weeds and soften the soil rather than hand-hoeing down each row of plants. Edwin would have availed himself of a cultivator or other machines as finances allowed because these things facilitated the farmer's ability to produce more with less time and effort. A farmer's most important asset, however, was their work ethic. Hard work and common sense led to Edwin's success in the goldfields, banking, and farming.[3]

There was hired help on the Winans farm in 1860, as evidenced by census records. It shows Edwin Winans, a farmer, Elizabeth Winans, George G, Juliette Kelly, and John Seese. The census shows John Seese as a farm laborer at the Winans farm. Juliette Kelly was possibly household help.[4]

A 400-acre farm required hours of work - more than Edwin could do by himself. In addition to John Seese as a laborer, Edwin probably also used local help on the farm. But Elizabeth also needed some help keeping house because she did not have the modern conveniences taken for granted today. She may have had a washing machine, but one without a motor. Some wooden barrel washers worked by turning a crank, but someone had to carry the water for everything from washing clothes to bathing.

Edwin liked farming; it was what he knew best, and even though he involved himself in many different vocations, he always had the farm to return to. Years of outdoor work gave Edwin a powerfully built physique. He prided himself on outworking hired help on the farm, pitching more hay and cutting more corn than anyone. "One over-exertion, however, brought a severe penalty. Passing where two of his neighbors were trying to roll a huge stone out of the roadway, he made fun of their clumsiness and offered to do it alone. He did it, but his right eye was so strained in the exertion that it had to be removed, though few people ever suspected that he wore a glass eye."[5]

Note: *There are few photographs of Edwin, but with the knowledge he had a glass eye, it is noticeable in some of them.*

Edwin reported the status of his farm to Livingston County in 1879. He reported 400 acres worth $16,000.00. He had farm equipment worth $500.00 and paid wages of $450.00 that year. The value of his livestock was $2800.00. He also reported in bushels his crops of winter wheat, Indian corn, oats, barley, and buckwheat. He ran a substantial farm worth more and more productive than many farms in the area.

Those were busy days. Both Edwin and Elizabeth worked hard to make the farm a success. Early in 1869, they knew they would have another child. His second son, Edwin Baruch Winans, Jr., was born on October 31, 1869. A new house was needed to accommodate another child, friends, and family. Edwin built the house on a bank overlooking Pleasant Lake (Winans Lake) across the street from the farm in Hamburg, Michigan. (The farm is now Lakelands Golf and Country Club) He hauled all the lumber required for the home from Flint, Michigan, 40 miles away, and built the house they would live in for the rest of their lives.[6]

Edwin's Early Days

Returning to Michigan and operating a farm was a natural thing for Edwin to do. As a young boy, Edwin lived on the farm with his parents in Unadilla, Michigan, before moving to Hamburg to attend elementary school. He lived in town with his half-sister, Nancy, and her husband, Leland Walker, while going to school. Nancy was just 16 years old when her father, stepmother, and half-brother moved to Unadilla from Avon, New York, in 1834. She moved with them - she married Leland Walker four years later in Hamburg. Another sister who probably also moved with the family, Harriet, married Gabriel Morehouse in Michigan five years after the move.

Note: *Edwin attended the Bennett Schoolhouse in District No. 2, and Horace Griffith was his teacher. "Griffith was a married man, and lived on the farm now owned by Orville Sexton, in the same school district."* [7]

Edwin admired his brother-in-law, Leland Walker. He said, "Leland Walker, the owner of the saw and flowering mills of North Hamburg, was a man who filled a large space in society; a man of acute mental power, he had much to do in shaping matters of public interest. For many years he was supervisor of the town and took a strong interest in all educational matters; late in life he took an interest in the study of medicine, and having graduated from a medical school, he removed to Dexter to practice his profession, but soon after died suddenly of heart disease. His death was a serious loss to the community." [8] Edwin, mentored by Leland, learned much and was influenced by this model of manhood.

The family was essential to Edwin. He came from a family who supported and cared for each other. Edwin Baruch Winans was the 8th child of John Winans and the only child of Eliza Way Winans. He was born on May 16, 1826, in Avon, New York. Edwin had six half-sisters and one half-brother. Chronologically, they were Mary, Louisa, Esther, Harriet, Theron, Emily, and Nancy. Their mother was Mary Betsy Bates Winans, who died in 1818. [9]

When John Winans died in 1842, Edwin had to get a job to support himself and his mother. He was just 16 years old when he began working for Seth Pettys. Mr. Pettys owned a woolen mill. Mr. Pettys paid Edwin ten dollars a month plus room and board. A year later, he moved into a log cabin with his widowed mother, and Pettys paid him an additional four dollars a month in place of the room and board. He worked for Mr. Pettys from 1842 to 1846 and completed his contract. Mr. Pettys owned and operated machinery for wool carding and cloth dressing. "Many a sack of wool I carded for the wives and daughters of this county, to spin and weave into cloth for men and women's wear, and many yards of flannel I have dyed and pressed for dresses, fulled and dressed for suits for the boys to go courting in. I took special care to have the cards clean to make the rolls for the girls of my acquaintance to spin because if they were knotty and did not run free, I was sure to hear from them in such a way as was not at all flattering to my vanity." [10]

The area around the mill became known as Pettysville. It is within walking distance of Pleasant Lake and the Galloway Farm, which later became the Winans Farm. Pettys extended and improved his business, and a little hamlet grew up around the mill to include a grist and flouring mill, a blacksmith, a carriage shop, two stores, a post office, a shoe shop, a school, and a church for the fifteen or twenty families who lived there.

Hamburg was a nascent, growing community when Edwin first lived there with his sister. He knew Ferdinand Grisson, one of the four brothers who came from Germany and had influence enough to name the town after Hamburg, Germany, a town they had memories of from their youth. Edwin said, "Mr. Grisson was the postmaster and justice of the peace. He makes himself so generally useful that, though a strong partisan and his party in the minority in our town, he can always be elected by a large majority. That is the kind of man he is. May he live a thousand years and his shadow never grow less."[11] Joyce DeWolf Terry states, "They (the Grissons) were the most versatile businessmen in town at that time. They purchased the Hammond & Gay sawmill, built and ran the first store, erected the hotel, and had the grist mill built." [12]

The hotel, Hamburg House, was built by George Grisson in 1835. It was built into a hill in Hamburg, and its two-story size was impressive. It was a place where a young girl could secure good, honest work. The guests the young women served came from places like Detroit and Toledo. Joyce DeWolf Terry reports there was even a barber shop in the hotel. The hotel changed hands several times after 1835.

Another acquaintance of Edwin's when he was growing up in Hamburg was Justus Bennett. Mr. Bennett owned a story-and-a-half farmhouse with a wing on each side that seemed to Edwin to be a mansion. The house was known as the Big White House. Edwin attended a party at the house and was impressed by the many rooms, nooks, angles, and corners of the house. Edwin's experience of home was very different than those of the Bennett's. Edwin's parents lived in a one-room log house in Unadilla. Edwin, when at home with them, slept in the corner of the cabin. It was a one-room cabin with no ceiling boards - it was open to the roof. Edwin could lay in his bed and listen to the sound of the rain hitting the roof or the birds chirping without the muffling of any insulation or flooring above him.

Another significant pioneer family was the Halls. "My first impressions were that Hamburg people were mostly Bennetts, Cases, and Halls, and it seemed to me in about equal proportions, and some of the Halls struck me as being very beautiful and attractive. Of course, I was young and my experience very limited; but though many years and some travel have enlarged my experience, I still shall insist that the elegantly furnished Halls of today have not the fascination and attraction or charm for me as had those young and beautiful Hall girls of Hamburg, in those days of my early manhood." Edwin said that Jesse Hall was wealthy for a pioneer, and "being of a social, hospitable disposition, many of the early settlers made his house their home till they had time to build a house of their own." Elizabeth's parents, the Galloway family, lived with the Halls until they built their house on Pleasant Lake, which Edwin and Elizabeth later purchased.[13]

Adjoining the Galloway farm lived Col. Edward Bishop, sheriff of the county. Edwin remembered, "The colonel was a man of remarkable memory and with the faculty of relating the events of his life. He could make a story as interesting as an Arabian Nights tale, and I have often been a delighted listener as he narrated the many incidents of his varied life. He was a wagon-maker by trade. I well remember the sign nailed to a tree in the woods at the forks of the road as you came west from Hamburg village, "E. Bishop & Son, Wagon Makers."[14]

Note: *It is probable that the wagon Edwin and friends took west on the overland trail and then again on the Idaho trip was a Bishop & Sons wagon.*

Then, there was George Mercer and his family. Edwin describes George as "a cultured English gentleman better fitted by birth and education to walk in more cultivated walks of life than to be a pioneer. For years, he was the bookkeeper and confidential clerk of William Maynard of Ann Arbor, but his family continued to farm. Mercer's accomplishments and qualifications were useful in building up and developing this county." [15]

Edwin says that the history of Hamburg would not be complete without a mention of Thomas J. Rice. He was "well versed in literature and history, and is himself an author; but modest, retiring, and unassuming, he hides his light in his study on the banks of Silver Lake, and unless he is dug out by his admiring friends he prefers to remain in retirement."

Note: *After making this comment about Thomas Rice, Edwin quoted Thomas Gray's* **Elegy Written in a Country Churchyard**:

"Full many a gem of purest ray serene,

The dark, unfathomed caves of ocean bear."

I find it interesting that in a presentation to the Livingston County Pioneer Society Edwin offered some poetry. The farmer, Hamburg Township Supervisor, and Probate Judge is a man who appreciates poetry.[16]

Edwin completed school in Hamburg and worked as a teacher in District 8. He taught school in 1846 and 1847. Edwin said he had 20 children from the Bishop, Galloway, Hendrick, and John Bennett families. When Edwin taught school, he lived with George Butler and his wife. Edwin states, "They made their home so pleasant for me that in my memory, the hospitality dispensed in the log houses of those days is not surpassed in the sumptuously furnished housed of these later times."[17]

In her book Memories, Joyce Terry shares a story about the Pettysville Store, aka Wiggin's. I easily placed Edwin and Elizabeth at a party like the one described because their farm was only a short distance from Pettysville. "Once inside the little store, the warmth of the pot-bellied stove soon made everyone shed about half their warm, wool clothing. Lanterns flickered and swayed above heads, and the big grey coffee pot set out an aroma that smelled of community fellowship. Abe and Pearl Haines were usually the first to arrive, for they were the entertainers and proud parents of one of the largest families. Pearl, quiet and almost silent as a conversationalist, could surely drum up a musical conversation when playing chords on the organ. Her hands would fly, keeping up an unbelievable pace. The tempo of every piece put the stiffest joint in a mood for dancing, and those no longer able would keep time in some fashion. It was contagious. She was accompanied by her husband Abe, who played the fiddle equally as well as Pearl did the organ. The one thing that Abe loved next to his wife and family was the fiddle. He'd don that perpetual smile, start the tempo with his foot, and the dance would be on its way. He'd swing in time, and Pearl would chord to his rhythm.

Square dance would be more popular than the waltz or the two-step. The sideline viewers could feel the floor almost rock-like an ocean liner as the seasoned boards vibrated and echoed the constant movement. There were always a few sets with the small fry or grandparents. Grandpa Burton was the best caller of all, but his little grandson of six could call equally as well when Grandpa needed a rest.

Around midnight or one a.m., lunch would be served. This was furnished by all who came. Sandwiches and cakes were of every description and flavor; there was plenty of everything. The young ones were never told it was bedtime but were allowed to stay up as long as they wished or were able. One by one, they would tire out, and with stomachs filled and energy spent, they would burrow themselves deep into the warm coats like hibernating bears. Moms, dads, big sisters, and brothers, along with grandparents, frolicked until they would see the streaks of a grey dawn. Someone would sadly announce, "It's getting light outside. Guess it's time to go home and feed the horses." [18]

Life in Hamburg was idyllic in those days, and the pastoral setting was one to admire, but the aesthetics were only one aspect - the rich culture and tightly knit community formed the bond that made it great. Edwin Winans' morals and goals evolved from the people he knew and admired in and near Hamburg, Michigan, people like his brother-in-law, Leland Walker, who "shaped matters of public interest," or one of the founders of Hamburg, Ferdinand Grisson, who "made himself useful and provided good honest work" for others. Seth Pettys taught Edwin the importance of commitment and perseverance. George Mercer was an example of building up and developing a community. Jesse Hall made an impression on the young Edwin of the importance of being hospitable - making his home a home for others. Thomas Rice was a model of a modest, unassuming person who left a mark on the community. When asked to talk about the history of Livingston County, these were the men Edwin chose to highlight.

Note: *Edwin risked his life searching for gold but stood up to the dangers in the Wild West to return home and make a name for himself. There was no doubt that he loved the farm, but Edwin had a need the farm did not fulfill. He was enticed by the controversies involving slavery and states' rights. There was a lot going on in politics in 1860, and Edwin wanted to be a part of it – even if it put him on the wrong side of the new president – Abraham Lincoln!*

Edwin's first job was at Pettys' Mill. Edwin carded
wool for Pettys to support his widowed mother.

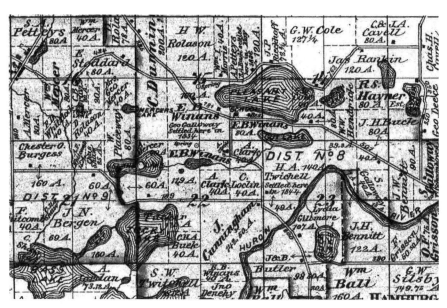

Map of the Winans farm on Pleasant Lake, later named Winans Lake.

Edwin purchased some land in Livingston County
on August 18, 1859. He purchased this piece of land
before he bought the farm from Elizabeth's brother.

Record of the purchase of the Galloway farm in 1866
from Stephen Galloway by Edwin Winans for $6,900.
Edwin and Elizabeth lived there the rest of their lives.

THE MICHIGAN LEGISLATURE AND
THE CIVIL WAR

E dwin was happy to return from California to his roots in Hamburg, Michigan, where he had many friends. Gold mining had vastly improved his financial status, and he could afford to purchase a farm he had admired for many years, the Galloway Farm. The purchase of the farm solidified his standing in the rural community. Still, the gentleman farmer had interests beyond the farm.

In 1860, when Abraham Lincoln was elected President of the United States, Edwin Winans was elected a Democrat to the Michigan Legislature.[1] The issue of slavery was a hot-button issue - there were anti-slavery societies, and the Underground Railroad was active in Michigan. An outcome of the anti-slavery movement in Michigan was the birth of the Republican Party in 1854. Citizens unsatisfied with the Democrats or the Whigs gathered in Jackson, Michigan, and rallied forces for a party supporting anti-slavery and some economic issues.[2] Edwin, as a Democrat, was also anti-slavery and he was also anti-war.

The people of the State of Michigan voted to elect Republican Abraham Lincoln with 57.23% of the popular vote, and when South Carolina confederate troops, on April 12, 1861, fired on the arsenal at Fort Sumter, Michigan readily supported the Union cause. They sent the first regiment from the western states to the District of Columbia. Lincoln reportedly exclaimed, "Thank God for Michigan!"[3] Edwin wished that cooler heads had prevailed because he thought there should be a solution short of war.

During Edwin Winans' time in the state legislature, the eminent issues were connected to war. Edwin's interest was in preserving the Union and saving lives, but Edwin was also engaged in what was happening with agriculture and the economy. At the beginning of the war, George Copway, a Methodist minister and Chippewa, proposed a regiment of Great Lakes Native Americans to serve in the war. The Michigan legislature dismissed his idea, but as the war dragged on, there was a federally imposed draft and quotas to be filled by each state. Thousands of Michiganders were already killed in the conflict, causing the state to reconsider and accept the native volunteers. Known as Company K of the 1st Michigan Sharpshooters, the natives fought valiantly. Antoine Scott was recommended twice for the Medal of Honor; Sergeant Thomas Kechittigo was known as the fighter "Big Tom." Garrett Graveraet and Garrett's father, Henry Graveraet, both gave their lives in the war. Company K fought at the Battle of the Wilderness and the Battle of Spotsylvania Court House. Many of them were captured and suffered at the famous Andersonville Prison. Including Company K, over 90,000 Michigan men fought in the Civil War.[4] Edwin believed these sacrifices could have been avoided.

Edwin, the Democrat, neither agreed with the Republican platform nor did he vote for Abraham Lincoln. After the election there were more differences of opinion. He thought Abraham Lincoln was a tyrant. This assignation resulted from Lincoln setting aside the rights given to Americans under a writ of habeas corpus. Newspaper articles informed the public that authorities arrested a Maryland man for attempting to hinder Union troops, and they held him at Fort McHenry. His attorney filed a writ of habeas corpus so he could come before a judge to have the charges against him examined. The government refused the writ, and he was kept in jail without trial.[5] Some of these cases came to the public's attention, but many more did not. Edwin thoroughly disagreed with imprisoning a man without giving him an opportunity to prove his innocence.

He also thought President Lincoln had no authority to issue the Emancipation Proclamation because he believed it unconstitutional. "As president, Lincoln could issue no such declaration; as commander in chief of the armies and navies of the United States, he could issue directions only as to the territory within his lines; but the Emancipation Proclamation applied only to territory outside his lines."[6] It was a declaration of freedom taking effect only as the military advanced. In addition, the proclamation didn't free all the slaves. It only applied to the slaves in the Confederacy "and not to those in the border states that remained loyal to the Union."[7]

Note: *Edwin never ran on being antislavery, but he certainly was against slavery in any form. Although what resulted from the Emancipation Proclamation was good, the eventual end of slavery, there were obvious reasons to disagree with the original document.*

Edwin was generally against the war because he thought the government should have negotiated a solution. "Many Democrats were concerned by the perceived threats to civil liberties, especially the revocation of habeas corpus, the use of military tribunals, and the shuttering of opposition newspapers."[8] Some called Edwin a Copperhead, a derogative name referring to "the snake that strikes without warning." The Copperheads were also called Peace Democrats because they wanted to end the bloodshed.[9] Some viewed Edwin as disloyal to the Union due to his negative votes on war legislation. Criticized about his position, he did not waver. Once he made up his mind, grounded in morals, he took the insults and held his ground.

Note: *The election of 1864 must have presented a difficult choice for Edwin. He was a Peace Democrat and wanted a reconciliation with the Confederacy. Abraham Lincoln also wanted a peaceful end to the hostilities. However, the Democratic candidate for president was George McClellan, a War Democrat, who wanted a hard line taken in the south. I'm pretty sure Edwin still would vote with the Democrats. He set that example when he backed Cleveland even though he did not agree with his monetary policy. He was a Democrat and that was that.*

Edwin wasn't the only Winans against the Civil War. Edwin's cousin, Ross Winans, was jailed for his anti-war stand - twice. Ross was on the secessionists' side and a solid states rights advocate. His opposition was noticeable because he was also a member of the Maryland legislature. He was arrested on May 14, 1861, while returning from a special session of the legislature in Frederick, where they considered but rejected secession. Lincoln's suspension of habeas corpus was employed, but the authorities released Ross through the efforts of others in the Maryland legislature.[10]

According to the census, Ross was wealthy; his worth was 300K, which would make him a multi-millionaire in today's economy. He was an inventor and owned a machine shop in Baltimore, Maryland. He built steam engines and did a lot of work for the railroads. His most famous engine was called the camelback locomotive. He also invented an unusual spindle-shaped boat, built in two sections, with a midship propeller powered by steam engines. These bizarre ships were known as cigar ships.[11] Major General Wool sent a message to Edwin Stanton, Secretary of War, on May 14, 1862, suggesting Ross Winans' iron steamer could be useful in the war. "It is the shape of a cigar and runs very fast. She would … into the Merrimack or any other vessels. She is at Baltimore."[12]

Note: *The Merrimack was a steamship salvaged by the Confederates and rechristened the Virginia. They armored her hull with iron, and she "virtually decimated a fleet of wooden warships." There were subsequent engagements against the Union ship the Monitor, but the battles were not decisive.[13]*

According to the American of April 23, 1891, "The works of the Misters Winans, the entire force is engaged in the making of pikes, and in casting balls of every description." Along with the stockpile of ammunition, there was also a steam gun. This steam gun had been invented, but not by Ross Winans, and brought to Baltimore for the defense of the city. The gun owners brought it to Ross Winans' machine shop, and the rumor mill added it to Ross's accomplishments. The gun looked impressive but eventually had no military impact.[14]

Ross and Edwin were cousins - their great-great-grandfathers were brothers, but there is no evidence to substantiate they had any personal contact with each other. However, Edwin was a Michigan legislator knowledgeable about current events right when Ross made such a splash in the news of the day as a Maryland legislator jailed for being a Southern sympathizer. Edwin, indeed, was aware of that incident.

Note: *At the onset of the Civil War, the abolition of slavery was not a goal of the war. The goal was the preservation of the Union. But as the* *war progressed, enslaved people headed by thousands to Union lines as the troops marched south, making emancipation a political and military necessity. Black people enlisted in the Union Army in large numbers. Three days before he died, Lincoln proposed that some black people, such as those who had enlisted in the military, deserved the right to vote.[15] Our view of right and wrong and our sensibilities have changed over time – but most will acknowledge Lincoln was a man with good intentions who did great things.*

Edwin Winans was no longer in the legislature at the end of the war when John Wilkes Booth shot Abraham Lincoln at Ford's Theatre. Such news would have been the talk of Hamburg, Michigan, and at the Winans farm. The Winans would have followed the newspaper articles on the escape and then the capture and killing of the assassin. There was much talk about whether the person hiding in the barn at a farm in Virginia and subsequently killed was John Wilkes Booth, but there is no evidence to support such rumors.[16]

As a legislator, Edwin Winans was most interested in issues surrounding the small farms of Michigan. Farming was a significant part of the 1860s economy, and much of the population were farmers. Wheat was an important crop, but Michigan farmers also produced fruit. Apples and peaches grew well along the shores of Lake Michigan; sugar beets and mint were also cash crops. Celery was grown in the marshes near Kalamazoo and Newberry in the Upper Peninsula. Kellogg and Post promoted cereal products in Battle Creek. Michigan State University required students to work on the school's farms as part of the curriculum and contribute to farming and agricultural research.[17]

Lumbering was a large-scale industry in Michigan. "The total worth of Michigan's forests far exceeded the value derived from the famed gold rush of California."[18] The harvesting of timber in Michigan led the nation and had a lasting influence on many communities. Edwin Winans likely knew Perry Hannah, a lumber baron and founder of Traverse City, Michigan, who was predominant in the lumber industry, as they were both involved in politics.[19] Perry Hannah left Chicago to come to Traverse City in 1851 with his partner Tracy Lay. They purchased land and a sawmill from Harry Boardman. They expanded the operation and shipped lumber down Lake Michigan to Chicago as much and as fast as they could. Tracy Lay eventually returned to Chicago, but Perry Hannah stayed to found the town and preserve a legacy.[20]

The Upper Peninsula mines of Michigan produced copper and iron ore in abundance. The state's natural resources boosted the economy, but the state needed human resources to operate the farms, mines, and other industries. Fortunately, immigrants from Germany and the Netherlands wanted to migrate due to poor economic conditions in their homeland. "Cornish miners, Finns, Swedes, Norwegians, and Italians provided the human labor necessary to support the mining and lumbering enterprises."[21]

A Place in Time: *In 1862, James Vernor, a pharmacist, was trying to create a new beverage when he left to fight in the Civil War. When he returned four years later, the drink he had stored in an oak case had acquired a delicious gingery flavor. The first soda pop made in the United States, Vernor's Ginger Ale, was created by accident in Detroit in 1866.[22]*

In the early 1870s, after leaving the state legislature, Edwin focused on his farm, family, and neighbors. He ran for the office of Hamburg Township Supervisor and was elected twice even though he was a Democrat, and most of his friends were of a different party. He also belonged to the Masonic Temple and the Episcopal Church in Hamburg.

As if running a farm was not enough, Edwin was elected one of one hundred delegates to the Michigan Constitutional Convention in 1866.[23] The convention met from May 1867 to August 22 that year, but all their work was for naught because the voters rejected the proposed changes in April 1868. One of the reasons the voters rejected the convention's modifications was the salary increases for state officers and circuit judges. Another reason voters gave for rejection was the clause allowing equal suffrage for white and black voters. Interestingly enough, equal suffrage was adopted not long after as an amendment to both the Federal and Michigan constitutions.[24]

While helping to write changes in the state's constitution, he was also a member of the Livingston County Fire Insurance Company and became their president in 1873. His continued interest in the farming community led to his membership in the Livingston County Agricultural Society; he was elected president in 1874. It is evident that others saw Edwin as a leader in a variety of roles and organizations.[25]

Edwin was busy running a farm and contributing to the local society, but he desired more. Spurred on to greater heights, Edwin decided to run for Probate Judge. He was surprised when he won the election because most of his friends were Republicans.[26]

Although the Winans farm was less than 20 miles from Howell, Michigan, where he worked as a Probate Judge, the trip had to be made by horse or horse and buggy, which consumed a significant part of the day. Edwin found it necessary to have a place in Howell to stay on occasion, as evidenced from the 1880 U.S. Census showing Edwin Winans, Probate Judge as a boarder of Wm. H. And Jerusha Gaines in Howell, Michigan.[27]

Edwin started out seeking the position to get a "handle to his name before he died,"[28] and although people referred to him as Judge Winans long after his term, he did not enjoy the work. Processing wills for probate turned out to be a tedious and confining activity he was happy to give up when his term, which began in 1876, was over in 1880, and the gentleman farmer then set his sights even higher.

Although Edwin Winans loved family and farm, he was always ready for the next challenge. He did look for opportunities, but sometimes the opportunities looked for him.

Ross Winans is Edwin's cousin and contemporary.
He was in the Maryland Legislature when Edwin
was in the Michigan Legislature during the Civil War.

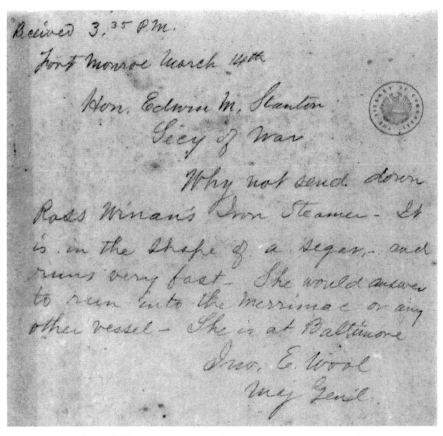

Received 3.³⁵ P.M.

Fort Monroe March 14th

Hon. Edwin M. Stanton
Secy of War

Why not send down
Ross Winan's Iron Steamer. It
is in the shape of a segar, and
runs very fast. She would answer
to run into the merrimac or any
other vessel. She is at Baltimore

Jno. E. Wool
Maj Genl.

Ross Winans invented the cigar boat mentioned
in this letter to Secretary of War Stanton.

The Winans family had a second home in Howell, not far from Howell Lake.

Edwin worked as a Livingston County Probate Judge
in Howell and subsequently owned a business there.

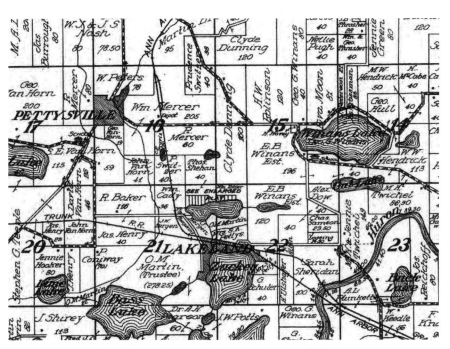

A 1905 Map of Hamburg shows the Winans
farm, and the lake is now Winans Lake.

The Congress of the United States

E dwin Winans identified as a Democrat early in life. In the gold-fields, he served the people of Rough and Ready, California, as a Democrat. He professed the ideals of the Democratic Party when he served the people of Michigan in the state legislature, in the Constitutional Convention, as Hamburg Township Supervisor, and as Probate Judge for Livingston County. His views did not change while serving in the Congress of the United States of America.

Note: The platforms of both Democrats and Republicans have changed since the 1890s, and what the public wants from their government has also changed. Edwin's views were provincial. They grew from hard work as a common wool carder, miner, and farmer. His focus was simple: he was fiscally conservative, promoted the coinage of silver and thereby the increasing the money supply, advocated in support of agriculture, and was attentive to the needs of the commonplace.

As a Democrat, he was in the minority among his friends and neighbors. Still, his reputation as a fair and reasonable man who looked out for the good of the ordinary person put him in public office repeatedly. He was at the Michigan Democratic Convention in 1882, where conferees declined several nominations for U.S. Congress. When Edwin Winans' name was proposed, he attempted to stand and decline, but the man seated behind him, Mr. H. Hooper of Howell, grabbed his coattail and jerked him back into his seat. "Unable to free himself quickly, he was nominated by acclamation. The convention quickly adjourned."[1]

Edwin was reluctant to be nominated but ran for office with vigor. He went to the Harland Mills to ask the mill hands to support him. Edwin got there "just as the men entered the hotel for their noon meal. He

101

sat down with them in his shirt sleeves, talking and joking throughout the meal. At the end of dinner, someone remarked that the Republican candidate was having his dinner in a private room upstairs. He arose and introduced himself to that group and asked for their votes. This friendly gesture may well have decided the election. He won by a majority of only thirty-two."[2]

Mr. Winans goes to Washington! The 48th Congress of the United States of America represented their districts from March 4, 1883, to March 4, 1885, while Chester A. Arthur was President. The approximate 500-mile trip from Hamburg, Michigan, to Washington, District of Columbia, was not formidable to Edwin. He was, after all, a veteran of the overland trail, but walking was not an option this time. Should he take his horse or a horse and buggy to Washington? If he took his own transportation, he would have to stable the horse and store the buggy during the session of Congress. A more likely choice would be to go by stage, train, or possibly both. After making his way to the Capitol, he also needed a place to stay during the months Congress was in session. Although some congressmen bought houses to live in, there is no evidence that Edwin purchased a house in Washington. His home was his farm in Michigan, and his time in Washington was transitory. There were boarding houses available, and there were hotels for members of Congress to use while serving their country.

Edwin and Elizabeth knew his commitment to being a congressman meant living in Washington from early December until late spring each year. Elizabeth followed Edwin wherever he served, but the 1883 Congressional Directory shows Edwin lived in Washington alone, indicating she may not have stayed in Washington all the time.[3] Edwin lived at 52 B Street N.E. while serving in the 48th Congress. B Street intersects 14th Street in the White House neighborhood. In 1883, the street went past the Department of Agriculture, the Smithsonian, and the National Museum before moving past the Capitol toward the East Branch of the Potomac River.

Note: *The map of Washington has changed significantly since 1883. B Street N.E. still exists, but the street name changes to Independence Ave as it heads east.*

Members of the Constitutional Convention created The District of Columbia so that no state would have more power due to its being home to the national government. The Constitution provides that the district "not exceeding 10 miles square" would become the seat of the government of the United States."[4]

In 1790, Congress passed the Residence Act to establish a permanent home for the government. George Washington picked the site.

The District of Columbia originally included the towns of Alexandria and Georgetown, but the people of Virginia were not happy with the cession of Alexandria, and people in Washington City were not satisfied with the inclusion of Alexandria in the district due to the slave trading there. Finally, in 1846, the Virginia Assembly passed a retrocession bill, which the governmental authority in Washington approved, and Congress signed legislation on July 9, 1846, to return Alexandria to Virginia. Georgetown, on the other hand, remained part of the District of Columbia.[5]

Pierre Charles L'Enfant came to America to help fight in the Revolution and, in the process, met the general who would become the first president. George Washington asked L'Enfant to survey the area designated for the nation's Capital and to recommend where significant buildings should be located. L'Enfant placed the capitol building on a hill overlooking the Potomac. Roads radiated from this center point in a grid system interspersed with public squares, parks, and traffic circles. L'Enfant's plan also included a mall going from the capital building to the President's house meant for use by the common people. Washington liked L'Enfant's plan, but there was some controversy over it. Eventually, Andrew Ellicott offered some changes to L'Enfant's plan, which city planners adopted, but Pierre Charles L'Enfant did not receive any credit for his effort.[6] It took many years for the plan to come to fruition, and by the time Edwin Winans arrived at the Capitol, there was still much to be done. The city Edwin arrived at in 1883 was not the Washington we know today, but already had some significant government buildings - the Capital Building was there, as was the White House, and the Washington Monument was nearing completion. The streets were tree-lined, and most were residential rather than business or governmental.

Edwin didn't live at the Hillman House Hotel but lived within a few blocks of the famous site once owned by George Washington. The Hillman House was within walking distance of the Capitol Building on Capitol Street. The hotel has a rich history, beginning with George Washington. Our country's first president bought the land and erected townhouses. President Washington was keenly interested in building the townhouses, but sadly, he died before construction was completed. His nephew, Supreme Court Justice Bushrod Washington, inherited the townhouses. The War of 1812, which resulted in the burning of the Capitol Building and the White House, also burned the townhouses down. George C. Washington sold the ruins in 1817. A new structure using the remaining walls became a boardinghouse. The property changed hands again, and eventually, Nelson J. Hillman purchased it and operated it as a hotel called "Hillman House" from 1876 to 1896 while Edwin was in Congress.[7]

Note: *The history of this property is such a little nugget of awesome it makes me wish I could say Edwin stayed there. The building was demolished in 1913, and on the bicentennial of George Washington's birth, the District of Columbia donated a historical marker placed at the location of the townhouses initially built by our first president.*[8]

When Edwin moved to Washington, D.C., from his farming community in Hamburg, Michigan, it had been ninety years since the founding fathers took steps to form the city where he now resided. I can picture Edwin walking the capital city streets, orienting himself to his new environment. He undoubtedly walked from near the White House, where he lived, down Pennsylvania Avenue to the Capitol Building. Edwin surely strolled around Lafayette Park and then across the park to St. John's church. St. John's is an Episcopal Church, so he likely attended services there while he was in Washington. The original church was completed in 1816 and added to in 1822, and again, when Edwin was there, James Renwick, designer of the Smithsonian Castle, worked on expanding the church.[9]

The Smithsonian would have been a place of interest to Edwin Winans. The building is as attractive in its structure and design as the history of its conception. It is constructed of red sandstone in a combination of Romanesque and Gothic styles and, therefore, was known as the castle.[10] James Smithson, "a man who never set foot in Washington, D.C., left his fortune to a nephew with the stipulation that, if the nephew died without heirs, the money would go to the United States of America to found an establishment for the increase and diffusion of knowledge." The original building held the entire institution. Edwin could have visited the gallery, the natural history collection, and even a laboratory - all in this historic structure.[11]

The Washington Monument was completed while Edwin was there. It was about time; it took nearly four decades to complete. In contrast, Baltimore, Maryland, erected their monument to George Washington in just four years. They ran a lottery to raise funds and got the job done.[12]

Note: *Washington, D.C., was a quagmire for decision-making and getting things done even in these early years.*

The laying of the first stone in 1848 was a big deal, with 20,000 in attendance. Lady Dolley Madison was there, as well as Alexander Hamilton's widow. There were controversies along the way, but the Civil War stopped any construction, leaving the half-finished stump. Mark Twain, in 1868, said, "The ungainly old chimney is of no earthly use to anybody else, and certainly not ornamental. It is an eyesore to the people. It ought to be either pulled down or built up and finished."[13]

In August 1876, Congress unanimously adopted a joint resolution that appropriated $2 million to complete the monument. Colonel Thomas Lincoln Casey, Chief of the Office of Public Buildings and Grounds, completed the memorial. His associate, George Perkins Marsh, had studied obelisks and concluded the height should be ten times its width at the base. The height was acceptable at 555 feet, including the 55 feet of the pyramidal apex - the angled point at the top.[14]

In 1880, the Otis Company installed a new steam elevator to aid the workers in construction. It lifted Rutherford B. Hayes and two members of Congress to the top of the shaft - 150 feet at the time. In 1884, the Brush-Swan Company added electric lighting to the shaft.[15]

On December 7, 1884, thousands cheered, and soldiers fired cannons in salute as Casey lowered the 3,000-pound capstone into place. Some spectators wore necklaces and brooches purchased at Karr's Jewelry Store on Pennsylvania Avenue and made from "genuine chips" of the monument's marble. At the top, the chief engineer placed the 5 1/2 by 9 1/2-inch tip upon the obelisk. Known as a "pyramid-ion," it was cast aluminum, a metal that would resist corrosion and act as a lightning rod, and so novel that Tiffany's had put it on display in New York.[16]

On February 21, 1885, the parade celebrating the monument's completion went down Pennsylvania Avenue toward the Capitol. After reaching the Capitol, the festivities retired to the house chamber. Edwin, as a member of Congress, would have been present for the commemoration ceremonies there, which included some descendants of George Washington. There were comments by Speaker of the House Robert Winthrop, who stated, "Its successful completion is…an unspeakable relief, as well as a heartfelt delight and joy."[17]

Because of the monument, Washington's citizens began to speak of their city as beautiful; they sometimes even mentioned it in the same sentence as London or Paris. "Washington has risen out of the dust and mire and clay which formerly was its abiding place and stands today in new and becoming attire infused with new life."[18]

The capital city of the country was growing exponentially during the 1880s. Government buildings were rising, housing for those working in the government was increasing, and the wealthy were building mansions. Dupont Circle was just a suburb in a wooded and marshy area, but it became an "attractive residential neighborhood after streets and utilities were installed in the early 1870s."[19] The circle was named in honor of Samuel F. Dupont, an officer in the Navy during the Civil War.[20] A statue of Dupont was placed in the center of the circle on December 20, 1884. Edwin was in Washington when the statue was dedicated. I think he was there - why would he refuse to attend such auspicious occasion?

Unique private homes were undoubtedly not restricted to the Dupont neighborhood. Commodore Stephen Decatur, Jr. and his wife built a spectacular home on the northwest corner of what is known today as Lafayette Square. The Commodore took his place in society, and the couple had lavish parties at their home, but unfortunately, the glory only lasted fourteen months because the Commodore was killed in a duel. As a result, Susan Decatur eventually had to sell the home. The home changed hands many times, and the Army used it as a headquarters during the Civil War. General Edward Beale owned the home when Edward was in Washington. The Beales redecorated the house and often hosted parties for the Washington elite. Edwin Winans, United States Congressman, may have been invited to a reception there.[22]

Along with the "gilded mansions" came churches funded by influential people. The Church of the Covenant was founded in 1883, and a small chapel was built in 1884. Construction of the main church began while Edwin was living in Washington, but the historic collapse of the bell tower occurred after he had returned to Michigan. Edwin read newspaper accounts from his home in Hamburg with interest in the cracking sounds that alerted a watchman and others of imminent danger. Blame for the collapse was pointed in all directions, but the official investigation ruled the cause was inferior materials. The mortar used was "practically useless."[23]

Mansions weren't the only gilded places in Washington - there was the Willard Hotel. The Willard Hotel already had a reputation for elegance before Lincoln was elected. He chose to reside at the Willard before his inauguration. "Nathaniel Hawthorne, who visited Washington in 1862, observed that Willard's Hotel could more justly be called the center of Washington and the Union than either the Capitol, the White House, or the State Department."[24] Mark Twain was also a visitor during the Gilded Age. The hotel was rebuilt in later years and is still considered an elegant establishment.

The man who walked 3,000 miles to California in search of gold was not the kind of person who spent his evenings behind four walls. Washington, D.C., was just 10 square miles, and Edwin Winans easily walked all over the city. The Rhodes Tavern would have been a building of interest for Edwin. It was the Washington Stock Exchange when he was in Washington, but it had functioned as a boarding house, a bank, a meeting house, and a polling place in addition to its original function as a tavern opened by William Rhodes in 1801. It was located at 15th and F Streets and was considered the oldest commercial building in the city. The Baroness Hyde de Neuville made a painting of it in 1820. [25]

Note: *I have a picture in my mind of Edwin strolling the streets of Washington, D.C., with his walking stick. Walking with the stick takes a certain amount of hubris, to be sure, but a person who has the courage to purchase or own such an accouterment would have the self-confidence to show it off.*

There were stories told in the city, some true and some not, regarding its colorful history. A lot of them, of course, were about George Washington. Where did he stop, and where did he sleep? Edwin would have heard about the place in Georgetown referred to as Washington's headquarters. Some people thought The Old Stone House was Suter's Tavern, dating back to the country's early days. It was where George planned the city with L'Enfant. It was where Thomas Jefferson drank Madeira or Sherry. The problem is that none of this myth can be substantiated with facts. The Old Stone House is now a National Park Service site, but no one knows where Suter's Tavern was.[26]

The events of April 14, 1865, have lived on in the country's history. After John Wilkes Booth shot Abraham Lincoln at Ford's Theatre and Lincoln later died, the government closed the theatre. The War Department continued controlling the site, eventually buying the building and gutting the interior - turning the space into an office building. When Edwin was in Washington, D.C., the "New Ford's Building" building housed a museum and offices.[27]

A Place in Time: "*Matthew Brady's photography studio was permitted to take crime scene photos of the interior of Ford's Theatre. These images were invaluable when the government restored the theater almost a century later.*[28]

During the day, Edwin would have been busy with congressional duties, but living in the city also came with domestic responsibilities. Edwin could have shopped at the Boston Dry Goods House on Seventh Street and Pennsylvania Ave. They advertised "One Price," meaning there was no haggling over price. This was an advanced concept at the time. People everywhere were used to haggling over cost. During his stay in Washington, the Boston Dry Goods House moved to the corner of 11th and F Streets and later was known as the Woodward and Lothrop Department Store. "The building was on the leading edge of department store design and was meant to serve as a prominent entertainment destination, impressing passersby and drawing them in. Once inside, the finest customer amenities were provided, including an elegant reception room on the mezzanine level, enclosed by an ornamental mahogany balustrade, where ladies could wait for their shopping companions to arrive before embarking on a romp through the isles. Shoppers could see evidence of the store's technological prowess in the Martin & Hill Electric Cable Cash Railway. a Rube Goldberg contraption that included a small track running in all directions throughout the building's four shopping floors. It transported cash from station to station in small "German silver Box cars" that raced about at fourteen feet per second. Mayhem ensued at least once a week when somebody's excitable pet dog, driven crazy by the zippy little boxcars, would break loose and go tearing after them barking loudly."[29] Witnessing a scene of barking dogs chasing a toy sized box car, and the resulting chaos would have caused Edwin, as it would have most people, to chuckle.

Whether Edwin lived where meals were provided or if he cooked his meals, he would have shopped at Marsh Market. It was halfway between the Capitol and the White House. George Washington designated the location of a market. It was known as Marsh Market and later as Central Market in the early days. Edwin could have purchased fresh fruit, vegetables, meat, fish, flowers, and much more from the local vendors there.[30]

Note: *When I found the chart showing where Edwin sat in Congress, I was so excited, I had to share it. The seat assignment for Congressman Edwin Winans in the 48th Congress was number 84 on the East side in the House of Representatives.*

As a United States Congressman, Edwin was placed on the Agriculture Committee and the Invalid Pensions Committee. The Agriculture Committee was a perfect fit for Edwin. His passion was farming, and he retained his farm in Hamburg, Michigan, while in Congress. As a farmer, he opposed protectionist tariffs. Farmers in the U.S. could undersell their competition elsewhere and did not need a tariff to protect their interests. However, the manufacturers pushed for protective tariffs. As a result, foreign markets retaliated by raising tariffs on agricultural goods and manufactured goods. This resulted in the loss of sales for farm products in foreign markets due to the costs added to their goods from foreign tariffs.

The pinch from protective tariffs was exacerbated in the 1880s because the government deposited large surpluses in vaults rather than banks where the money would be recirculating in the economy. A shrinkage of the money supply made it harder to get a loan and affected the farmer's ability to do business. Farmers also wanted an increase in the money supply by adding silver coinage to gold. An act of Congress in 1873 omitted the silver dollar from the list of authorized coins. By adding silver to gold coinage, the money supply would increase, and prices inflate, benefiting farmers." The collapse of land and farm prices beginning in 1887 increased the demand by farmers for the unlimited coinage of silver."[31]

On August 13, 1886, the Detroit Free Press reported on the remarks made by Congressman Winans at the Livingston County Convention. "The Democratic Congressmen from Michigan had gallantly fought for the much needed reforms. His votes were in sympathy with the toiling masses, while the Senate composed of millionaires were the especial legislators of monopoly. The Michigan Democratic Congressman had worked unceasingly for tariff reform, for the free coinage of silver and for the Morrison resolution relating to the surplus. The speaker was very determined in his assertion that the surplus over $100,000,000 should be used in payment of that portion of our public debt now due. He thought, too, that the customs would soon be lowered, as the amount now received daily from internal revenue and tariff customs was some $1,000,000...and was far more than what was needed. ...Mr. Winans did not believe in hoarding up the people's money in the public treasury, he much preferred it would be in their, the people's, pocket. In short, the speaker's remarks as his votes in Congress had been, were sensible and elicited the closest attention and hearty applause of the convention."[32]

The Detroit Free Press reported his endorsement by the Greenback-Labor Convention on September 2, 1882. "He (Edwin Winans) is especially prominent in agricultural circles, has been for years an active member of his county agricultural society - one of the most prosperous in the state - and for two successive terms its President. A staunch

Democrat, he is essentially a man of the people, and his nomination will command popular support that few candidates can command. Endorsed as Judge Winans is by the Greenback-Labor Convention, he will make the campaign in his district exceedingly musical for the Republicans.[33] The Greenback Party supported Edwin's positions on silver coinage and tariffs. Edwin supported the policies of tariff reform, silver coinage, and not hoarding treasury funds, and at the same time, was working diligently for invalid soldiers and their pensions.

The government granted pensions to Civil War soldiers who could provide proof of time spent in the military and a disability that occurred while in service. The first pension program wasn't working well. Therefore, Congress passed the Pension Act of 1879 to correct some problems. While Edwin was in Congress, President Cleveland vetoed another bill that was proposed and passed through Congress. The Detroit Free Press reported Edwin's position on October 26, 1884. "Dear Sir - You ask me if I am in favor of the Robison Bill, pensioning prisoners of war. Yes, if I cannot get a better one, which I think Col. Watson's substitute is, for the reason that it is more liberal to the soldiers. The substitute provides for the widows of those who died in rebel prisons and for all soldiers now disabled, no matter where or when. It also pays those detained in prison after their term of enlistment expired. I consider it far more liberal and just to the soldier than the original bill. In the case of a prisoner of war, no proof is required except the certificate of any reputable physician that disability exists from any cause. The Pensions Committee of the G.A.R. said it was preferable to the original. Both bills are before Congress. I would vote to pass either. I am very truly yours, Edwin B. Winans."[34]

Note: G.A.R. is Grand Army of the Republic - an organization of veterans who served in the Civil War.

Edwin Winans was supportive of benefits for military service members, and he would have been aware of the history of the Arlington Estate. The Lee family abandoned the Arlington Estate at the start of the Civil War. The U.S. Army seized the property due to its strategic location. The government built three forts on the property, and in 1863, they established a Freedman's Village. The government set up the Settlements for formerly enslaved people - refugee camps. "They evolved into a unique and thriving community with schools, hospitals, churches, and social services. While intended to be temporary, the community remained on the land from 1863 until 1900 and left a legacy."[35] The first burial on the property in 1864 resulted from other local cemeteries running out of room. It was initially not considered an honor but ensured a funeral and proper burial for service members.

A Place in Time: *Some contemporaries of Edwin Winans were Henry Wadsworth Longfellow and Samuel Langhorne Clemens. Longfellow was popular during Edwin's lifetime; his poem 'The Song of Hiawatha was published in 1855. The setting for the poem is the shore of Lake Superior, and the feats of Hiawatha are mythic.36 Samuel Clemens was a gifted humorist and a serious author who wrote under the pseudonym Mark Twain. He used his life in Hannibal, located on the Mississippi River, his experience working in the printing business, and his time as a riverboat captain to turn his fantasy into something believable.37 Mark Twain shared what he knew when he wrote "Life on the Mississippi," "The Adventures of Tom Sawyer," and "Adventures of Huckleberry Finn." His grounding in hard work and perseverance was something Edwin would have admired.*

Edwin ran again for U.S. Congress from the Sixth District of Michigan. The Oakland County Campaign rallied in Pontiac, Michigan, on November 1, 1884. "About 2 p.m. the horse brigade with the speakers, leading citizens and accompanied by six bands and numerous banners, flags, and emblems marched through the streets, which were filled with a vast multitude of visitors. At half-past 2 p.m., speaking began on the fair ground which was crowded with people who could not be discouraged by the inclemency of the weather. ...In the evening there was a torchlight procession far exceeding anything ever seen in Pontiac. One-thousand men zealously carried torches through the muddy streets, and the large horse brigade enhanced the splendor of the parade. The stores and many residences were beautiful decorated, and the sky was all ablaze with fireworks during the parade. Nothing ever witnessed in Pontiac could compare with it in splendor and brilliance. The music of the six bands and the multiple transparencies with appropriate mottoes were magnificent."[38] An estimated ten thousand people attended, and

Hon. Edwin B. Winans was one of the speakers at this event. Anyone would be overwhelmed after a full day with speeches in the afternoon, parades, food, shaking hands, and kissing babies. Edwin must have felt he had come a long way from the one-room log cabin in Unadilla.

Others thought so, too. The Detroit Free Press of September 26, 1884, offers: "The Hon. Edwin B. Winans, who has been renominated for Congress has been an able and clear-headed representative of his constituents. He has proved an industrious legislator and can always be found at the post of duty. He always votes intelligently and conscientiously and has proved a satisfactory representative. His record has been fittingly endorsed by the Union forces, which paid him the high compliment of a unanimous renomination last week. He is a strong man with the people, and everything indicates now that he will be reelected by a handsome majority."[39]

There was a coexistent relationship between Edwin Winans and Josiah Begole, the 19th governor of the State of Michigan from 1883 to 1885. Josiah had changed parties and ran for governor as a Democrat, but by the time Edwin ran for office, he identified as a Republican. Josiah was an antislavery man and promoter of women's rights. Their strongest agreement was on the use of currency and its effect on the economy. They were both for increasing the money supply and including silver for currency.

When asked, in October of 1884, what chances Winans had in the election for congressman from the sixth district, Ex-governor Begole said, "I believe that Judge Winans will be re-elected by some 400 majority. That district is naturally ours (Republican) by 200 majority. Two years ago, when Judge Winans first ran, he was a stranger to many of our people. But this year, Judge Winans is better known. He has made a good record as a congressman and is making an active canvass. The things that worked to his disadvantage before do not appear in this canvass, and he will be re-elected by an increased majority."[40]

Note: Edwin Winans's relationship with Josiah Begole was professional. They did agree politically on some issues, but they were from different parties. Josiah Begole is an example of someone who, even though he sometimes disagreed with Edwin Winans, respected him.

Grover Cleveland was President of the United States during the 49th Congress, from March 1885 to March 1887. Some issues close to Edwin's heart were under consideration. One of the issues before Congress was election law, and the other was agriculture. The point of how to elect the President and the Vice-President of the United States was contentious. Before the Revolutionary War ended in September of 1783, it was evident the Articles of Confederation were insufficient to meet government needs. Valiant men then gathered to construct a constitution for the 13 states in the union at that time. After a hard-fought war, the next battle would be to devise government rules the majority could agree upon.

One of the last issues the writers of the Constitution resolved was how to elect the President and Vice President. Some thought that the House of Representatives should choose those two offices, but then that would make for too cozy a relationship between the Executive and Legislative forms of government. A standing president would do whatever he could to curry favor with Congress in preparation for the next election. The convention members then offered the solution of a popular vote. The problem with this idea at the time was that citizens were not able to make informed decisions. Not every city had a newspaper, and many of the population were not educated - they could not even read. It would be difficult for candidates to reach the electorate with their message. The compromise was for an intermediary between a popular vote and the House of Representatives vote. Thus, the Electoral College. The electors in each state would come together to weigh the facts and decide their votes. The founders did not foresee the development of political parties that resulted in votes along purely political lines. The system did not always work smoothly, but in 1876, difficulties arose with nearly a constitutional crisis. Due to the controversy about whether Samuel Tilden or Rutherford Hayes had won, Democrats rejected the result and began to filibuster. The filibuster only ended after some backroom deals, making Hayes the President-Elect. Edwin Winans was a member of the 49th Congress who voted on the bill to correct this flaw in the system - the Electoral Count Act of 1887. The act addressed the role of state government in the Electoral College while allowing

Congress to challenge a state's votes. This involves a House member and a Senator to make the challenge in writing, resulting in a joint session of Congress with a two-hour limit to the discussion, followed by a simple majority vote.

The Electoral College remains in dispute, but facts show the "party in power typically benefits from the existence of the Electoral College, and the minority party has little chance of changing the system because a constitutional amendment requires a two-thirds supermajority in Congress plus ratification by three-fourths of the states."[41]

The Agricultural Experimentation Act of 1887 was legislation within Edwin's expertise. This law provides that land-grant colleges do agricultural research. Those colleges came into being due to the Land Grant Agricultural and Mechanical College Act of 1862, but the Hatch Act of 1887 gave federal funds to the land-grant colleges to create agricultural experiment stations. These stations would share what they learned about soil minerals and plant growth.[42]

Michigan Agricultural College was "chartered under Michigan State law as a state land grant institution before being designated as the federal land-grant college for Michigan in 1863.[43]

Edwin was familiar with Michigan's land grant college; his Hamburg, Michigan farm was only about 27 miles away from the Michigan Agricultural College. The Grand River Road, just as many other roads in the state, was once a Native American trail following the Cedar River. In 1852, the Lansing Central Plank Road Company built a plank road over the Lansing and Howell Road, and tollgates were distributed along the road every four to six miles."[44]

To reach the Michigan Agricultural College, Edwin would have traveled north to Howell and west on Grand River Road or the Lansing Howell Road. The route would become familiar to him because after a short respite at the farm he reached for the highest office in the state.

U. S. Capitol building as it looked when Edwin was there.

Map of Washington, D.C. Edwin lived at 52 B Street
N.E. in Washington, D.C., while in the 48th Congress.

The Washington Monument was completed
when Edwin was in the U.S. Congress.

When Edwin lived there in the 1880s, Dupont Circle
in Washington, D.C., was becoming an upscale neighborhood.

Henry Willard founded the Willard Hotel, which was a
favorite of Abraham Lincoln and is still a luxury hotel.

The Rhodes Tavern was built in 1799 and sold or rented to
Williams Rhodes in 1801, who operated a tavern there until 1805.

The Old Stone House is one of the oldest
structures in Washington, D.C., built in 1765.

Freedman's Village—Before the military cemetery
was established at Arlington, some of the land was used from
1863 to 1900 as a temporary settlement for Civil War refugees.

200   *Congressional Directory.*

Name.	Post-office.	City address.	Page.
-*Taylor, Joseph D_____	Cambridge, Ohio _____	933 G street, N. W_____	71
¿‖Thomas, John R_____	Metropolis, Ill ____ ____	1321 N street, N. W _____	22
Thompson, Philip B., jr_____	Harrodsburg, Ky _____	1013 E street, N. W_____	32
Throckmorton, James W_____	McKinney, Tex _____	525 Sixth street, N. W___	87
Tillman, George D_____	Clark's Hill, S. C_____	412 Sixth street_____	81
*Townshend, Richard W____	Shawneetown, Ill _____	221 4½ street, N. W_____	22
*¿Tucker, John Randolph ___	Lexington, Va _____	McPherson House _____	91
¿Tully, Pleasant B_____	Gilroy, Cal _____	National Hotel _____	11
Turner, Henry G _____	Quitman, Ga_____	523 Thirteenth st., N. W__	16
*¿Turner, Oscar _____	Woodlands,OscarP.O.,Ky	Willard's Hotel _____	31
*Valentine, Edward K_____	West Point, Nebr_____	National Hotel_____	53
Van Alstyne, Thomas J_____	Albany, N. Y_____	3 B street, N. W_____	61
*¿Vance, Robert B_____	Asheville, N. C_____	230 First street, N. W ___	67
*Van Eaton, Henry S_____	Woodville, Miss _____	917 Sixteenth street, N. W.	48
*Wadsworth, James W_____	Genesee, N. Y _____	821 Fifteenth street, N.W_	63
Wait, John T _____	Norwich, Conn_____	Hamilton House _____	12
Wakefield, James B_____	Blue Earth City, Minn__	704 Fourteenth st., N. W__	45
Wallace, Jonathan H _____	New Lisbon, Ohio_____	Ebbitt House _____	71
Ward, Thomas B_____	La Fayette, Ind _____	7 Grant Place _____	24
Warner, A. J _____	Marietta, Ohio ____ ___	18 Grant Place _____	71
- Warner, Richard _____	Lewisburg, Tenn_____	410 Sixth street, N. W___	85
*Washburn, William D_____	Minneapolis, Minn____	Arlington Hotel _____	46
Weaver, Archibald J_____	Falls City, Nebr_____	304 Indiana avenue _____	52
*Wellborn, Olin_____	Dallas, Tex_____	1706 L street, N. W_____	87
Weller, L. H _____	Nashua, Iowa_____	230 First street, N. E ___	27
*¿Wemple, Edward _____	Fultonville, N. Y_____	1408 N street, N. W _____	61
*‖White, John D _____	Manchester, Ky _____	1014 Seventeenth st., N. W.	33
·White, Milo _____	Chatfield, Minn _____	National Hotel_____	45
*Whiting, William _____	Holyoke, Mass _____	Riggs House _____	42
* Wilkins, Beriah_____	Urichsville, Ohio _____	Welcker's Hotel_____	71
Williams, Thomas _____	Wetumpka, Ala _____	Metropolitan Hotel _____	6
*Willis, Albert S _____	Louisville, Ky _____	Metropolitan Hotel _____	32
Wilson, James_____	Traer, Iowa_____	National Hotel _____	27
Wilson, William L_____	Charlestown, W. Va____	1008 N street, N. W _____	93
Winans, Edwin B _____	Hamburg, Mich _____	52 B street, N. E _____	43
* Winans, John_____	Janesville, Wis _____	Arlington Hotel _____	94
Wise, George D_____	Richmond, Va _____	1327 G street, N. W_____	91

Directory of Congress

THE HOUSE OF REPRESENTATIVES.

Directory of Congress Seating Chart

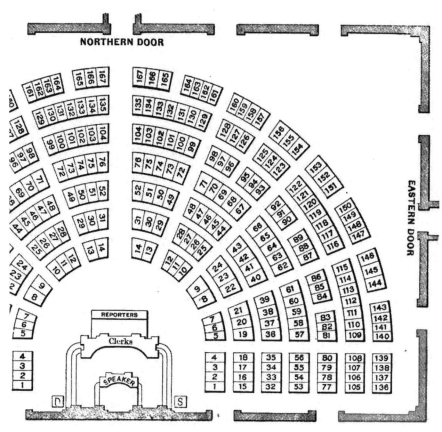

Directory of Congress Seat Numbers for 48th Congress

The Nomination and the Campaign

After completing two terms in Congress, Edwin returned to farming, but soon, friends pleaded with him to run for governor. His chances were not good; there had not been a Democrat in the governor's office since before the Civil War.

His party needed a candidate who was the epitome of honesty and integrity, and Edwin fit the bill. The Republican candidate for governor, James Turner, was accused by J. F. McElroy and others of unethical behavior. He allegedly benefited from his position on the Blind School Board by being involved in the sale of building materials to them. When accused of inappropriate and possibly illegal activity, he resigned from his post.[1]

James Turner could easily also be accused of poor judgment. When questioned by Methodist leaders about renting houses to prostitutes, he said he would not kick the prostitutes out because they paid their rent. The Methodists were outraged at his response and proceeded to do everything they could to campaign against him. Neither the Republican candidate, Turner, nor his party recognized the hornet nest they stirred up by antagonizing the Methodist voters and, by extension, the Christian voters of every denomination in Michigan. By offering the electorate a candidate with a reputation for being a gentleman who demonstrated unquestionable ethical and honest behavior, the Democrats knew it increased their chances of a win. Edwin B. Winans was the answer. "In every precinct, two or three Republican voters shifted to the Democratic column, and thus Winans, a Democrat, was elected governor - a feat almost impossible then."[2]

When Terence R Shields of Howell nominated Edwin B. Winans for governor, he referred to him as a scholar and a gentleman. He said he had always served with fidelity and wisdom. He is an "honest man, a good neighbor, a pure citizen, and a farmer. A farmer whom farmers delighted to honor and whom the voice of the people had called time and time again like Cincinnatus of old from the handles of his plow to the halls of legislation."[3]

At the Democratic Convention, two names were offered for consideration for the nomination for governor: Frank A. Dean of Eaton County and Edwin B. Winans of Livingston County. As the time was nearing for a vote, it was evident that most of the convention was in support of Edwin Winans, and then Frank Dean stepped up to the podium to say that he believed it to be in the best interests of the Democratic Party of Michigan that the nomination of Edwin B. Winans should be unanimous. "The nomination of Edwin B. Winans for Governor was then made by acclamation."[4]

Although Edwin was never known for using foul language, a ward heeler was able to prompt a swear word from his mouth. This man asked Edwin for money in return for promised votes. Edwin politely refused his offer, but the man insisted. Edwin had no intention to buy votes or have anyone think he did such a thing. He wrote to the man: "Before I send you one cent, I'll see you farther in hell than a pigeon can fly in a week." I guess that's far because he did not hear from the man again.[5]

Edwin was an outstanding campaigner, going from county to county, giving speeches and offering his opinion. The Coopersville Fair hosted him as a speaker on Democratic Day, "speeches to commence at 10 o'clock so as not to interfere with the races in the afternoon." The people of Grand Rapids were encouraged to attend the fair on Friday for a unique combination of speeches, horse racing, and a wedding.[6]

The Northeastern Fair in Saginaw Valley, where Edwin received a warm reception, provided an audience of nearly 4,000. He said he was not there to give a speech, but as a farmer, he was interested in the agricultural show. He was sure people would find value in attending the fair, which he described as a great educator. He was impressed by the advances in ingenious and labor-saving devices that benefit farmers and their wives. He and other distinguished guests stayed for the races and watched comfortably on cushioned benches provided for them in the grandstand.

He was also greeted enthusiastically by more than 2,000 people at the fair in Port Huron before traveling to his next political event in Detroit. The big event in Detroit was at the Detroit Rink. "The capacity of the building is so great that it takes many people to make a respectable showing of attendance, but in this case, the seats on the main floor were at a premium, and the galleries were well filled by voters who brought their wives and children to hear the words of the speakers."[7] Judge Winans had to be more than pleased with such a large crowd. On the campaign trail, he told voters why he was against the McKinley Bill and misuse of the tariff, how important it was to have the free coinage of silver, and how he felt about taxation and election law.

William McKinley of Ohio wanted to protect American industry from foreign products. His tariff bill raised the taxes to 50% on some products from foreign markets and eliminated it altogether on others. His law had unintended consequences. Farm prices continued to decrease, and prices for essential items increased, causing a double tax on the American farmer. They were earning less and had to pay more for basic goods. The supporters of the protectionist tariffs believed that these taxes were paid by the foreigners sending goods to America, but what happened is the American people were paying the taxes with increased prices of the goods they purchased from foreign markets. "There are very few of the necessities of life the prices of which are not increasing on account of the McKinley tariff."[8]

Edwin Winans used his candidacy to promote the free coinage of silver. He strongly advocated this issue because increasing money in the economy decreased borrowing costs. This was a huge boon to farmers who depended on loans to operate their farms.[9]

The State Republican September 12, 1890
"Edwin B. Winans of Livingston, the democratic nominee for governor of Michigan, is personally a fair man, and he was one of the few

125

democrats in Congress who kicked when Dictator Cleveland plied his party lash, strangled all legislation in favor of silver, and knocked the silver plank out of the democratic platform of 1888. Mr. Winans and his party claim to be in favor of free silver now. In this they are radically opposed to Mr. Cleveland. Why, then, do they place Mr. Winans on a platform that 'points with pride to the prudent, wise, and statesmanlike administration of Grover Cleveland?' It is a gratuitous insult - a deliberate slap in Mr. Winans face, which he cannot fail to notice."[10]

Note: *The language of the 1890s differed from how people converse in the 21st century, but somehow, twisted political messages remain the same. This article took a fact - Edwin Winans was for the free coinage of silver, and Grover Cleveland was not - and reported it as a slap in the face of Mr. Winans because the democrats of Michigan had included support for President Cleveland in their platform.*

Edwin's views on taxation are best described in the Detroit Free Press article dated August 30, 1890, titled "For Winans and Success." It states, "He (Edwin Winans) believes that no money should be exacted from the people except such as is absolutely necessary for economically carrying on the necessities of government; opposed to all bounties, subsidies and special legislation in the interests of the few and against the many."[11]

Regarding elections, Edwin Winans was a strong proponent of privacy of the vote - ballots should all look the same. There should not be separate ballots for each party and of different colors - everything should go on one ballot so the person standing in the voting line behind you has no idea how you voted. Also, the voter has a right to mark their ballot in privacy. These voting basics were not the standard before 1891. [12]

The Detroit Free Press backed Judge Winans. Their editorial stated, "As a man of ability, principle, integrity, industry, and one earnest for tariff reform, Judge Winans, in my opinion, stands ahead of any candidate mentioned: and he can carry Michigan. If you will ask any resident of Livingston County (no matter what his politics) what his record is as a Member of the State Legislature, Judge of Probate, president of the agricultural society, and four years in Congress, you will find the same answer, viz.: faithful, honest, a hard worker, and attending to every duty great or small in earnest, kind and unassuming manner."[13]

Howard Hovey told a story about Edwin Winans. "It's a small world," said Mr. Hovey. Years after Edwin's return from California gold fields he was talking to a group at Flint. He mentioned how he and his partner occupied a small cabin with a dirt floor. The place was infested with rats. One night he shot at a rat and saw something shine where the bullet struck the dirt. He investigated and found a quantity of gold coins. While the two men discussed the find, a stranger walked up, told how he had feared robbery by some companions and had hidden the coins in the cabin. He named the exact sum and told such a straight story that the coins were returned to him. When the Governor had finished Judge Newton, of Flint, arose in the audience and said, "And I, Mr. Winans, was the man to whom you returned that money."[14]

But not everyone was singing praises of Judge Edwin B. Winans. His detractors called him a Copperhead. Although he probably preferred Peace Democrat, Edwin did not let name-calling bother or influence him. He had been called a Copperhead since his time in the Michigan legislature. Criticism arose because, as a state legislator, he voted against a resolution in support of the war, but the truth was that out of two resolutions, both offered by Republicans, Edwin voted for one and not the other. The resolution he supported was "with the purpose of presenting Michigan to the national administration and the world in solid and unbroken harmony and unity in support of the government for the suppression of the rebellion and the preservation of the Union. The other set of resolutions, Winans thought, was only intended to score a partisan advantage."[15]

The legislator who wrote the bill Edwin voted against, S.W. Fowler, says that he proposed the resolution several times and finally passed by only two votes in the Senate and became law. Prominent Republicans did not support it, and when the war was over, the Supreme Court declared the law unconstitutional. S.W. Fowler said, "I think it unfair to blame Democrats for voting against the measure when most of the leading Republicans fought it tooth and nail in the Senate and in the House."[16]

Then again, when he was in the Michigan legislature, Edwin voted for the following resolution: "Resolved, That the numerous arrests without complaint or process of law, caused by the President of the United

States, of loyal citizens of loyal states and the arbitrary suspension of the writ of habeas corpus, where courts are devoted to the Union, and have ever been faithful to the constitution and laws, constitute a most high handed and daring assumption of power, which is without parallel in the history of constitutional governments and dangerous to the constitutional liberty of the American people; and that the long incarceration of citizens so arrested, in filthy and unhealthy forts and prisons, distant from their homes and friends, without examination or trial, constitutes a degree of remorseless cruelty, more benefitting the character of a Turkish despot than a President of the American Republic."[17] Edwin's stance on habeas corpus caused some to think he was not loyal to the Union, but to Edwin, it was not a matter of loyalty. It was a matter of holding to a principle worth protecting. Edwin believed that people are innocent until proven guilty - a founding principle and one fought for in the Revolutionary War.

Regarding Edwin Winans loyalty to the Union, a man who served with him in the Michigan Legislature, J. B. Welch, stated, "I had the pleasure of making the acquaintance of Mr. Winans during the war, being associated with him in the Legislature of the state of Michigan during the sessions of 1862, 1863, 1864, and 1865. I can testify to his loyalty to the old flag and to his being a true patriot for the Union of the states - a true war Democrat. Any man asserting anything to the contrary misrepresents the man."[18]

Nepotism was another complaint against Edwin Winans. When he served in Congress, he secured several positions for his family members and a friend, whom the paper incorrectly called an adopted son. These facts are not disputed, but the article fails to state how many other positions he recommended for non-family members.[19]

Despite many, especially those from the Republican Party, who disagreed with the positions taken by Edwin, there was a landslide victory on election day.

The headline in the Detroit Free Press on November 6, 1890, was **STORMED**[20] and went on to list:

- The Democrats Capture Each Branch of the Michigan Legislature
- This is the First Democratic Legislature Since 1853

- The Greatest Political Overturning Any State Ever Received
- The Senate Has a Snug Democratic Majority
- And in the House, the Democrats Have Nearly Two-Thirds
- With Edwin B. Winans in the Executive Office
- And John Stoner, Jr., Presiding Over the Senate

It wasn't until November 22, 1890, that the Interstate News-Record of Ironwood, Michigan, reported: "The returns of the late election in this state are practically all in, says the Tribune, and show the dimensions of the Republican defeat. ...All the Democratic candidates on the state ticket have been elected by majorities ranging from 12,000 for the governor down to a few hundred for state treasurer. ...A study of the returns will show that the Republicans have themselves to thank for their defeat. They have been beaten by their own apathy. ...In round numbers 100,000 Michigan voters stayed away from the polls this year."[21]

Note: *How many loyal Republicans stayed home because they didn't want to vote for James Turner but, on the other hand, didn't want to vote for a Democrat?*

The election was over, the results were in, and the celebrations commenced. On November 7, the Democrats rejoiced in their victory at the Detroit Rink. Governor-elect Winans was there, as well as Lieutenant-Governor-elect John Strong. "There was noise, music, and enthusiasm enough about the Detroit Rink last night to have stocked half a dozen ordinary political meetings. The rockets went up like Democratic majorities and the sticks came down like Republican hopes. The band played and the crowds gathered for an hour before the advertised time of the meeting and, when that time came, there was no room for the people who wished to join in the congratulation of the people ever the most fortunate political result that the State of Michigan has ever known. ...It was a great victory, and the celebration of it was no less great."[22]

Among other celebrations was the "Jubilee at Flint." It began at the railroad station where Governor-elect Winans and Lieutenant-governor John Strong were greeted by an "immense concourse of people." There was a band, and G.A.R. veterans from the Army and Navy fired salutes from canons. As the group made their way up the street, the sidewalks were thronged with cheering people. Banners hung across the streets reading, "Welcome to Gov. Winans, Welcome to Farmer Winans, Welcome to All." Mayor Patterson of Flint presented the keys to the city to Governor-elect Winans, after which the group went to the Crystal and had an enjoyable dinner. The group re-formed at the public park where Governor-elect Winans said: "The result of the election and the joyful demonstration which he witnessed here convinced him that the people of Genesee County thought it was high time they should be first in the management of public affairs. Everywhere, Republican rule and policy had been condemned. The McKinley Bill and the legislation on silver were against the interests of the people, and it was time for the people to take the management of affairs into their own hands. The people of Michigan may well rejoice that they have chosen so many good Democratic Congressmen to represent them in Washington. (Applause.) The Democrats rejoice, but Democrats cannot assess to themselves the whole credit of the victory. It belongs to the people. It is known that the Democratic Party has long been in the minority in this state. The patriotism of the people of Michigan has combined to place it in the majority because it represents principles which will promote their welfare. Therefore, to the farmers, and to the Patrons of Industry the good result was largely to be credited. The intelligent and industrious people of this country had considered the questions before them and many of them had taken their places in the ranks of the Democratic Party. As a farmer he bade them welcome and thanked them for their strong assistance, hoping they would ever persevere in the good work. (Cheers.)"[23]

It is possible that all the celebrations over his election, or mingling with crowds, caused the newly elected governor to be ill. The Parsons Daily Sun on December 16, 1890, reports: "Detroit, Mich., December 14 - Democratic leaders here are greatly alarmed over a report from Hamburg that Edwin B. Winans, the first Democratic Governor elected in Michigan since 1852, is dangerously ill with pneumonia."[24] This was not the only serious illness Edwin had during his two short years as governor.

Drawing of Edwin Baruch Winans

THE GOVERNOR

E dwin Winans' term as Governor of Michigan began in January 1891 and ended in December 1892. The State's constitution determines term limits for officeholders, and since the beginning of statehood in 1837, there have been two-year terms for governors.[1]

A Place in Time: *June 1891: Minutes, Annual Meeting 1891; Historical Collections, Michigan Pioneer and Historical Society "Judge Albert Miller said: "My good friend Felch in 1847 was Governor of the State. I was a member of the legislature that year. That was the legislature that located the capital of the State in the wilderness, I believe, where there was one log house and a sawmill. I advocated the location of the capital here with all the force I had because I knew that if the capital of the State was located here, somebody would know something about the interior of our State. Nobody did, but the few who were scattered around in the vicinity knew anything about the value of it. But if the capital was located here to get people in, our State would get settled, and it resulted as I anticipated. And now we shall be here but a little while to see all this, but it is a great gratification to me that I have lived to see the improvements, the anticipations more than filled, of my early days."[2]*

Inauguration

January 1, 1891, was the new Governor's first day on the job. Edwin Baruch Winans took the oath of office that day, but the formal ceremony was on January 8. The previous evening, January 7, the Governor and Mrs. Winans received guests at a "grand reception in the executive parlors beginning at 7:00 local time, and to continue until a late hour. An orchestra will give forth music from the center of the rotunda and dancing in the corridors will be one of the main features of the evening." [3]

Note: *Did the Governor shake hands in the receiving line? We know that a miner mangled a finger on his right hand in a fight in California over water rights. Howard Hovey described his finger as appearing that he had caught it in some machinery. Maybe he wasn't vain about the finger, but the painting in the state capitol building shows no damage to the fingers on his right hand. This poses the question - was this his choice or the artist's?*

"Thousands of people gathered in Lansing for the inaugural celebration. Train excursions arrived from around the State carrying bands and drill teams along with spectators. Women and the way they dressed confirmed the ceremony's significance. For example, Elizabeth Winans' attire for her husband's 1891 swearing-in-ceremony helped establish the Governor's position without distracting from it. Her dignified black and rich brown cloak with fur collar reflected, in its quiet elegance, the event's importance. The only mention of Michigan's First Lady in the newspapers was of her place beside her husband on the receiving line."[4]

A Place in Time: *The juxtaposition of the image of Elizabeth in her fine clothing at the inauguration to the one of war with Big-Foot-Mniconjou occurring on the same day is eye-opening. January 8, 1891: From The Livingston County Daily Press and Argus - Fighting Indians: Big Foot's Band Start A Massacre In The Bad Lands. "These Indians under Big Foot were among the most desperate there were. Thirty-eight of the remainder of Sitting Bull's following that joined Big Foot on the Cheyenne river and thirty that broke away from Hump's following when he took his band and Sitting Bull's Indians to Fort Bennett making in all nearly 160 warriors. Before leaving their camps on the Fort Cheyenne River, they cut up their harness and broke their wagons and started south for the Bad Lands, evidently intending not to return but to go to war."*

Note: *The infamous Massacre at Wounded Knee had just occurred in December of 1890.*

Making Appointments and Accepting Resignations

Edwin's first few days as Governor involved accepting resignations and appointing his supporters. On his first day, "the Governor's office was crowded with prominent Democrats during the entire day, and many were the tales related to the chief executive concerning the qualifications of prominent Democrats for positions within his ability to gift."[6]

When a party was elected to govern, the newly elected party replaced employees who had served the previous administration. The new administration rewarded the people who had helped them get elected by offering them positions in the government. It was referred to as the spoils system - to the victor go the spoils.[7]

"Margaret Custer Calhoun, the sister of General George A. Custer and Captain Thomas Custer and widow of Captain Calhoun, is now prominently mentioned for the office of Librarian, to succeed Mrs. J. E. Tenney, who has filled the position for many years."[8] Harriet Tenney became state librarian in 1869 upon the retirement of her husband Jesse E. Tenney. She served as State Librarian for 22 years and was a voice to the legislature and the public regarding the importance of a State Library. Harriet also introduced significant reforms in the system. Her assistant, Mary Spencer, wrote of her, "The library was her life and her joy; she loved the books as the mother does her child and watched them closely."[9] The Democratic party initiated Harriet Tenney's systematic discharge. It was through no fault of hers and seemed unjust.

That first day was a busy one for Edwin and his family. That day, he signed a commission making George G. Winans, his son, private and military secretary to the Governor. Sometime later, he also hired Howard Hovey as executive clerk to the Governor during his term. "Mr. Hovey was practically adopted by the family as a youth and has since been in contact with the family and their relatives."[10]

Note: *Edwin appointed George and Howard because he could. He knew what kind of a job they would do - he only had two short years to make a difference and needed people he knew would accomplish those things that would lead to the completion of his goals. As it turned out, some of his appointments were not as useful as those of George and Howard and did not support or lead to completing his goals.*

At Home in Lansing

Edwin Winans maintained his farm in Hamburg while serving as the 22nd governor. During the time he necessarily spent in Lansing, he resided at the Downey Hotel on the corner of Washington and Washtenaw streets. He only had a few blocks to walk from the Capitol to the hotel, or maybe a carriage picked him up and delivered him.[11]

Note: *Did he saunter from the capitol building to the Downey Hotel with the walking stick? The walking stick has been passed from generation to generation in the Winans family. The ferrule of the stick shows wear, so the Governor must have used it because those who inherited it were not inclined to walk about town with a fancy walking stick. Anecdotally, the stick goes to the eldest son unless there is a child named Theron Winans, and in that instance, Theron inherits the walking stick. Edwin passed his elegant walking stick on to his brother's family, but the question is who Edwin passed it to? His brother, Theron S. Winans, died in 1862. Edwin was in the Michigan State Legislature then, and we were in the Civil War. I don't think it was a time in Edwin's life that he would be passing the artifact along. The next Winans in line would be Theron's son, Nathaniel H. Winans, and that is certainly a possibility. Still, I think the walking stick went directly to Nathaniel's son, Theron. Edwin wanted Theron the younger to have it in memory of Edwin's brother by the same name, and thus, any future Theron is first in line to inherit. We know that the walking stick went to Theron-the-younger's son, Case Winans, from Case to Gerald Winans and Gerald to David Winans.*

Governor and Mrs. Winans lived some of the time in Lansing and returned to the farm periodically. Even though their farm and home on the lake were 38 miles away in Hamburg, they felt at home in Lansing because some of their family lived nearby. Edwin's half-brother, Theron S. Winans, had lived near Lansing before he died in 1862. His son Nathaniel H. Winans lived with his wife and children in Lansing on Main Street when Edwin was Governor, a short walk from the capitol building and a shorter walk from the Downey Hotel. Nathaniel owned a dairy on Main Street and established a milk delivery route in Lansing in 1888.

Edwin's uncle, his father John's brother, had also relocated to Michigan from New York, and his son, Edwin's cousin, George Albertus

Winans, lived in the Lansing area but died in 1878 at age 35. However, his wife, Susan Kinney Winans, worked as a clerk at the capitol building before Edwin's governorship. Susan was a Republican, and her job ended just as her friend Mrs. Tenney's ended with the new administration. S.K. Winans, a republican clerk of the state department, "stepped out today to make room for reformers." [12]

Note: *I wish we could go back in time and chat with Susan K. Winans. She surely knew how Harriet Tenney felt about being replaced by Margaret Custer Calhoun. Susan lived in the same boarding house as the Tenneys, as shown in the 1880 census. Susan and Harriet were both auxiliary members of the G.A.R. (Grand Arm of the Republic) Susan was a member of the auxiliary because her husband had been a member of the G.A.R. The Lansing Tri-Weekly Republican on June 5, 1883, reported: "Mrs. S. K. Winans of the office of the secretary of state has recently presented to the G.A.R. post at Ovid a fine crayon portrait of her deceased husband, Capt. Geo. A. Winans for whom the post was named. The portrait was accompanied by a letter from Mrs. Winans, in which she thanked the post for the honor done to the memory of her husband, and begged an acceptance of it as a slight testimonial of the good will which she bore towards all who followed the old flag during the hour of the Nation's peril."[13] Susan K. Winans was a Republican - can we assume George A. Winans was also a Republican?*

The spoils system frustrated both workers and administrators. Workers were unsure at each election whether they would keep their jobs. Politicians enjoyed gifting jobs to supporters, but when the people they appointed did not perform well, it made the government, and the politicians look bad. Also, some felt entitled after working hard to get someone elected. After a frustrated office-seeker assassinated President Garfield in July of 1881, there were calls for civil service reform. The reformers called for job standards and a competitive application process. They wanted civil servants who would be politically neutral. Patronage workers were not motivated to do a good job, and many were inefficient. The Pendleton Civil Service Act of 1883 was a start but only applied to ten percent of the positions in the federal government. Michigan did not enact any civil service reforms until the 1930s.[14]

The Record-Union of Sacramento, California. February 1, 1891.
"Edwin B. Winans, who is the first Democratic Governor that Michigan
has had in thirty years, is a conservative, bald-headed old farmer, with a
neatly trimmed beard and kindly eyes beaming out of gold spectacles." [15]

The Capitol Building

The office of Governor Edwin Baruch Winans was in Michigan's
third capitol building. The first building was in Detroit, the territorial
Capitol of Michigan before Michigan became a state and remained the
Capitol until the legislature decided to move the capital to Lansing in
1847. The second capitol building was in Lansing but was an unassuming wooden structure. The third building is exceptional by any standard.

The rotunda has a glass floor supported from below with iron pil-
lars and is spectacular from the floor to the exquisite iron dome with
its platinum and gold leaf stars at the top. The precarious feeling from
standing on the glass floor lifts as the eye turns skyward and beyond to
the universe in the dome.

Back to terra firma, the black and white tile found in the corridors
on three floors originates in Vermont. The tiles are irreplaceable – their
quarries are depleted. The white tiles are marble, but interestingly, the
black tiles are limestone. By looking carefully fossils may be seen in them.

Throughout the building, the use of color and design in murals and
the gallery portraits of former governors makes the visitor feel as though
they are in an art museum. Visitors to the building and the people who
worked there could appreciate the gas chandeliers featuring native elk
and shields of the State.[16]

An unusual feature of the building was the elevator. It moved from
floor to floor by water displacement but was unreliable. Most days, the
Governor took the stairs to his office on the second floor. The Governor's office and parlor were spacious and had a luxurious appearance.
The woodwork throughout "appears to be walnut - and almost none
of it really is. Most of it is pine or other inexpensive woods, carefully
hand painted to mimic walnut. Called "good graining," this technique
involves applying seven layers of paint by hand. Every line of grain - and

even the pores in the wood - are painted by hand!" Edwin undoubtedly loved this money-saving feature.[17]

Let's Have a Party!

A "Governor's Levee" was held in February 1891 and hosted by the Detroit Light Infantry, one of many militia groups in the State. The Governor's reception honored the new Governor, past governors, and high-ranking military. The event was the climax of the social season. The Detroit Free Press describes it as "in every particular the most finished, interesting, and important affair of the kind ever seen in the Peninsular Commonwealth,"[18] so I guess it was a pretty big deal. The guests moved from the reception line in the Armory to the "rink," an acre-sized building decorated with palm trees in baskets, ferns, and foliage. The decorating committee added strips of red, yellow, and blue bunting, which they draped down from the center of the room. At one end of the room was a large likeness of Governor Winans flanked by portraits of past governors. There were bands at the north end of the gallery and at the south end. There was also another area where the guests could go for "supper." The supper was served sometime after 11 p.m. There were oysters, sandwiches, and desserts. Thousands of people attended this extravaganza - the "ticket price was $5 for a gentleman and a lady; extra ladies' tickets are $1 each. This includes everything, admission, supper, checking, etc." [19] "Mrs. E.B. Winans wore black faille silk, with a side panel of black lace over lavender satin; corsage garnitures with black lace, and diamonds."[20] This event firmly established the Governor as the commander-in-chief of the Michigan Militia. Although the Detroit Light Infantry was hosting, representatives from nearly every military organization in Michigan were there. From the private sector came professionals, manufacturers, and all branches of commerce - a representation of the people - thousands attended this spectacular occasion.

The Marshall Statesman March 13, 1891, Michigan's Governor Very Ill and 'Tis Thought He Will Die

"Gov. Winans is thought to be dying. He has had hiccoughs for thirty-six hours. A dispatch says: Gov. Winans of Michigan, has been afflicted with hiccoughs, from which his physicians have thus far been unable to give him more than temporary relief. Unlike those attacks which are usually the result of nervousness, the Governor's trouble returns after he has had long seasons of refreshing sleep. The attending physicians expressed considerable alarm at the Governor's condition. They fear that there is something serious back of the hiccoughs because of their constant recurrence. In December last Gov. Winans was very sick for several weeks with a stomach trouble, and the doctors apprehend that the present difficulty is due to the same cause. There is no concealing the fact that both the Governor's physicians and his family fear that the alarming feature of his illness has not yet fully appeared, and it is not improbable that he is afflicted with a fatal malady and may never again enter upon the active discharge of duties."[21]

Note: *Years after the death of the Governor, we know hiccoughs that last 48 hours or more may be indicative of a heart problem.[22] The Governor did return to work and completed his term of office, but the doctors were prescient in their fear that there was something more serious in the Governor's condition.*

In April of 1891, Edwin found another benefit of the governorship was to be entertained by the Marine Band. When "Director Sousa took his stand the enthusiasm of the crowd was evinced by royal applause. Handsome and magnificently formed, Mr. Sousa was an ideal director. He controlled the small world of music about him with graceful moves, usually with one arm, a nod here and there, and frequently with but a side glance to his men. The program included numbers by Wagner, Rossini, Rubinstein, and Gounod. A composition by Mr. Sousa styled the "Chariot Race" elicited two encores. At the close of the concert the band serenaded Gov. Winans at the capitol."[23]

Note: *John Philip Sousa was the Marine Band's 17th leader. He not only conducted, but composed - in 1888, he wrote "Semper Fidelis" traditionally known as the official mark of the Marine Corps. When he serenaded Gov. Winans, the band was on their first tour - a tradition which has continued since that time except in times of war." [24]*

The State Republican July 21, 1891: "Gov. Winans expects to be through haying and will have, his farm work far enough along to return to the capitol and devote a few hours to business on Thursday."[25]

What's On the Agenda?

Edwin had some specific things he wanted to accomplish in the two years ahead of him. He had an ambitious agenda for this short term of office. The Governor intended to reform election law, reduce expenditures, equalize taxation, establish a system and standard for road repair, and reduce the number of state boards. He had to surround himself with the right help to get even a portion done.

"Governor Winans read his inaugural to the Legislature Thursday. It was by far the most radical message presented by a Michigan Governor in many years. It advised a sweeping change from the present system of managing the State's institutions and recommended the abolition of the State Board of Health. He also advises that the State Board of Correction and Charities and the office of Game Warden be abolished, favors the cottage system for the care of the insane, an appropriation for Michigan's exhibit at the world's fair, the Australian system of voting, the establishment of a general system for good road making, and the county system for collecting taxes on land." [26]

Election Law: It took until July 1, 1891, to pass the election law based on the Australian system. Edwin approved the election law passed by the previous administration but did not feel it went far enough. The new law provided that the names of all candidates be printed on one ballot. Under the previous system, people at the polls could quickly determine how others were voting based on the ballot they chose - the ballots were different sizes and colors. According to the new law, the ballots must be printed at the county level, not by the Secretary of State. The election officials would distribute the ballots, and no one could take ballots out of the voting precinct. Edwin Winans was a proponent of the private vote and approved the new law, which preserved booth voting.[27] The passage of this law put Edwin's agenda on the way to completion.

A Place in Time: *June 5, 1891: From The News Palladium of Benton Harbor, Michigan*

On July 7, 1866, Benton Harbor became a town. Thirty-four years later, a movement developed for a merger with St. Joseph. There was a hassle over a combined name: some people suggested Zalediscoffokesonischi. St. Joseph won the favor of the state legislature, and a charter was prepared that would doom the name of Benton Harbor. Enraged Benton Harborites fought for their identity with protests that made legislators relent. On June 5, 1891, the pen of Governor Edwin B. Winans severed the consolidation as he signed bills granting separate city status to each village. This gave Benton Harbor and St. Joseph common birthdates as cities!

Road Repair: The roads in Michigan in the 1890s were not good and adversely affected the entire population. The State had spent a large amount of money without positive results. Edwin called for a general system of roadmaking with "competent supervision" that would gradually improve the quality of the road structure in Michigan. According to the Weekly Expositor in Brockway Centre, Michigan, the Governor appointed a highway commission to recommend a plan for improving the highways to the legislature. The Governor will send the report to the legislature and inform the public of their recommendations.[29] The Governor did not fix the roads during his tenure. It took his full two-year term for the commission to develop their plan.

Note: As a lifelong Michigander, I wonder what is so difficult about making and keeping good roads. It seems it should be a straightforward process, but it's government, so it quickly gets complicated. Edwin suggested a working system to ensure it is done consistently and correctly with competent supervision, and voila - good roads, but here we are more than 130 years later with the same problem, only more of it.

Judicious Expenditure: "There should be an effort made to reduce taxation and spending. The demand that only careful and needed expenditures be authorized is imperative and should be heeded," said Edwin. During Edwin's administration, the tax was a property tax - there was no income tax at the time, so farmers were most affected by the rate of taxation. Governor Winans said, "Our system of State taxation needs a thorough revision for the purpose of equalizing the assessment on property. Every industry, business and property interest should bear its just share of the burden of taxation. There seems to be no good reason why property owned and used by railroad, mining, telegraph and telephone companies, and other associations for private purposes should be exempt from general taxation. I doubt the policy of exempting any property from equal taxation. The granting of special privileges to any class affords just cause of complain to the masses." [30] Based on the governor's recommendation, the State Board of Equalization met and compared how property was valued around the State. Their proposed goal was "to make the equalization upon an equitable basis, and the fairest in the history of the state." [31]

Governor Winans also followed through with his declared intention to reduce spending by vetoing some legislation. The Governor vetoed the appropriation of $1,200 a year for two years to the Home of Discharged Prisoners. He was unequivocal in his reasoning: "The institution is a worthy one, but not more so than hundreds of others in the State which depend for support upon the free offerings of individuals. Charitable institutions are almost invariably poor, and money donations are peculiarly acceptable to them. The State, however, cannot afford to extend aid to all the deserving - we speak, of course, of those which are private in their character - and it has no right to make invidious distinctions or to single out one or more to be the recipients of state aid. That the power may reside in the State to make such an appropriation as the one in question may for the purpose of this argument be conceded. It was exercised two years ago in the case of this same institution, and there is probably no real doubt that it is clearly within the legislative discretion, the necessary two-thirds vote being obtained. It rests with the judgment and conscience of each legislator to say for himself whether such an appropriation of public money for private purposes is justifiable and right." [32]

The Governor stood firm in his defense of what should be paid for by the taxpayers of Michigan. He vetoed the bill appropriating $30,000 to the Grand Army of the Republic, making him the "most cordially hated man in the State." [33] (Harrisburg Telegraph. Harrisburg, Pennsylvania. May 28, 1891). "While this bill was pending in the House, Detroit appropriated $50,000 with the proviso of the State making a grant. The bill passed the House by a two-thirds vote of all the members, and then Winans vetoed it, killing the Detroit appropriation at the same time unless the bill was passed over his veto. His reasons as given in the veto, are that it is granting public money for a private purpose; that it is a scheme on the part of Detroit to make money, and the Grand Army men have no more right to it than a political convention or the General Assembly of Presbyterians now in session in Detroit." [34]

The veterans held a grudge, and the old soldiers were hissing the name of the Governor at the national encampment in Detroit. A Petoskey Democrat responded that they should blush with shame. "For four years, Edwin B. Winans was a member of the select committee on pensions, and month after month, he worked until after midnight four days a week arranging evidence and preparing reports to secure pensions for union soldiers. We know whereof we speak when we say that he did more work on the pension committee than any other two members of Congress and that hundreds of deserving soldiers, scattered all through the land, owe their pensions to the patient, honest work of this same Edwin B. Winans, who is now being denounced by a conscienceless partisan press as an enemy of the soldiers." [35]

The bill returned to the legislature, requiring a two-thirds vote of representatives and senators to pass over the Governor's veto. The votes were there to pass the bill in both houses, but then one of the legislators made a speech to allot the money and verbally attacked the Governor. "One of the leaders who had prepared a speech advocating the bill now sprang to his feet and defended the chief executive who had been so maligned for doing what he considered his duty. He advised that the Governor be sustained in his veto, repudiating the statements of the previous speaker and expressing the highest esteem for the chief executive. In a flash, a bill which was as good as carried was lost. Such loyalty, such a spontaneous expression of regard toward a leader, is a rare thing in politics," and there were tears in the Governor's eyes when he learned of the action in the House.[36]

Consolidating State Boards: The Governor kept his promise to combine state boards. The prisons and reform school operations by legislation came under the control of a single non-partisan board. The single board was an effective and saving approach to running these institutions. The reports from the individual institutions presented savings in expenditures and increased earnings to the State. The prison was able to provide the inmates with comfortable living quarters and, at the same time, maintain discipline.[37]

The Governor's policy reduced three boards to one for the State Public School at Coldwater, the School for the Blind, and the School for the Deaf. The "opportunities afforded a single board of using the knowledge and experience gained in one school for the advantage of prices of supplies assists in reducing expenses and promoting efficiency."[38]

In addition to reducing boards, the Governor looked for other ways to reduce spending. An expenditure in each year's budget included $8,000 for a geological survey. The State Board of Geological Survey had not provided a report on the State's geology in years, and Edwin recommended that it be completed, or the board abandoned. Once again, he focused on not wasting the citizen's tax dollars.[39]

Looking Out for Public Welfare: Edwin was also concerned with the growing popularity of Building and Loan Associations. He believed that the subscribers of these organizations had no means of knowing that the associations would be able to meet their obligations. Edwin thought the stockholders should be protected by having the business placed under competent state supervision so that the financial condition of these associations may be known by those asked to invest in them.[40]

The State Republican: June 22, 1891, *Falling Chandelier.*
"One of the large chandeliers in the west corridor of the Capitol fell down with a crash this afternoon that brought the occupants of the offices to the scene with a rush, thinking a cyclone had struck the building. The strong wind from the west, blowing through the open doors had swayed it loose from the ceiling fastener and down she came. A number of the globes were smashed and the framework somewhat bent

and broken. Luckily, no one was passing at the time, or the papers would have recorded a death." [41]

The State Republican August 10, 1891, Annual Report of Board of State Auditors for the Year 1892 Lighting: Chandelier "Board of State Auditors paid bills $40.29 for repairs to chandelier - probably hall chandelier - required man and two helpers to repair and rehang." [42]

The Columbian Exposition

In the test of time, some world fairs are memorable, and some are not. The fair held in Chicago from May to October 1893 was remarkable for several reasons. The setting was spectacular. The fairgrounds met up with the beautiful inland sea; the entertainment was unusual because no one had ever seen a Ferris wheel before; the inventions were novel and astounding, and the opportunity to showcase what industry and government had to offer the world was unprecedented.

By statute, Governor Winans was very much involved in the planning for Michigan's contribution to the Columbian Exposition. "The Act to create a Commission, define its duties and powers, and appropriate $100,000, for the purpose of making an exhibit of the manufactures and products of the State of Michigan at the World's Fair in 1893 became a law July 21, 1891. It provided that the Commission should consist of six residents of the State, two of them to be women, with the Governor an ex-officio member. The six members and the Secretary of the Board to be appointed by the Governor.[43]

The organization of the fair ensured its success from the outset. The planning started early, from international boards to the boards established for each organization represented at the fair. In Michigan, the Governor was responsible for appointing people to boards that governed not only the construction and decorations for the Michigan building but also the many exhibits that would represent business and industry in the State. Republicans criticized him for appointing only Democrats, but the Governor had the authority under the law to make the appointments as he desired. Governor Winans understood the benefit of exquisite exhibits to impress visitors from other states and the world.

He wanted tourists to come away knowing what Michigan had to offer regarding resources and people.

The festivities began on Columbus Day, October 21, 1892, months before the fair was ready to open. Celebrations honoring Columbus were nationwide, and it was the perfect day to dedicate the exposition grounds.

"Whereas, the President of the United States has by proclamation recommended the observance of that day by public demonstration and by suitable exercises in the schools and other places of assembly throughout the land."

"Now, therefore, I, Edwin B. Winans, Governor of the State of Michigan, hereby commend and request the observance by the people of Michigan of the said 21st day of October 1892 as a general holiday, that business be suspended, and that civil and military organizations join in the celebration. In testimony whereof I have hereunto set my hand and caused to be affixed the great seal of the State, this first day of September, A.D. 1892. Edwin B. Winans, Governor."[44]

The Governor attended the ceremony in Chicago along with 42 members of the Owosso Light Infantry as his guard. The special train they traveled on was parked in front of the Mining Building. The Mining Building was about 500 feet from their quarters. The soldiers ate their meals at the Agricultural Building and were disgusted with the food, which they said seemed to worsen daily. When they returned home, they acknowledged that they were impressed with the "vast and extensive World's Fair Buildings and the wonderful city of Chicago." [45]

The International Fair Board chose Chicago because they could provide railroad transportation to bring millions of visitors to the fair, and the financial support provided by Chicago's millionaires was also a factor. The professional planners of the fair had nearly 700 acres to lay out their beautiful white buildings separated by canals and perched on the banks of the unsalted sea. Architects met and collaborated to develop a vision for the fair buildings.

The result was fair architecture that influenced construction in the United States for decades. The Neo-classical European revival in white was stunning. Add electricity, and it became a fairyland at night.

Fair voyeurs could take a boat taxi from downtown Chicago to the wonderland in white. They could travel through the acres on Venetian gondolas, and replicas of the Nina, the Pinta, and the Santa Maria were reminders that the fair was in recognition of the 401st anniversary of Columbus' discovery.

For those fairgoers who wished to walk, there was the midway with offerings of food, entertainment, and souvenir purchases such as "a new-fangled postcard to send to their friends." [46] Walking the midway was new to the world's fair experience, and added to that was the thrill of riding on the gigantic wheel invented by George Ferris. The wheel was 250 feet in diameter, and a rider sat higher than the top of the Statue of Liberty at the highest point. It was Chicago's answer to the Eiffel Tower from the 1889 Paris fair.[47]

The fair showcased many spectacular inventions, but the most spectacular was electricity. In 1893, electricity was still not known by most Americans. President Cleveland pushed a button to electrify the fair. Lightbulbs provided by the Westinghouse company lit up the fairgrounds, and alternate current electricity became the standard in the United States due partly to its use at the fair.[48] Fair goers could witness the amazing machinery powered by electricity: electric incubators for chicken eggs, an electric sidewalk, electric irons, sewing machines, and laundry machines. Thomas Edison's Kinetoscope was there, the first moving pictures to astound attendees. Some products that debuted at the Chicago World's Fair were Cream of Wheat, Juicy Fruit gum, and Pabst Blue Ribbon beer.[49]

Note: *It is unknown if the Governor sampled the Cream of Wheat or the Juicy Fruit gum, but I'm pretty sure he did not try the Pabst Blue Ribbon beer because he was known not to drink. It is also pretty sure that he was not an electricity user in his lifetime. The capitol building did not have electricity until about 1900, and electricity was not a commodity on a farm in the countryside where Edwin and Elizabeth lived.*

Much of the fair's funding came from federal and State governments. However, private citizens served in appointed positions, and businesses and private citizens donated money and goods.

The headline was: MICHIGAN AT THE FAIR - Plans for a State Building Selected by the Commissioners. The Commissioners received eight plans for the building, and the contract was awarded to Mortimer L. Smith & Sons of Detroit. Smith & Sons was an established firm in the State, having already designed the J. L. Hudson store, among other buildings in Detroit. An issue of importance in deciding who would receive the contract was the shortness of time before the fair was to open. The design had to be locked in because Detroit, Grand Rapids, Saginaw, and other cities had been assigned a room they would finish using "particular woods and finishing materials of which they are the producers."[50] All of these things required time, and time was getting short.

The result was a "structure one-hundred by one-hundred-forty-four feet in dimensions, three stories high, and partly surrounded by broad balconies to the first and second stories. In the center of the west front rose a tower, pierced with windows, one-hundred and thirty feet in height. The grand tiled reception hall was sixty-two feet wide and the entire depth of the building. There were the usual offices for officials and a series of finely furnished rooms for visitors, beautifully finished in Michigan woods - having great fireplaces with carved oak mantels."[51]

A journalist, Marian Shaw, attended the fair. She wrote articles on her observations daily and submitted them to her employer. Her view of the Michigan building follows: "In the chaste and elegant Grand Rapids and Saginaw rooms of the Michigan building, one is fain to linger and listen to the soul-filling strains of the grand organ, which, at night, illuminated by 500 incandescent lamps, delights both eyes and ears. The Grand Rapids room is in Louis XIV style, in white and gold with old colonial fireplace. The walls are everywhere adorned with exquisite tapestries and paintings." [52]

The World's Columbian Exposition held in Chicago in 1893 was a significant event during the tenure of Edwin Winans as Governor of Michigan. He was involved in the process by appointing people to boards with oversight. He took a personal interest by attending the dedication of the grounds. He viewed participation in the exposition as beneficial to the State and fully supported this magnificent cultural event.

The Russian Famine

Another significant event during the Winans' administration was the famine in Russia. A drought in the Volga River region caused the Russian famine of 1891 - 1892. The famous writer and Russian Count Leo Tolstoy wanted to do whatever he could to help those most affected by the famine. He organized free food kitchens and wrote articles, spurring others to respond. The government of Russia wanted the issue silenced - they did not even want the word famine spoken. Tolstoy countered with a letter-writing campaign to get the attention of anyone outside of Russia to help the people. The famine became world news, and aid increased. Within two months, American financial contributions reached a total of $500,000.[53] The United States Minister to Russia requested help, saying that many thousands would die if they did not receive help soon. The President, Grover Cleveland, then asked the states for help. Governor Winans responded by issuing a proclamation and appointing a committee for the organization and execution of the response. In part, the proclamation read: "Now, therefore, I, Edwin B. Winans, Governor of the State of Michigan, do hereby recommend a prompt response by the people of our State to this appeal…Supplies of flour, cornmeal, cured meats, canned or dried fruits, and other provisions, as well as money contributions, are asked for and named above and marked "For Russian Famine Relief." Most newspapers printed the proclamation, rousing the population to support the people of Russia.[54] The failure of the grain crop and mismanagement of resources by Russia's government led to the Marxist revolution. It is approximated that millions of people were affected by the famine, and from 375,000 to 400,000 people died.[55]

Note: *Although the Governor disapproved of using tax dollars for causes such as aid to the Russians, he was happy to support and encourage others to voluntarily support this effort personally. (See picture/document of thank you to Governor for the $100.00 contribution.)*

The Democrat and Chronicle of Rochester, New York February 24, 1892

"Governor Edwin B. Winans of Michigan, is not very widely known outside of his State, for unlike many western governors, he does not often go East to visit cities and mingle with men in hotel corridors. He is a man of commanding appearance, with a tall, straight, military figure, iron-gray hair, and a mustache of like color. He is usually at his desk by 8 o'clock and is a hard worker." [56]

The Miner Law

The election of 1890 in Michigan not only established Edwin B. Winans as Governor but also resulted in a Democratic House and Senate. The new majority had the votes to pass anything they wanted. One of the first pieces of legislation they passed was the Miner Law, named after State Representative John Miner of Detroit.

Before the Miner Law, the presidential candidate winning the majority in the general election received all 14 electoral votes from the State of Michigan. The 1891 Michigan Legislature and the Governor, Edwin Winans, did not support this method as it disenfranchised the minority. If 49% of the State voted for the candidate in the minority, their votes essentially did not count.

To yield a more "exact expression of the preferences of the people," the Miner law established that in 12 congressional districts, the voters of each district would elect one elector. Two districts were established; each district was composed of six congressional districts, and the voters of each were to choose an additional elector. The State was entitled to a total of 14 electors.

Edwin Winans was firmly in favor of the Miner Law. He argued his reasons in support of the law in the North American Review. First, the Constitution of the United States provides, "Each State shall appoint, in such manner as the legislature thereof may direct, a number of electors equal to the whole number of Senators and Representatives to which the State may be entitled in the Congress." The method of choosing electors differed from State to State. In some states, the legislators picked the electors; in some, it was by popular vote in a general ticket, and others by district. There were different ways to set up districts as well.

Edwin gives several reasons in support of the bill. When the Constitution was written to include an electoral college, the presidential electors were not pledged to a specific candidate. They were free to choose the candidate who reflected the desires of the section they represented. Often, electoral votes were split between candidates. Governor Winans argues that if the intent was for a state's votes to go to one candidate, there would be no need to appoint electors. "The Presidential votes of a State could then have been cast by one officer as well as twenty."

By choosing electors based on the result of a general election, the majority decides even when the minority may represent 49% of the State. Therefore, if districts chose the electors, the votes would be equitably divided.

To those who argued that splitting up the electoral vote weakened the political power of the State, Edwin said, "If popular sentiment in a State is divided her electoral vote ought to be divided whatever the result."

Another argument was that the districts could be gerrymandered. The district lines were established to the benefit of one party. To that, Edwin said, "But if we condemn the gerrymander because it lessens the representation of the minority, what is to be said of a system which excludes the minority from any representation whatever? Yet this is the exact result attained by choosing Presidential electors on a general ticket."

The argument made by Edwin Winans in the North American Review (see Appendix B) gives you, the reader, an excellent impression of him, of how he thought and why he fought for the bill.

The bill as passed in 1891 was appealed to the Supreme Court of Michigan and found to be constitutional. However, the next administration passed a law negating the Miner Law.

Note: *This topic is as relevant today as it was in the 1890s. Some agree with Edwin Winans that we should get rid of the Electoral College because it doesn't represent the authentic voice of the people. Still, one of the reasons for the College was to offset the tyranny of the majority. Without an Electoral College, the states with the largest populations would run the country, and the minority views would be ignored. What is good for New York or California is not necessarily good for Michigan.*

The Miner Law appeals to many in Michigan because in a Presidential election, our biggest city, Detroit, carries the State, and often, the Upper Peninsula votes for the opposite candidate or policy. The minority vote in the northern part of the State is thus nullified.

I wish we could bring back the Miner Law to provide more equity in the system. Today, our polarized political parties would never allow a Miner Law. Both parties are more concerned with political power than they are a better-represented constituency.

The Governor's Window

Some prestigious guests visited the Capitol, and the Governor invited them into his apartments and private room. The Governor took the guests to the south window, which gave them a view of two churches. The Governor said, "Come here and look out. This is the window I look out of when I feel wicked." The guest, a clergyman, said, "Governor, I wish you could get the present legislature a window to look out of and see its wickedness." [57]

Note: *The churches the Governor referred to are no longer there. The 1st Presbyterian Church was on the corner of Capitol Avenue and Allegan. There is a parking ramp there now. The Plymouth Congregational Church was next door on Allegan Street.*[58] *(See postcard photo)*

Scandal

Accused of scandal, the Winans administration quickly responded. When the Governor learned of the accusations of misappropriation of state funds by the Secretary of State, Daniel E. Soper, he acted. He ordered three people, including one Republican, to investigate and give an accounting of the situation. Mr. Soper then resigned and admitted to guilt.

Detroit Free Press December 29, 1891,

"Gov. Winans' prompt and determined course in dealing with the Secretary of State's charge with malfeasance in office has greatly reduced the supply of wind in the sails of the calamity howlers on Republican tripods. They were prepared to picture wholesale corruption with banded conspirators behind it, but the Governor has said that the most thorough investigation must be had, no matter what the truth may involve, and that no whitewashing will be tolerated. The party that will punish its own wrong doers is a revelation so startling to the political freebooters who are in possession of the Republican machine that they stand in silent amazement." [59]

Beer for the Militia

Edwin Winans made his decisions based on evidence and experience, and once he made a decision, he was resolute and did not care if public opinion was against him. He decided it was acceptable for the militia to have beer at their encampment. Rev. J. M. Barkley of Detroit and others criticized him for that decision. Response to these critics is best in the Governor's own words. "I suppose this man Barkley is a good, conscientious man," said the Governor last evening when discussing the Barkley article, "but his ideas as to the advancement of temperance, as far as the state troops are concerned, at least, differ greatly from mine. Now, some people think it is a great harm to take a glass of beer, and perhaps it is, but I fail to see it. I think it was clearly demonstrated that the last encampment was a great improvement over that of previous years. There was less drunkenness and rowdyism, and I attribute it mainly to the fact that it was not necessary for the boys to sneak into camp their beer and other liquor or go to some town in the vicinity of the camp, there to remain until intoxicated, destroying property and getting into all sorts of trouble and perhaps the guard house. But instead, they were given the privilege of purchasing what beer they wanted right on the ground and were contented to remain within the lines and attend strictly to business. That the canteens, or saloons, as Mr. Barkley has seen fit to term them, were a success and exerted a good influence over the boys, is demonstrated from the fact that not a drunken man was seen on the grounds during the whole encampment."

"Then you would recommend the continuance of the canteens at future encampments, governor?"

"I certainly should; it is but following out a custom adopted in the regular army, and I think their usefulness is no longer doubted by any practical man of the world."

"How about Sunday, Governor? Would you not recommend that they be kept closed on the Lord's Day and no liquor sold?"

"As I understand it, the boys in camp have the same duties to perform on Sunday as any other day, and I see no reason why they should be deprived of any benefits that can be derived from keeping the canteens open. Fully 10,000 visitors were on the grounds the Sunday the boys were in camp, and yet no bad effects were noticed from the sale of beer. Not a particle of drunkenness was noticeable, while in other years, with liquor smuggled into camp from all quarters, drunkenness and rowdyism was apparent on every hand."

Governor Winans is frank if not politic."[60]

Note: *As demonstrated in his interview with the reporter, the Governor had thought out reasons for his decision to allow beer at the militia's encampment. The Governor shut down the "gotcha" question about Sunday beer drinking with more good reasoning.*

Detroit Free Press October 27, 1891: Notes from Hamburg "Hamburg, October 26 - The fine rains and recent cool weather have materially changed the condition of growing wheat in this vicinity. It is getting a fine start, and the ravages of the insects are not so apparent.

Governor Winans will abandon his farm for the winter, and he and Mrs. Winans will spend the winter in Lansing with a probable trip to Mexico and California. The Governor desires to look upon the land that was the scene of his early struggles. Lieut. Edwin B. Winans, Jr., who reported for duty on September 30 at Fort Supply, I.T., has been ordered to the field, not to fight Indians but to drive off the vast herds of cattle that are grazing unlawfully on the Cherokee strip." There is no evidence the Governor and his wife went on this probable trip.[61]

The Detroit Free Press of Detroit, Michigan October 27, 1892, Headline: Gov. Winans at Yale

"Yale, October 25 - Gov. Winans delivered a very able address to a crowded house here this afternoon. His remarks were confined principally to state issues, showing clearly that the present administration has been more economic than the one preceding it. His remarks on the tariff were so clear and concise that no one could help understanding him. Mr. Winans made many friends while here. A large hickory pole was raised here today." [62]

Vice-President Winans?

Governor Winans acted quickly to enact his policy of reducing government expenditures. Just as quickly, he was viewed as a government reformer nationwide. In an article in The Times (Philadelphia, Pennsylvania) July 18, 1891, *Farmers to the Front*, Winans is suggested as the Vice-Presidential running mate for Grover Cleveland. Farmers cast forty to forty-five percent of the ballots in the country; they contribute three-fourths of our exports. They are the principal consumers of imports, the news stated, and they wanted Michigan's farmer governor on the ticket.[63]

The State Republican August 16, 1892: Edwin Winans, He will not attend the State Convention
"The Hon. I.M. Weston, ex-chairman of the democratic state central committee, was about the corridors of the Morton last evening and extended his hospitality to the early arrivals in the field of the democratic convention battle. To a reporter, he expressed himself as confident that the proceedings of the convention would be carried out in a speedy and harmonious manner. When questioned as to the probability of the ticket, Mr. Weston said in substance that there was no possibility of a contest for Governor and that Winans would be nominated. Referring again to a leading question as to Morse's candidacy and a letter of withdrawal, Mr. Weston was of the opinion that it would be taken in good faith."
"The Winans boom will not be carried to Grand Rapids by any member of the family. The Governor has decided Lansing is a good enough place for him just at present and will split all his political good

right in the executive office. Major George will also be conspicuous at the convention by his absence, and if the nomination comes their way, it will be on the traditional silver platter not soiled by administrative hands and unsought for." [64]

Governor Winans Throws a Bomb

"That long-drawn-out conference in the Governor's office yesterday morning was not without fruit. As a result, Gov. Winans, late yesterday afternoon, sent the following message to Chairman Campau.[65]

To the chairman of the democratic state convention, Grand Rapids, Mich.

Dear sir - It is apparent that there will be in your convention a division of opinion in regard to who should be nominated for Governor. I have felt that owing to my views upon the financial question, I was not in entire harmony with all democrats and could not command the active and hearty support of a united, harmonious democracy if nominated. As I am an earnest, life-long democrat I desire to see the party successful, believing it will in the end settle all public questions for the best interests of the people. In the interest of harmony, therefore, I do not desire a renomination and would not accept it if it was tendered to me.

I am very respectfully yours,

Edwin B. Winans

Lansing, Michigan, August 16"

The State Republican August 17, 1892, Out of It: Gov. Winans Throws a Bomb Into the Grand Rapids Convention In the Shape of a Letter of Withdrawal. The Nomination Will Now Go To Morse. Gov. Winans Could Not Swallow Dickinson Rule and the Silver Plank.

"Gov. Winans positively refused to deny or affirm the rumor that he had sent a letter of withdrawal to the democrat convention last evening, but this morning, he felt different, and to the Republican said:

"Yes, sir, I am out of the race. You are welcome to a copy of my letter."

"Is there anything you desire to say or could say on the situation, governor?"

"Nothing. The matter was fully and fairly considered, and there is no string to it."

"It is rumored, governor, that you might be induced to accept a nomination for United States Senator."

"As regards that matter, you can say there is nothing politically that would tempt me. I am tired of public life and anxious to retire to my home, there to spend the rest of my days in peace. There is no public office in the gift of the people I would accept."

"Maj. Winans was asked this morning if his father's withdrawal meant his retirement for good from politics. "As far as office holding goes, yes," was the reply. "He is a Democrat, however, and will be found in line this fall." [66]

According to the August 17, 1892, article in The State Republican, including the Governor's withdrawal, the Governor could not 'swallow' Dickinson's rule. Donald Dickinson was a leader in the Democratic Party and considered an effective Democratic Organizer, but Dickinson "preferred the sound money policies of the Republican Party." Dickinson supported Edwin Winans as Governor for a second term, but with a 'sound money' plank. Edwin Winans was, without any doubt, a proponent of free silver. Edwin's letter of withdrawal said, "I have felt that owing to my views upon the financial question, I was not in entire harmony with all democrats and could not command the active and hearty support of a united, harmonious democracy if nominated." Edwin could see that the free silver plank was dividing the party, and a divided party would serve no one.[67]

"The free silver plank called for the unlimited coinage of silver, which would have effectively increased the money supply and inflation. The idea was popular with farmers and other debtors, who would have benefited from higher prices. However, creditors opposed it, who would have been hurt by subsequent inflation. The free silver plank was the most important issue in the 1892 election and was a major factor in Cleveland's victory. After the election, Cleveland worked to enact the policy, but he was ultimately unsuccessful. [68]

Note: *The Governor's letter should be taken at its face value, but I also think that part of the reason for withdrawal was Edwin's health. In hindsight, we know he had a bad heart. I think he was just too tired and ill to fight an uphill battle over free silver - especially within his own party and against another Democrat.*

First lady Elizabeth Winans wore this fur-trimmed cloak (from left) in 1891. Lt. Gov. Martha Griffiths wore this outfit in 1983 when she was sworn in. Lt. Gov. William Milliken wore the four-piece morning suit for President Nixon's inauguration in 1969.

Elizabeth's cloak is shown in a newspaper report on the inauguration in 1891.

Elizabeth's cloak she wore at the inauguration.
Courtesy of the Michigan History Museum

Hotel Downey was the residence of Edwin Winans during his administration from 1891-1892. The site later became the Knapp's Building.

The head of the walking stick is a quartz nugget
veined with gold, held in a gold mounting.

Walking stick leaning against a desk of the period.

Photograph of Edwin B. Winans – possibly taken when
he was Judge of Probate for Livingston County, Michigan.

First Capitol Building of Michigan

Second State Capitol Building

Michigan State Capitol Building 1890.

Governor Edwin B. Winans

1879 view of the inside of the governor's office.

Postcard picture of the two churches the
governor could see from his window.

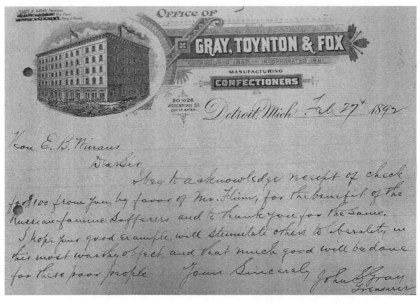

Acknowledgement and thank you for the $100.00
the governor donated to the Russian Relief Fund.

The Michigan Building at the Columbian Exposition of 1893 in Chicago.

Governor Winans with the Michigan National Militia 1891.

FARM AND FAMILY

The heart of Edwin and Elizabeth Winans life was the farm in Hamburg, Michigan. They were farmers by choice. Edwin would leave the farm to serve the town, the county, the state, and the country, but he always returned to the comfort of Elizabeth and the farm. "During the term he served as governor, Edwin continued his practice of going back to the farm whenever he could, and so was called the Farmer Governor."[1]

In April of 1893, a newspaperman from the Detroit Free Press happened to run into Edwin at the Hotel Cadillac. When the journalist approached the ex-governor, he said, "I have a little business here which will keep me two or three days. Politics is not my forte now, I am farming. Look at my hands, don't they prove it? I have been planting 700 fruit trees to take the place of the old orchard on our place. It was there when I first occupied the farm and I intend to leave as good an orchard when I go."[2]

Elizabeth must have been exuberant when they bought the farm she grew up on from her brother Stephen. When Edwin built the house overlooking the lake, she was comfortably happy in her role as lady of the house. She was co-steward of the property, and it was against her rules to cut down any trees unless it was absolutely necessary. "This created a primordial forest, so to speak, around the house."[3] The house Edwin built was an exceptional place with its serene setting on the shore of Pleasant Lake (Winans Lake). Based on census reports, the Winans never lived alone - in addition to the hired help, they opened the door to friends, family, and young people. Their home was a welcome destination for many.

Elizabeth was "an educated, refined woman, whose mental attainments and social qualities fit her for the position which she occupies as hostess of the Gubernatorial Mansion. The reference to the Gubernatorial Mansion was, of course, the Winans home." [4]

Elizabeth Galloway Winans was as much a leader as her husband. Her duties as a politician's wife took her from Hamburg to Howell and from Lansing to Washington D.C. before her obligations as First Lady of Michigan returned her to Lansing. She was "endowed by nature, education, and training with those qualities which made her a fitting helpmate through all the career of her honored husband."[5] Whether she was shaking hands in a receiving line or sewing gold coins into her dress, she was always his partner and companion. She fulfilled professional roles with dignity, but her favorite place was the farm where she was born. Elizabeth oversaw preserving the harvest from the farm; there were vegetables to can and apples to store in barrels. She must have entered items at the county fair and shared recipes with friends. She was an active member and leader with her husband at St. Stephen's Episcopal Church.[6]

Edwin returned to Michigan, after five years in California, on a mission to find a wife - Sarah. Knowing Sarah had been his first choice was disregarded by Elizabeth because she recognized something in Edwin that convinced her he was the right one for her. When she agreed to be his wife after her sister, Sarah, turned him down, Elizabeth made a covenant with Edwin that lasted the rest of their lives. Elizabeth went with Edwin across the continent, and although they both knew she would rather live in Hamburg than Rough and Ready, they stayed there for three years. However, moving back to Michigan was probably as much Edwin's idea as Elizabeth's because the gold business was slowing down there, and miners were moving to areas with more promise, resulting in dwindling bank business.

Note: *The little bit we know about Elizabeth Galloway Winans reveals her as a strong and opinionated woman. It takes a confident and loving man to appreciate those qualities in a woman, and Edwin loved and appreciated Elizabeth. They were so well matched that what we know about one tells us something about the other.*

Ed and Lib had a long and fruitful life together. They experienced the essential things in life: birth, death, success, failure, disease and health, and most of all, enduring love. They enjoyed the passion of youthful lust, learned the meaning of true love, and moved on to the closeness old age brings.

The Sons

George Galloway Winans, the eldest son of Edwin and Elizabeth, was born in Rough and Ready, California, in 1856. He was very young when they returned to Hamburg in 1858 and grew up on the family farm. George stayed close to home most of his life. He was active in helping with the farm but lived, according to the 1880 census, in Howell. The census shows George living in a hotel run by William H. Gaines in Howell, and his occupation is a bank clerk. Edwin also had a residence in the hotel for a time.[7] George was also undoubtedly involved with a business his father owned in Howell. That business burned down in a fire in 1892.

October 6, 1892: From the Detroit Free Press of Detroit, Michigan
Headline: **A Fatal Fire**
Howell, October 5 - (Special) "The most disastrous fire since March 1857 started about 1 o'clock this afternoon and burned until 5, destroying one whole block except the Topping brick store on Grand River Street. The stores were owned and occupied as follows: Corner stores owed by Greenaway and occupied by Monroe Bros., dry goods, building, and contents insured. Double store, owned by Gov. Winans. Dry goods, clothing, boots, shoes, etc. A heavy stock, but it was well insured. As soon as the fire became unmanageable, help was telegraphed for, and the fire department from Lansing responded as soon as a train could fetch them, but the fire had burned to the street, and the walls of the last building were falling before they could be of any service. They did good work in helping to save other property, and if they had been here two hours earlier, they could have saved much property and one or more lives." [8]

Later - "The smoking ruins of Hickey & Goodnow's store have given up their dead, blackened, and burned almost beyond recognition, and it is worse than at first supposed, there being two, instead of one, so far discovered."[9]

Note: *Traveling back and forth from Hamburg to Howell by horse and buggy took significant time out of a business day. Instead of living in a boarding house, Edwin built a house in Howell, giving the Winans family a place to reside while doing business there. The well-maintained house still sits on a large corner lot and is currently divided into apartments. The carriage house is still there but in need of repair.*

George Galloway Winans married Catherine Valentine on December 26, 1889. Their son, Edwin Valentine, was born in 1893, and their daughter, Elizabeth, was born in 1891. George Winans was what could be called a "jack of all trades." He was a farmer on his father's farm and one he owned. George followed his father to Lansing when Edwin was Governor to act as private and military secretary to the Governor.[10] George G. Winans was a member of one of the state militias and attained the rank of major. He was also a customs collector in Detroit for a time.[11] George had a postal route as well. He was active at the State Fair with the poultry exhibit in his spare time. It seems George was handy at just about anything.[12]

Edwin Baruch Winans, Jr. was born on October 31, 1869. The following year, his father built the house on Pleasant Lake where Edwin Jr. and his brother George grew up. Elizabeth and Edwin would live there for the rest of their lives. Growing up on the farm with a father of some prominence - Edwin Sr. had served in the state legislature and a constitution convention - did not mean little Edwin was a privileged child. His parents were comfortable but certainly not wealthy. The 1870 census shows their real estate was worth $16,000, and their personal estate was worth $10,000. Their total worth in 2023 would be over 600,000 - Edwin Sr. was not a millionaire.[13]

Edwin Jr. attended the Orchard Lake Academy from 1884 through 1887. He played the triangle in the band there. In his last year there, he worked as a professor; he must have been a very bright student.[14]

Edwin entered the United States Military Academy at West Point at 18 and graduated in 1891. Edwin, Jr. married Edith May Auman at Fort Supply, Oklahoma, on June 1, 1892. She was the daughter of Captain William Auman. They were the parents of two children: Catherine was born 7-17-1894 at Ft. Supply, Indian Territory, and Elizabeth was born 6-15-1902 in San Francisco, California.[15]

His distinguished career took him from West Point to the Philippines, from the Arizona-Mexico border into Mexico with an expeditionary force. "During World War I, he served in France commanding the 6th Infantry. He was awarded the Distinguished Service Medal and the Silver Star."[16] He was superintendent of the U. S. Military Academy, commanded the 10th Cavalry, and retired due to age on November 1, 1933. After retirement, he served on a League of Nations Commission.[17]

Major General Edwin B. Winans, Superintendent of the Military Academy at West Point, was involved in a brouhaha with Admiral Nulton, Superintendent of the Naval Academy, over eligibility rules for collegiate sports. The admiral "thinks three years of intercollegiate athletics should be the limit allowed a transfer student in the service schools. The general thinks there ought to be no limit."[18] Since the two superintendents could not agree, there was no Army vs. Navy game in 1927, 1928, or 1929. Play resumed in 1930 after differences were reconciled. General Winans moved on to other assignments before play was resumed.

The sons of Edwin and Elizabeth were accomplished and valued citizens. As a family, they attended St. Stephens Church in Hamburg. Elizabeth and Edwin schooled their sons in religion and what it meant to be a responsible member of society. Their parents guided their lives and influenced them to be their best. Family was the core of their existence, and their family not only included biological connections but others as well.

Extended Family

The Winans household was a place that was welcoming to all and a home to some. The Winans took in an orphan of seventeen in 1875. He appears in the 1880 census as part of the Winans household. Howard

Hovey lived at the farm and was considered a part of the family. He remembers life at the farm was simple and wholesome. "Mrs. Winans was a woman of character and culture and a competent and thrifty housewife. She would allow no other cook in her kitchen, the table was always bountifully supplied with good things, and there was always room and a welcome for a friend or a chance wayfarer." [19]

Howard Hovey remembers "Ed Winans" as having an even temper and a cheery disposition. "While a man of great force of character, he did little governing of the younger members of the family, good conduct was inspired not by fear of punishment but by the satisfaction of winning his approval." [20]

Howard Hovey married Helen Galloway, the daughter of Stephen and Eliza Galloway. Stephen was Elizabeth Winans' brother, and his marriage connected him to the family by marriage. Howard also served the Winans Administration - the Governor hired him on his first day in office day as his executive clerk. [21]

The lives of both Edwin and Elizabeth Winans touched many others with their concern and their example. Life on the farm was memorable, where friends and hired help learned it was necessary to work hard if they wanted the approval of the "judge."

Harry Kislingbury was a student at Orchard Lake Academy with Edwin Jr. and became acquainted with the Winans family. Harry's mother, Agnes Bullock Kislingbury, died in 1878, leaving Harry an orphan when his father died. Harry had a guardian while he was a student at Orchard Lake, but the guardian committed suicide. [22] Harry had a tragic early life and found empathy and guidance at the Winans home. Harry had a famous father, Frederick Kislingbury. He was a member of the Greely Expedition to the North Pole in 1881. The Greely Expedition got stranded and then forgotten. Those responsible for sending the expedition supplies did not send any because they thought others were doing it. The group managed to survive for three years. Frederick did not survive. To add to this tragedy, after Frederick's body was returned to the United States it was discovered he had been cannibalized. [23] It is no doubt that Elizabeth and Edwin were heartsick with the knowledge of what young Kislingbury had been through and offered him the warmth and love he greatly needed. The relationship between Harry and the Winans family is evident in his correspondence with them.

An example of Harry's correspondence with Governor Edwin Winans:[24]

Los Angeles, Calif.
Dec 27th, 1891
Dear Judge:
"Your most kind letter came duly to hand, it being forwarded to me from Riverside, and as you see by the heading I have moved over here in hope of getting steady work. Have at last succeeded and I go up to Newhall, in the morning, but will have to leave my family here for the present. Newhall is situated about thirty miles north of here. Am going to work on grain ranch, one dollar per diem and board, but still this is much better than doing nothing. Have been here three weeks and this is the first work that I have succeeded in getting. Have had a hard time of it I assure you, being utterly without funds. But thank God, I have work, such as it is. However, it is enough to support us and perhaps something better will turn up. I sincerely hope that you or Gen. Schofield will succeed in obtaining a permanent position in Washington. I shall be most grateful and will endeavor to give satisfaction. When you go to Washington you can tell Gen. Schofield, just exactly how I am fixed. To be plain, I am here and broke and with work just sufficient enough to support my family. You see there is such an influx of people…(unintelligible) that it is next to impossible to get a situation, and I being a stranger it was so much the harder for me. If anything of war turns out of the Chilean squabble, I shall certainly go to the front. I hold a Captain's Commission in the N.G. of Arizona. Have held it for the past two years. Shall keep up a good heart however and will probably come out on top yet. Regards to Mrs. Winans, yourself, and George, and best wishes for your health."
I am truly yours,
Harry Kislingbury

Harry Kislingbury knew the Winans family and has given us an insight into their character. He knew the family because he attended Orchard Lake Academy with Edwin Jr. and then felt confident enough in his relationship with them to ask Edwin Sr. for help obtaining a job. Harry contacted the "judge" because he knew Edwin as an advocate and friend.

And the Rest of the Story

Elizabeth was a wife to Edwin, a hostess at the mansion, and a loving mother to her sons, George and Edwin Jr., and to Howard Hovey, whom some called an adopted son. She was also a grandmother to Edwin Valentine Winans, and a granddaughter, Elizabeth, children of their son George. Sadly, little Elizabeth died in February of 1894, months before the death of Edwin in July of that year. After Edwin died, two more granddaughters were born, daughters to her son Edwin Jr., whom she called "Ned." Elizabeth did not see Edwin Jr.'s girls often because they moved around the country with the military, but the neighborhood children also called Elizabeth "Grandma Winans." One of those children later remembered that she was a very gracious woman and not too large." [25]

Elizabeth's sister, Sarah, lived in the Oklahoma Territory with her husband and two daughters, according to the 1890 census. The 1890 census for Hamburg was destroyed in a fire, but we know that Sarah died in Hamburg in 1899. An article in The Fort Worth Daily Gazette, June 21, 1891, states: "Sarah Galloway's husband, whom she married in preference to Winans, died and left her an invalid with two children. She has ever since made her home in the hospitable mansion of Governor Winans, to whom she promised in the long ago to be a sister." [26] Sarah's husband died in Edmond, Oklahoma, on August 9, 1890. It is reasonable to think Sarah returned to Hamburg after his death and lived with the family in the mansion on Pleasant Lake.

Note: *Interestingly, Sarah would not go west with Edwin when he wanted her to marry him and move to Rough and Ready, but then she married Milton Reynolds and moved west with him. She evidently changed her mind about moving west, but the evidence of her regard for Edwin is that she named one of her daughters Edwina.*

Sarah's daughter, Susan Reynolds, was interviewed in 1937 by the "Indian-Pioneer History Project for Oklahoma. She relates the story of her father staking a claim in Oklahoma Territory. She stated, "The first year of our life in Oklahoma was quite hard. We did not have too much to eat. That year, my uncle, who lived in Michigan, sent us quite a lot of canned fruit and vegetables and a large barrel of apples." [27]

Note: *Their first year in Oklahoma was 1869, and I believe Edwin Winans is the uncle who sent the food to Sarah's family. Although Stephen Galloway was also her uncle, Edwin owned a large farm and orchard and was more likely to have the goods to send from his farm and the ability to afford the cost of transportation.*

The 1900 Hamburg census shows Elizabeth as head of household and her sister, Julia, living with her. Julia was an invalid and cared for by Elizabeth and George for the rest of her life. The 1900 census shows George G. as the owner of his own farm in Hamburg.[28] By 1920, George was living at the family farm and listed as head of household, and it was quite the household. Living there was his wife Catherine, their son Edwin V, daughter-in-law Ethel, and their son George; Elizabeth lived there - she was 84; Elizabeth's sisters, Julia and Mary, were also living there.[29]

The Governor's mansion burned to the ground on January 20, 1924. George Winans was there and helped his mother, who was sick, away from the burning building. Neighbors helped to save some of the contents of the building, but the house was destroyed.[30]

Elizabeth was the last of her sisters to die on February 2, 1926. George retired and moved his family to Montana in 1925.

Eventually, the property was sold, and the Daughters of the American Revolution placed a bronze plaque on a large boulder at the site commemorating where the home of the 22nd governor of Michigan had been.

Left to right: Julia Galloway, Elizabeth Winans, and Mrs. Bode on the porch at the governor's mansion in Hamburg, Michigan.

The Winans' home in Howell, Michigan.

Edwin Winans, Jr. – a cadet at Oakwood Academy.

Harry Kislingbury – a cadet at Oakwood Academy.

General Edwin B. Winans, Jr.

Plaque at the site of the Winans home on Winans Lake.

PRAISE FOR THE GOVERNOR

In August 1893, the Detroit Free Press reported that friends had commissioned a portrait of the ex-governor. Although it was customary for governors to present a picture of themselves to be hung in the capitol, they usually had to buy and present the portrait themselves. "During his term as governor of this state, Edwin B. Winans, of Hamburg, made for himself a small army of friends - friends of the enduring sort with whom politics cut no figure. These friends have taken it upon themselves to show their appreciation of his worth; it will take the form of a portrait, in oil of himself, to be hung in the executive chamber of the state capitol. The fact that Mr. Winans' friends have done this for him is an extraordinary act showing the universal esteem in which he is held." [1]

When his term as governor was over, Edwin returned home "prepared to settle down to rural quiet - to become what he proudly called himself, "a practical farmer," and devote himself to his duties there. "I want to pass the remainder of my days peacefully, though actively, on my farm," he said, among my friends and in a community where I have known persons for many years." [2]

Edwin Winans had seen much of the North American continent from Michigan to California by land and then from the Pacific to the Atlantic Ocean via the Isthmus of Panama. He lived intermittently in Washington, D.C., on the East Coast during his time as a congressman. As governor, Edwin traveled all around the state. He had seen unique geographical artistry all over the continent. However, he most appreciated the incredible beauty of the area he called home. Livingston County was prime farmland, growing abundant crops of corn and wheat. The

187

forests and orchards were first-rate. The rolling hills interspersed with little lakes made the scene even more picturesque. His love for the land and those he served could only be exceeded by his love for his family, especially his lifelong companion, Elizabeth Galloway Winans.

On July 3, 1894, Edwin kept an eye on the young men spreading Paris Green on potato plants in the garden. He had been diagnosed with pneumonia and advised to stay in bed but chose to be out and about near activities on the farm that day. He overdid himself and ended up back in bed. The next morning, Tuesday, July 4, 1894, "he sat up in bed and read the newspapers and talked with friends at his bedside until a few minutes before he died" at 4:30 in the afternoon." [3]

Words chosen to describe the life of a person after death leave for perpetuity a reflection of them locked in time. "The deepest gloom is spread over the entire community, as the governor always had a pleasant word and a smile for everyone he met. Governor Winans was a clear-headed, modest man who possessed to an unusual degree the confidence of the agricultural and business interests of the state. In politics, he was an uncompromising Democrat, and in his public declarations, he has always been an advocate of tariff reform and the free exchange of silver." [4]

Although sorrow for the passing of the much-loved governor spread across the state and the country, his closest neighbors and friends were most affected by the loss. "Hamburg, Mich., July 5 - (Special) This village is mourning the death of ex-Gov. Winans. The news was a shock to every person for miles around, as the governor's genial disposition had endeared him to all. While the funeral tomorrow will be private, nearly everyone here will attend. The greatest sympathy is expressed for Mrs. Winans." [5]

Note: *I pause to consider the statement, "While the funeral tomorrow will be private, nearly everyone here (Hamburg) will attend." Nearly everyone in the village was considered a friend and invited to the funeral. I want to put an emoji heart right here.*

Howell, Michigan, was a place where Edwin was well known and where he chose to build a second home. He served as Probate Judge at the courthouse in Howell and operated a business from there. "All flags that are unfurled today are at half-mast and a feeling of sadness hovers over the whole village. Political preferment meant to him a public trust, and while holding such trust, he considered himself no better than when he was swinging a pick in the mines of California or working on his farm in Hamburg." [6]

The Funeral

"Upon the lawn in front of the house were about a couple of hundred residents of the vicinity. The remains were placed in the hall, and all the friends from the immediate locality and elsewhere filed in to glance at the pallid features, which had changed little with death. The body was in a heavy red cedar casket covered with broadcloth, and beneath it was a handsome placement of flowers, with the words, "At Rest." [7]

"The Episcopal funeral service was read by Rev. M. Stones of the Hamburg Episcopal church. After the regular service to the dead, the rector announced that a few remarks would be made by Rev. W. H. Osborne, and Judge Newton. The former said that he had known the late ex-governor well when he attended St. Paul's Episcopal Church during his sojourn as chief magistrate in Lansing. A high tribute to the Christian character of the deceased was paid by the reverend gentleman, who dwelt upon the importance which should be attached to the belief in the fatherhood of God by persons holding earthly positions of trust." [8]

Judge Newton was an old friend; "they had met in California in days when the gold fever was at its height." He described Edwin as "tender as a child and tolerant in the extreme. He knew what his rights were and what were the rights of other men. Devoid of prejudice, the welfare of the people of all classes and parties was dear to him." [9]

The funeral train, consisting of open vehicles of all descriptions, extended over a mile. Beneath the shadow of a tree in the graveyard, the casket was lowered into the earth after the usual preliminaries of the Episcopal church, and sadly, the mourners and their friends turned from the spot. It was an ideal day. The country never looked more charming. The simplicity of the services made a lasting impression on everyone.[10]

Not only the services but also the man himself made a lasting impression. A Detroit Free Press writer reminisced about his relationship with the ex-governor in his article *He Is Dead* in the Detroit Free Press of July 5, 1894: "Those who served with the governor in 1891 and succeeding years when he was Michigan's chief executive remember well his uniform courtesy and kindness. He would never injure the feelings of anyone and would take many an extra step to serve a friend. Of his integrity, his associates in the state offices and the legislature entertained the highest respect, for he was known to be a man who would not deviate in the slightest from what he considered was right. His aim was to serve the people to the best of his ability and their interests he took to heart. In January 1891, at the beginning of his administration, he said to the writer of this article: "My aim shall be to save the people in every possible direction in the matter of taxation. Persons in the cities are apt to underestimate the importance of economy in a state administration, but in the rural districts it is of much moment how much money is expended annually." [11]

Note: *I don't know how many governor's of Michigan can say, without using some fancy accounting tricks, that they decreased spending while in office, but I'm pretty sure it's a low number.*

The Crawford Avalanche in Grayling, Michigan, July 12, 1894:

"Mr. Winans was clear-headed and possessed good business common sense. While not originating any great measure while in the Legislature or Congress, he was always much consulted by his colleagues on account of the confidence they had in his good judgment. He was very hospitable, and his residence was always a gathering place for friends, who were not confined to any one party. He was conservative, but a strong believer in tariff reform. He was not an eloquent speaker, but pleasant, conveying the impression of truth and sincerity to his hearers. Not only have the Democrats lost a strong man, but the state has lost one of its best citizens." [12]

Note: Edwin was described more than once as clear-headed. It strikes me as an adjective not used much, but it appropriately describes him. He was consistently clear-headed. He did not have to "step outside" to clear his head. He was all the synonyms - perceptive, sensible, rational, and recognized as such.

The Lima News, Lima, Ohio. July 5, 1894:

"Mr. Winans was born in New York State in 1826 and was a resident of Michigan since 1834, with the exception of eight years spent in California in the '50s, since when he has been a prominent farmer of Livingston County. He had always been a radical Democrat, and, besides his term as governor in 1891 and 1892, served as member of congress and of the state legislature. His administration as governor, while conservative and economical, gained the respect of all and the commendation of his constituency quite generally regardless of politics." [13]

It is my hope that the governor has gained your respect regardless of politics.

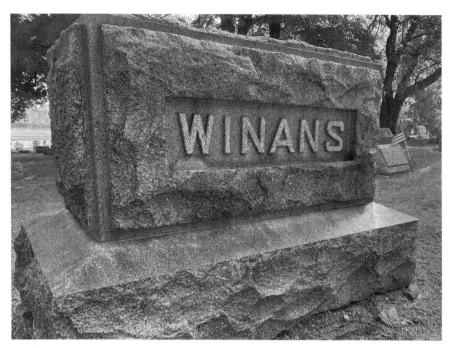

Winans family marker at Hamburg Cemetery.

EPILOGUE

Research on Edwin Baruch Winans, 22nd Governor of the State of Michigan, led me down unexpected roads. I met some folks I never expected to meet. I came serendipitously across some sweet little nuggets of history I could not resist adding to the book and some obscure enough to be left out. The most significant thing I learned was that the dead can still live. Edwin will continue to live in this book and in the hearts of readers who learn to like him, as I did, and what he stood for. In my list of desired reincarnations, Edwin is near the top. I wish I could have interviewed him - maybe that's another book.

The goal of this book is to introduce you to this great man and for you to learn something from him. Consider his arduous overland trail adventure and success in the stampede for gold when many were not successful. Reflect on his return to Michigan and the fateful change in his choice of a bride. Give thought to how his sound judgments and integrity led to accomplishments in both politics and as a practical farmer. Then, we add all the events surrounding this story - the Civil War, Washington, D.C. in the 1880s, the Chicago World's Exposition, and the Russian Famine. The laws passed during his administration in two short years, the Voting Law and the Miner Law, were radical new concepts. As Governor, he reduced expenditures. Yes, he cut the spending. He got his money's worth in a geological survey. He sent out a team to equalize property values. He did not fix the roads. They are still not fixed.

Edwin said that he wanted to run for Probate Judge to make a name for himself, and that was only the beginning. After years in politics, the name he made for himself was that he was a man who valued hard work, was trustworthy and kind, made good decisions, and then stuck to them. Even people who disagreed with him respected him. The name he made for himself was his legacy. Edwin Winans left this heritage to his sons, George Galloway Winans and Edwin Baruch Winans, Jr., as both were examples of integrity and hard work, and his legacy continues to affect his descendants 130 years after his passing.

As the Governor's walking stick was passed on to each new generation of Winans men, they stopped to consider who the man was who originally owned this stick. The first to receive the gift of the walking stick knew its significance and why the Governor chose to pass it to his brother's side of the family, but the message did not remain as pristine as the walking stick. Making up a good story has always been a talent the Winans men have, but there are a couple of things I know- the walking stick belonged to the Governor, and he passed it on to his brother's descendants, but I do not know which nephew was the first to receive it. What I know is that Edwin passed on more than the stick.

As I researched *The Extraordinary Life of Edwin Baruch Winans*, I saw glimpses of what I would call Winans attributes in Edwin's descendants. I briefly knew Case Winans, who was much like the Governor - a man recognized as honest, hardworking, and kind - a man of principle. Case Winans was a store owner and well thought of as a trustworthy entrepreneur and businessman in the Lansing area. He loved a practical joke and delivered them with a twinkle in his eye. I know that Case passed the stick to his son, Gerald. Case's son Gerald "Jerry," was much like his father - his light-hearted love of joking was a big part of who he was. *I think Edwin must have been the same jovial appreciator of a good joke. His portraits are all serious because there were not cameras everywhere snapping up emotions, but I'll bet you good ole' Uncle Ed laughed heartily at a well-done practical joke.* Jerry, like his Uncle Edwin, was community minded. He was president of the local school board for years and was so well regarded a school was named for him in Lansing just as a school had been named for his uncle in Hamburg. I know that Gerald passed the walking stick to his son David. David is known as a jokester and has also led a life of community service. He served as a volunteer firefighter for 47 years; most of those years, he worked full-time for the Department of Corrections. He devoted many hours to educating children on fire safety. He was honored as the recipient of the Governor's Volunteer Award for his service in public fire education, and so Edwin's legacy continues to prevail. There are many outstanding people with the name Winans, and I wish I could have given all of them a paragraph, but this would not have been a completed book in my lifetime.

The lesson is if you want someone to write a book about you 130 years after your death or even have a thought about you after that period, you need to be a moral person who cares about others, works hard, and with perseverance attains great things.

Gerald N. Winans School, Michigan Ave. Lansing, Michigan.

Winans Lake School. Courtesy Hamburg Historical Society.

TIMELINE

1826   Edwin Baruch Winans born May 16, 1826, in Avon, New York. Edwin is the 8th child of John Winans, and the only child of Eliza Way Winans. Edwin had six half-sisters, and one half-brother. Chronologically they were: Mary, Louisa, Esther, Harriet, Theron, Emily, and Nancy. Their mother was Betsy Bates Winans who died in 1818.

1834   Moved with parents John and Eliza Winans to Unadilla, Michigan, and then to Hamburg to live with his sister, Nancy, and go to school.

1842   Edwin's father, John Winans, dies December 2, 1842.
Edwin begins working for Seth Pettys carding wool. Edwin and his mother move to a log cabin. Edwin completes his contract with Seth Pettys.

1846 -
1847   Attended and graduates Albion College.

1847 -
1850   School teacher

1850   In March Edwin leaves for California with two friends, four horses, and a wagonload of supplies. Arrived in Placerville, California in July.

1853   Success in mining enabled Edwin to invest in the Randolph Hill Mine and the Rough and Ready Ditch Co. Then opened a bank with a partner - they bought gold from miners and sold it to the mint.

1855   Returned to Michigan via the Isthmus of Panama
When he reached Hamburg, he learned of the death of his mother. Eliza Winans died July 1, 1952.
Asked Sarah Galloway to marry him and she refused.
September 4, 1855, married Elizabeth Galloway.
Returned to Rough and Ready, California

1855 -
1858   Edwin and Elizabeth lived in Rough and Ready, California

The Extraordinary Life of Edwin Baruch Winans

1856   George Galloway Winans born July 20, 1856.

1858   Return to Michigan

1858   Returned West with friends in a venture they hoped would be profitable. Fell off a stagecoach and shot himself in the shoulder. Treated for his injury in Salt Lake City, Utah, and returned home weeks later.

1862   Edwin's brother, Theron dies in DeWitt, Michigan on April 12, 1862.

1860 -

1865   Michigan State Legislature. Second Capitol Building. Civil War.

1866   Edwin bought farm from Stephen Galloway.

1867   Edwin is a member of the Constitutional Convention.

1869   Edwin Baruch Winans, Jr. born October 31, 1869.

1872 -

1880   Probate Judge of Livingston County - the Court House he worked in later burned to the ground.

1883 -

1887   United States Congress - 48th and 49th Congress - Edwin was on the Agriculture Committee and on the Pension Committee.

1890   Campaign for Governor

1891 -

1892   Governor of Michigan:
                Election Law
                Miner Law
                Columbian Exposition
                Russian Famine

1894   Edwin Winans dies July 4, 1894.

1924   Farmhouse burns down. January 20, 1924.

1926   Elizabeth Winans dies February 2, 1926.

Appendix A

Messages of the Governors of Michigan Vol. 3 1869-1897
Michigan Historical Commission, Lansing. 1927
Michigan State Archives

Biographical Sketch

Edwin Baruch Winans, only child of John and Eliza Winans, was born at Avon, New York, May 16, 1826, and died at his home in Hamburg, Michigan, July 4, 1894. At the early age of eight years, he removed with his parents to Michigan, where they settled upon a farm at Unadilla, Livingston County. There he attended the public schools which at that time were of course very primitive. While yet a lad his father died, and his mother moved to Pettysville, a little hamlet which had nothing to recommend it but a good waterpower, on which had been erected a flouring-mill and a wool-carding and dying establishment. There the lad found employment, grinding grist for the farmers, and dyeing and pressing the domestic flannels for the farmers' wives.

But Edwin Winans had higher ambitions, and at the age of twenty he entered Albion College. There the same industry characterized his efforts. Early and late, he was found at his tasks, and no amusements diverted him from his studies. It was his intention, as soon as prepared, to enter the Law Department of the University of Michigan at Ann Arbor, but the discovery of gold in California changed his plans. In March 1850, he started for California by the overland route, with a respectable outfit consisting of four good horses and a wagon well filled with supplies. What privations he suffered, and perilous escapes from the attacks of Indians and wild animals will never be written in history nor fully. Understood except by those who were fortunate enough to accomplish the same hazardous journey. But his experience brought him in closer sympathy with the toiling masses who were struggling for bread and homes. After weeks of weary traveling, the horses became disabled, footsore, and reduced to mere skeletons. It was found necessary to put the provisions on the back of the best-preserved horse. Finally, it could go no farther, and young Winans, making a packhorse of himself, took the necessary supplies on his own back, and left the faithful animal on the bleak plains. After four months, footsore and weary, and in an almost exhausted condition, he arrived at Placerville. As soon as sufficiently recuperated, he commenced digging in the mines for the precious metal, at which he labored with varied success for a considerable time. Later he was one of the principal stockholders of the Rough-and-Ready Ditch Company, at the same time engaging in a bank in the town of Rough-and-Ready.

In 1855, he returned by ocean steamer and then went to Hamburg, his former home, to find that his mother in the meantime had passed to the Great Beyond. In September of the same year he married Miss Elizabeth Galloway, daughter of one of the early pioneers of Livingston County, and soon after, with his wife, he returned to California. Mrs. Winans, however, was not in love with her California home, and in 1858 he sold out his business there and they sailed for their Michigan home, where they settled on the farm on which Mrs. Winans was born.

But the restless spirit of adventure would not be quieted. With the Idaho excitement Mr. Winans started overland to what then was a far-off country, at that time a perilous undertaking. On one occasion he came near losing his life because of the accidental discharge of his own gun, on his return trip by stage. The country was overrun by robbers and outlaws, and scarcely a stage passed over the route without being way-laid and robbed. Everyone went heavily armed. When he loaded his gun for the trip he remarked to a friend, "The man that gets that will get ____." The roads were over the roughest country, and the drivers were reckless and daring. In passing over a dangerous part of the road the stage was upset, and Mr. Winans received the contents of his own gun. He was badly wounded, and five days ride from the settlements. After arriving at Salt Lake City, he had the medical attendance and care necessary for his recovery, and after a few weeks was able to continue his journey homeward.

Mr. Winans now quietly settled down upon his farm, where he continuously resided thereafter, save when called upon by the people to represent them in the State and National capitals. He was elected to the State Legislature in 1860, and re-elected in 1862, and in 1867 was a member of the Constitutional Convention. He was a judge of probate of Livingston County from 1877 to 1881. He was also elected to the forty-eighth and forty-ninth Congresses, where as a member of the Pension Committee he was influential in helping old soldiers in the advancement of their claims. On September 10, 1890, he was nominated for Governor of Michigan in the Democratic State Convention at Grand Rapids and was elected by a plurality of about 12,000. He had always been a Democrat. He believed the tariff to be a tax paid by the people, and that it should be levied for revenue only. He was an advocate of the free coinage of silver. On temperance he was with his party, though he did not use liquor or tobacco. On the subject of the justice of equal suffrage he was silent. He was a slow, conservative thinker, but on most practical subjects he had a clear head and sound judgement. He was in sympathy with labor. The same hand that signed the executive documents scattered broadcast the seeds that produced the crops on his farm. Governor Winans was a Mason. He and his family were members of the Episcopal Church. He had two sons: Major George G. Winans, and Lieutenant Edwin B. Winans, Jr., of the Fifth Cavalry, United States Army, who in the war with Spain was a Major in the thirty-fourth Michigan Infantry, United States Volunteers, and as such took part in the siege of Santiago, Cuba.

In private as well as public life Governor Winans was a man of sterling integrity. His talents were varied, and he used them fearlessly and earnestly in public and private service. His bitterest opponents respected him. He was of the highest type of American manhood.

1891
January 12, 1891

From *Journal of the Senate,* pp. 58-65
GENTLEMEN OF THE SENATE AND HOUSE OF REPRE-
SENTATIVES:

The people of Michigan have entrusted to you the legislative control of public affairs for the next two years.

I cannot doubt that you feel the great responsibility which comes to
you with the power to make laws affecting the varied interests of two million people, and that you will strive to exercise this power in a spirit of
equality and fairness to all. Coming, as you do, direct from the people, a
part and parcel of those whom you represent, with like experience and aspi-
rations and material interests, and with intimate practical knowledge of their
needs, you have only to be true to yourselves to serve well the interests of
your people. The magnitude of the trust reposed in you will become more
apparent as you proceed and should be a constant incentive to give your
best thought and energies to the faithful discharge of your duties.

Custom and the Constitution make it my duty to bring to your
attention such matters of public concern as seem to me to require legislative action. To outline a sound public policy, or to propose wise course
of legislation, would require large public experience and great political
wisdom. I can lay claim to neither, but I trust we are all actuated by the
same motive, how best to discharge our official duties and serve the true
interest of the people. In this spirit let us strive together to correct abus-
es and remove inequalities where they exist, and to make such needed
reforms and regulations as experience and the voice of the people point
out and demand at our hands. If we do this, we shall accomplish the object for which we were chosen, and justify the confidence reposed in us.

My predecessor has so fully and concisely laid before you the condition of public affairs that I can add little or nothing to the information
you now have. His diligence and fidelity have made him familiar with
the management of the various public institutions, and the measure of
success or failure in their administration. I commend his conclusions
and suggestions to your careful consideration.

I have visited the State Prison, the State University, the State Normal School, the School for the Deaf, and the Eastern Asylum, all of which seem to be in admirable condition. It was my intention to visit the other State institutions, that I might have some personal knowledge of their management and needs, but I have not as yet been able to do so. The growth of our institutions is vigorous, and their wants beyond their means. The question will be, not how much could they use, but how much can you grant. Most of them could make good use of more than they ask, but I feel sure the the various estimates have been made in the spirit of economy, and in view of the popular feeling against increased public expenditures.

STATE UNIVERSITY.

In submitting their estimates for the next two years I think the Regents of the University have acted in a spirit of the strictest economy. Their request is for $18,000 less than they asked two years ago, and $5,000 less than was then granted, yet the needs of the University, owing to largely increased attendance, are necessarily greater, and more room and accommodations are required. While visiting the institution observation convince me that utility was the aim in all expenditures, and if the same policy is continued, as I think it will be, every dollar you may grant will be carefully and judiciously used.

The University of Michigan takes high rank in the educational world and exert a powerful influence on the intellectual life of the State and nation. I commend its interests to your favorable consideration.

STATE NORMAL SCHOOL.

The State Normal School is well organized and managed for its especial work, and results are satisfactory.

The State Board of Education estimates its needs at $104,960 for the next two years, as against $102,150 for the past two years. While there is an increase of students, I think its efficiency can be maintained without additional cost. Some additional ground and some sewerage improvements are needed, but the necessity is not imperative at this time.

SCHOOL FOR THE DEAF.

The School for the Deaf is doing as satisfactory work as any of our public institutions. The class of children gathered there appeal strongly to our sympathy and should have your substantial support. The board ask for an increased appropriation over that of the past two years. In view of the public demand that taxation be lowered I think the material interests of the school need not suffer if their full request be not granted.

AGRICULTURAL COLLEGE.

I have been unable to visit the Agricultural College, but the State Board of Agriculture have sent me their estimates for the next two years, aggregating $52,620. While this does not seem a large sum for so important a school, the college has a substantial endowment fund, and if the board can, without injury to the college, prune their estimates, the farmers will appreciate the effect upon their taxes. The college is so near that I trust your committee will personally investigate its needs and thus be able to do justice both to the college and your constituents.

OTHER INSTITUTIONS.

I commend also to your committees the interests of the School for the Blind and the Reform School. Opportunity will cheerfully be given for a full understanding of their respective needs. I regret my inability to visit them in person.

The State Public School, the Industrial School for Girls, and the Soldiers' Home, will, I trust receive your earnest attention. I am unable to speak of them from personal knowledge, but they belong to our system and are justly entitled to their share of your attention.

ASYLUMS FOR THE INSANE.

At the Eastern Asylum I met members of the other Asylum Boards, and the needs of the three institutions were discussed. It was agreed that more room is required in all our asylums. This seems imperative, unless some plan can be devised to relieve them of a large class of patients who are harmless but incurable. It is obvious that if this class are returned to their friends, patients who could be benefited by treatment might be received. If the present practice is adhered to, the demand for more room will be continuous, and the cottage system will be far more economical than the multiplication of separate institutions. The reports submitted by the trustees give full information, and the care of our insane will require your serious consideration.

Michigan is advanced in her treatment of the mentally diseased, and one has only to visit our asylums to be convinced that these unfortunate people receive every needed care and comfort.

ELECTION LAW.

All are agreed as to the desirability of ballot reform, and our new election law is generally approved as a step in the right direction. The booth feature gives every voter an opportunity to be alone with his ballot, and absolute secrecy is the best guaranty of purity in elections. A practical test of our law has shown that some amendments are needed to render it entirely efficient and satisfactory. I suggest the following:

1. Let the law apply to all elections.
2. Let the distribution or using of ballots outside the booths be prohibited under the severest penalties.
3. Let the ballots be printed by the county clerks under the supervision of the party committees and be delivered by the county clerks to the inspectors of elections. Let the ballots be paid for in township and municipal elections.
4. A more expeditious method of counting should be adopted.
5. I favor the Australian system, or some modification which would render unnecessary the use of slips or posters.

PRISONS AND REFORMATORIES.

The Prisons and Reformatories are among our most important institutions, not only as regards the value of the plants and the character of their work, but also as regards the policy which would control them. Successful prison management requires special qualifications in the Warden and his subordinates. Questions other than the confinement and support of convicts are involved in prison government, and long study and familiarity with criminal classes and their conditions are necessary to fit men to deal with them wisely. Believing that our prisons should have the best executive and business talent obtainable for their management, I have elsewhere recommended that all our penal institutions be placed under the control of a single board. This board should, so far as possible, be non-partisan, and should appoint the wardens and have general supervision of the institutions. The wardens of our prisons are the only officers at the head of State institutions who are appointed by the Governor. The other executive heads of institutions are appointed by the respective governing boards, and sound policy demands that the prison appointments be non-political.

WAGON ROADS.

I call your attention to the necessity for some change in the laws relating to the highways of the State.

The condition of all wagon roads last winter was sufficient proof that our present system of road making is a waste of time and labor. Roads ordinarily the best were last winter as bad as those on which little or no work had been done. Good wagon roads all the year round would be more to the general advantage, would add more to the value of farms, and yield comfort, convenience, and profit to a larger number of people than any other work for which public money is expended. We claim to be a practical people, but surely our road building has been a failure. A vast amount of labor has been annually expended upon our roads for many years, but it has been done without system and without competent supervision. As a result, the labor is largely wasted and yields no final improvement. The establishment of a general system of road making which would gradually, even if slowly, result in permanent good roads throughout the State would be a wise and beneficent reform.

TAXATION.

There is a general feeling among all classes, but more pronounced, perhaps, among the agricultural and industrial people, that public expenditures have increased much more rapidly than the ability of the people to pay, and that our civilization is becoming very expensive. Greater simplicity would better accord with the present circumstances and condition of our people.

There is no desire to lower our standard of civilization or impair the efficiency of our various institutions, but the people believe that simplicity and wise economy promote, rather than impede, human virtues and improvement. Our people are willing to support generously those public expenses which tend to the general welfare, but they also believe that State taxes are too high, and that no public institution need suffer if less tax was levied. Taxation has steadily increased year by year, while the ability to pay, at least by the largest class of taxpayers, the farmers, has diminished. There should be an effort made to reduce taxation. The demand that only careful and needed expenditures be authorized is imperative and should be heeded.

Your own wisdom and experience will suggest ways and means of affording relief, but I call attention to some features of our present system which seem to me to need correction.

Our system of State taxation needs a thorough revision for the purpose of equalizing the assessment on the two classes of property, that subject to specific tax, and that subject to local taxation. Every industry, business, and property interest should bear its just share of the burden of taxation, but, under our present system, that vast amount of property which pays a specific tax, pays at least one-half less in proportion to its value than the property subject to direct and local taxation, thus adding to the burden of those least able to pay, and favoring the corporate wealth of our State.

Another just cause of complaint is that much property is now exempt from taxation that ought not to escape. There seems to be no good reason why property owned and used by railroad, mining, telegraph, and telephone companies, and other associations for private purposes should be exempt from general taxation. I doubt the policy of exempting and property from equal taxation. The granting of special privileges to any class affords just cause of complaint in the masses. I commend this subject of exemptions to your careful consideration.

Many who have given thought to the subject favor a return to the county system for the collection of delinquent taxes. I believe it would be less expensive and more efficient than the present system, which is, in my opinion, cumbersome and costly.

If each county were required to pay to the State its proportion the State tax, and then given full control of all proceedings to enforce collection by the sale of land, etc., I believe a large saving to the State would follow, and it would make the officers of the townships and counties more watchful of their duties in seeing that the tax is properly and legally laid, and the enforcement of the law would be more certain.

Another feature of taxation which should have your attention is the taxation of real estate on which there is mortgage encumbrance. Justice to the owner of the real estate forbids levying a tax on a larger interest than he may have in the land, yet, for various reasons. It may be difficult to ascertain his exact interest. All agree that the mortgage should, between them, pay taxes on the full value of the property. California has a statute under which the full tax may be paid by the owner of the land, and such proportion of the tax so paid as the indebtedness bears to the assessed value becomes a legal set-off against the mortgage. As our law stands, the owner of the land pays tax on the full value, be his real interest great or small, while the mortgagee, who is usually the better able to pay, either escapes taxation, or pays another tax on the same property. If the mortgagee is a non-resident of the State he pays no tax. Which is a discrimination against our own people who have money to loan. In the interest of equal taxation, I call your special attention to this feature.

I consider this question of taxation the most important with which you have to deal. Nearly all questions would be easy of solution if the cost was not to be considered, but every move cost money, and in the end the people must pay. The time has come when our people demand that unnecessary taxation must cease. State taxes must not increase. Let every request for public aid be sternly denied unless it can be shown that the money is needed for public purposes.

STATE BOARDS.

In this line of economical thought, I call your attention to the number of State boards of from three to six members now authorized by law. There are fifteen ex-officio, and thirty official boards, the latter comprising more than one hundred different members. No salary is paid by the members, but many of them receive expenses and per diem compensation, and some are allowed a secretary or clerk at a fixed salary. Aside from the question of expense, I believe the public interest would be better served by abolishing many of these boards. I favor having one board of control for all our prisons and reformatories, instead of one for each institution, as at present. Such a board would have the advantage of being able to compare financial and reformatory results in the different institutions and could establish a uniform system of bookkeeping so as to make such comparisons available. Clerical force could be reduced, and more economical and efficient administration of these institutions secured. Such a board would be as well qualified to advise in the matter of pardons as the board now organized for that special purpose and could also perform the duties now entrusted to the State Board of Corrections and Charities. A single board controls the prisons of England, another those of New York State, and I am informed the same policy is followed in most other states of the Union.

A similar board could control our educational institutions. We already have a State Board of Education whose principal duty is the management of the State Normal School. I believe good results would follow if all our State schools except the University and the Agricultural College were managed by the State Board of Education and their present boards of control abolished.

With a third Board of Control for our asylums and charitable institutions we would have five boards instead of a dozen or more for the management of the institutions named. The establishment of a single Board of Control for each class of institutions, penal, charitable, and educational, with full control over and responsibility for their proper management would secure better supervision of these important interests. The business of the State should have the best executive talent obtainable, and, so far as practicable, the officers should not be liable to interference except for business reasons. It is for the interest of every citizen that the business of the State be done correctly and economically and based upon true theories.

The duties of the State Board of Health consist largely of the collection of statistics of sickness and meteorological conditions which affect the health of our people, and of scientific experiments relating to the nature and causes of disease. Provision is already made for the collection of many of these statistics in other ways, at public expense, and such other information as is useful could be collected and published by the Secretary of State.

The last Legislature appropriated more than $8,000 for a State Weather Service which if continued should give us the meteorological statistics needed. The Medical Department of the State University is supplied with an able corps of professors, and with all the facilities needed for experiment and instruction in the nature, causes and prevention of diseases, and thousands of intelligent physicians, educated under these advantages, are scattered throughout the State. The State Board of Health costs the taxpayers $15,000 or more annually, and I suggest that you consider whether the discontinuance of this board would be injurious to the public health.

INSURANCE POLICY COMMISSIONER.

We have an Insurance Policy Commissioner, who, with the Commissioner of Insurance and the Attorney General, form a commission to provide a standard form of insurance policy. I suggest the discontinuance of this commission and that the Commissioner of Insurance be required to perform its duties.

STATE GAME AND FISH WARDEN.

The preservation of our game and fish from wanton and unnecessary destruction should be wisely guarded by law. The present law provides for the appointment of a State Game and Fish Warden, at a fixed salary, whose duty it is with the aid of certain deputies, to enforce the statutes relating to birds, game and fish. There seems to be no valid reason why this class of laws cannot be enforced, like any other, by the proper prosecuting and police officers of the counties. I am informed that the Game Warden has very rarely conducted a prosecution in person, but it is done by the local prosecutor at his request. Without such request it is still the duty of a prosecuting attorney to see that all offenders are punished.

The Deputy Game Wardens must get their pay through the Boards of Supervisors, and in many cases the boards have refused any reasonable compensation, and hence the law has been un-enforced.

I recommend that the law be so amended that the constables, sheriffs and deputy sheriffs of the counties be specially entrusted with its enforcement, such officers to receive the same fees that are allowed them in other criminal matters. If the changes suggested are made, the office of State Game and Fish Warden would seem unnecessary, and in such case, I suggest its discontinuance. The opportunity you have for the discontinuance of appointive offices, without being charged with partisan motives, should be improved where it will serve the public good.

THE WORLD'S COLUMBIAN EXPOSITION.

The World's Columbian Exposition, to be held in a neighboring city, will be an event of great interest to the world at large, and particularly to the citizens of the United States. The federal government has liberally aided in providing the funds needed by the management, and Michigan is honored in the selection of one of her most esteemed citizens as President of the World's Fair Commission.

Our importance as a State, and the great variety and abundance of our products and resources, suggest the propriety of our being represented at the World's Fair by an adequate exhibit, and you will doubtless be asked to appropriate funds for that purpose. It will be for you to decide what will be for the interest of the State in this matter.

CONCLUSION.

Let us bear in mind, in all our official acts, that we are exercising delegated authority and are sent here to enact the popular will. Public

sentiment plainly indicates that our people will no longer patiently submit to the steady increase of public expenditures which has continued
through the past twenty-five years. They demand economical administration of public affairs. They demand the abolition of every unnecessary
office. They demand that all who enjoy the protection of our laws shall
contribute to the cost in just proportion to their means.

Our fidelity to the interests and rights of the masses will be the
measure of our success. If we give to our public duties the care and zeal
we give to our own affairs, the people will be quick to see and approve.

I assure you of my earnest desire to co-operate with you to the extent
of my power in expediting your work and promoting the public good.

A business session, short and economical, will command popular approval.

EDWIN B. WINANS

May 11, 1891

From *Journal of the House of Representatives,* pp. 1561-1562
GENTLEMEN OF THE HOUSE OF REPRESENTATIVES:

I respectfully return, without my approval, a bill entitled "An act making an appropriation for the benefit of the Home for Discharged Prisoners."

This home is a private enterprise of a benevolent character, and, as such, is a very worthy and laudable charity. It is in charge of Mrs. Agnes d' Arcambal, a most lovely and estimable lady, who devotes her life, service and means to the good of the unfortunate.

This Home for Discharged Prisoners is not, however, in any sense a state institution. It was not established by the State, and its managers and executive officers are in no sense State officers or subject to State control.

This appropriation raises a question of State policy of grave importance. The home is one out of hundreds of equally worthy private charities existing in the State. So far as I am informed, it is the only one to which it is proposed to extend State aid. If the aid asked is granted, many other benevolent institutions will feel equally entitled to State aid, and either invidious discriminations must be made, or all similar requests be granted. State aid was first granted to this Home by the Legislature of 1889. If the example set then should be followed by your honorable body, it will be cited hereafter as the settled policy of the State that deserving private charities may receive money from the State treasury. It is true that only the modest sum of one hundred dollars per month is now asked, but, that granted, the need for more will follow as the Home grows, and thus, step by step, the State will be committed to a policy of large expenditures not contemplated, and which would not have been approved at the outset.

I am thus constrained to present my objections to this measure because, while the expenditure in this case is small, an important principle is involved. Once approve the policy of granting public aid to private purposes, and you enter a field which finds expression in the general demand for reduced public expenditures. Our taxpayers have their own wives and children to support, and their duty is first to them. Let their contributions to private charity be voluntary, and not enforced through the taxing power of the State.

Respectfully,
EDWIN B. WINANS

May 13, 1891

From *Journal of the House of Representatives,* pp. 1578-1579
GENTLEMEN OF THE HOUSE OF REPRESENTATIVES:

I respectfully return without my approval a bill entitled "An act for the relief of the Supreme Court by providing for the appointment of stenographers or copyists for the justices thereof."

My objections to the bill are as follows:

First, It purposes to create five new officers at an annual salary of eight hundred dollars each. Experience has shown that it is easier to create five new offices of doubtful necessity than to abolish a single unnecessary one. If these offices are once established at the expense of the State the salary named will soon be found inadequate to secure competent stenographers versed in law, and increased salaries will be demanded and granted, until they will involve a permanent annual tax of at least six thousand dollars.

This additional tax is to be levied to relieve the justices of the Supreme Court from clerical labor. It is not alleged that the work is behind or that the interests of our people are neglected by reason of the inability of the court to dispatch the business brought before it. The apparent object of the bill is not that the public may receive better service, but that the judges may be relieved of a portion of their work. It will be remembered that quite recently relief was given the court by increasing the number of judges to five, and by increasing their salary from four thousand to five thousand dollars each per annum.

The office is a highly honorable and desirable one, and its attainment the goal for which hundreds of able and ambitious lawyers are striving. The term of office is ten years, the salary liberal, and the personal expenses incident to the office are not large. For these considerations good service is due the State. The people are not penurious, but public sentiment is rightly opposed to multiplying offices.

Second, another questionable feature of the bill is the method provided for appointment to the proposed offices.

Sections 10 and 12 of article 6 of the constitution authorizes the Supreme Court to appoint a reporter and a clerk, and section 10 concludes as follows: "But no judges of the Supreme Court or circuit court shall exercise any other power of appointment to public office."

It is true the bill does not provide that each judge shall appoint his own stenographer, but that they shall be appointed by the court as a whole, but it is difficult to see how the court can appoint, without the judges exercising the power of appointment. The bill requires the persons to be appointed to take and subscribe the constitutional oath of office. They will therefore be public officers. Hence the bill authorizes the Supreme Court to exercise a power expressly denied the judges by the constitution, and if this is not a direct violation of its terms, it is a questionable way of avoiding the natural interpretation thereof.

I feel confident that your wisdom can devise some plan for affording the court all needed relief without the creation of five new and permanent offices.

Respectfully,
EDWIN B. WINANS

May 26, 1891

From *Journal of the House of Representatives,* pp. 1718-1719
GENTLEMEN OF THE HOUSE OF REPRESENTATIVES:

I respectfully return herewith, without my approval, a bill entitled "An act making an appropriation to aid in suitably providing for the twenty-fifth national encampment of the Grand Army of the Republic to be held in Michigan."

My objection to this bill is based on the ground of public policy and justice to the taxpayers. The power of taxation, which reaches directly or indirectly all classes of people, may be rightfully exercised only for public purposes. The determination what is and what is not a public purpose belongs in the first instance to the legislative department. Let us consider all before we employ taxation for new and unusual objects.

All taxation is burdensome, and its justification can be found only in the benefit, direct or indirect, which the taxpayers receive in return. In this case it cannot be maintained that the general public are to be in any way benefited, nor is the appropriation in aid of charity, to help the unfortunate or relieve the distressed. The bill proposes to take money earned by the hard work of labor and saved by the economy of patient wives and mothers and use it for a social entertainment and a general good time. Not one in a hundred of the people who are forced to contribute will participate in the pleasures of the occasion. A political convention or the Presbyterian General Assembly now gathered in Detroit would be equally entitled to State aid. On no principle of right or justice can this use of the people's money be defended. We are here as the servants of the people, to enact their will, and I am fully convinced that if the proposition to vote this money had been submitted to them, twenty votes would have been cast against it to one for it.

No public purpose is to be subserved by the expenditure. The money is taxed from the hard earnings of a people already justly complaining of oppressive taxation. Any measure which unnecessarily adds a feather's weight in this burden is a great wrong, and more especially when done by those whom the people trusted, and who promised to relieve and protect their interests by more economical legislation. In this State taxation has steadily increased year by year, and always the specious plea was urged for new expenditures. "It is only a cent or five cents for each individual, and it will not be felt, or the people will not care." But the time has come when the people do care, and we, their servants, should heed their just demands that the State treasury should not be used for private gain or individual pleasure. This bill proposes to take from the State treasury thirty thousand dollars to be used to help entertain the veterans of the Union army who may attend the grand encampment at Detroit. These men are patriotic citizens. They know their duty as such and would scorn individually to add one cent for their entertainment to the burdens of the taxpayers. They one and all pay their way wherever they choose to go, and if it is to meet again old comrades in arms, they do not ask that it be at public cost. It is not the veterans who rallied at their country's call who are asking for this measure, as the many remonstrances from them to your honorable body show. The demand comes from those who hope to receive indirect benefit from the expenditure of the money. The sum appropriated, if saved to the treasury, will defray the total cost of this legislature for thirty days or more. In a former communication I expressed to you my belief that our fidelity to the interests and rights of the people will be the measure of our success, and that every request for public aid should be sternly denied unless needed for a public purpose.

On behalf of the taxpayers of our State I earnestly and respectfully urge that you reconsider your action in this matter.

Respectfully,
EDWIN B. WINANS

June 9, 1891

From *Journal of the Senate*, pp. 1203-1204

TO THE SENATE:

I respectfully return herewith to your honorable body for reconsideration two bills originating therein, entitled respectively "An act to authorize the village of Manville, Tuscola county, Michigan, to borrow money to make public improvements in said village," and "An act to authorize the village of Fremont, Newaygo county, to raise money to make public improvements in said village, to issue bonds therefore, and provide for the levy of taxes therein to pay the same."

These two bills are similar in character and are alike objectionable in that they fail to specify the particular public improvements intended. They authorize the boards of trustees of the villages of Maryville and Fremont to levy taxes for public improvements and leave it for these boards to determine what these public improvements shall be. There is nothing in these bills to prevent these boards of trustees, after the people have voted the tax, from giving the money as bonuses to private enterprises. No argument is needed to show that such use of village funds is unconstitutional, for our supreme court has so held repeatedly. It has been well said that money raised by taxation constitutes a trust fund to be expended for a public purpose and no other, and the diversion of it to any improvements other than those in which the title vests in the public, is a misappropriation and betrayal of the trust. The time has come for the practice and enforcement of economy, and one of the prime essentials is to limit public expenditures to public and necessary purposes.

The taxpayers are entitled to know the exact purposes for which they vote taxes, and to be assured that their earnings shall not be used as gifts for private benefit.

I owe the Legislature an explanation of my action in heretofore approving two Senate bills and three House bills similar in character to those I now return. The bills referred to were approved before I discovered that the term "Public improvements" was liable to be interpreted as bonuses to private enterprises.

Respectfully,
EDWIN B. WINANS

June 17, 1891

From *Journal of the Senate,* pp. 1305-1307
TO THE SENATE:

I respectfully return without my approval a bill entitled "An act to regulate the uniformity and provide textbooks in all public schools throughout the State and the distribution of the same, and to repeal all statutes and acts contravening the provisions of this act."

The bill contemplates a radical change in our present schoolbook system, and the underlying motive seems to be to protect the people from the extortion of book rings. In seeking to escape one evil we ought carefully to guard against flying to a greater one. The bill provides that the State board of education shall prepare or select a uniform set of textbooks for use in our public schools and cause the same to be printed and bound at State expense, unless in their opinion the board can obtain them cheaper by contracting with publishers.

The State is to sell the books to the school districts at cost.

The bill thus gives to this board full and unlimited power to decide what books may be used in our schools, and without any limit as to what the change shall cost. Experience teaches that all public printing costs far more than private, yet under this bill the board may inaugurate a publishing house at State expense, with no limit to the expenditure. I regard this as a serious objection. The plan of state publication has been tried in California, and the results were thus stated by the present State Superintendent of Schools, in December last:

"For over four years this plan has had a fair and impartial trial in our State. I came into office, a believer in the project, and every aid which I could give to its successful issue has been freely rendered throughout my administration.

"But now in the light of my experience, I must acknowledge that the results have not met my expectations.

"In the first place, the expense has been great. Over $400,000 having been appropriated thus far for the compilation of the series and the manufacture of the first fifty thousand copies of each book. Ten books have so far been issued and 3 more are yet to come to complete a full series as required by law.

"In the light of our experience after 4 years of trial, I am therefore compelled, with personal reluctance, to acknowledge to the comparative want of success in our California experiment in making and publishing schoolbooks. Taking into consideration the large appropriations made, and the further and constant outlay for revisions, new plates, etc., the same number of books can be purchased in the open market at whole-sale prices for less than it costs the State to manufacture them. I am therefore constrained to admit that I would not advise any other State to enter upon the publication of schoolbooks."

Such is the experience of the only state which has thus far tried the experiment of State publication. Our present law provides for free textbooks, optional with districts, and so far as I know is satisfactory wherever adopted.

I am informed that about 600 school districts in our State have adopted the system. Under the proposed law the books now in use throughout the State would have to be discarded, thus destroying the value of a large amount of property.

Uniformity is the ostensible object sought by this bill, yet it defeats that object by exempting from its operation the schools in all towns and cities having a population of over 4,000, which towns contain about one-third of the children in our schools. This seems to be a serious objection, for if uniformity is sought why exempt one-third of the schools? It seems to me that it is not so much uniformity that is needed as that satisfactory textbooks at fair cost may be furnished to the scholars.

Under this bill choice is taken from the people, where now they can avail themselves of all improvements in school literature or any reduction in price from competition.

If the Board of Education should decide to contract rather than publish, an opportunity would be afforded for undue influence and jobbery, and here again the experience of other states shows that the people to not gain by having the State buy books under contract.

It is estimated that fully one million books will be needed, and it will require a large force of clerks and assistants for the work of distribution. I think it unwise to enter upon any scheme which involves an indefinite expenditure of public money, and this bill seems to me fairly open to this objection.

I therefore return it for reconsideration.

Respectfully,
EDWIN B. WINANS

June 25, 1891

From *Journal of the House of Representatives,* PP. 2114-2115

GENTLEMEN OF THE HOUSE OF REPRESENTATIVES:

I respectfully return herewith, without my approval, a substitute for House joint resolution number 31, entitled "Joint resolution directing the Board of State Auditors to settle the claim made by Joseph Schefnecker against the State of Michigan for services and money expended by him in recruiting and organizing the fourteenth regiment of Michigan Infantry Volunteers."

My attention has been called to the fact that the original title of House joint resolution number 31, was "Joint resolution relative to authorizing the State Board of Auditors to examine the claim of Alphonzo Button and audit the same for payment."

The resolution as passed by the House and concurred in by the Senate makes no reference to the claim of Alphonzo Button but relates to an entirely different subject matter. No House resolution relative to settling the claim of Joseph Schefnecker was introduced within the fifty-day limit, and the practice of using a title properly introduced under which to legislate on subject matter not introduced within the fifty day limit is a violation of the constitution, and, if continued will create a great amount of litigation. A recent decision of our Supreme Court has left no doubt upon this point. In the case of Sackrider vs. The Board of Supervisors, 79 Mich., p. 59, it was held that article 4, section 28, of the constitution, which provides that "No new bill shall be introduced into either House of the Legislature after the first fifty days of a session shall have expired," is violated by the reporting of a new bill after said fifty days as a substitute for a pending bill introduced within the constitutional period, the subject matter of which has no connection with the subject matter of the new bill.

I am further convinced that Mr. Schefnecker has no legal claim against the State. Would a legal or equitable claim be allowed to sleep for thirty years with no effort made to collect it? Michigan has all these years been able to pay all just claims against her, and it cannot be claimed that the State administration has been unfriendly to claims of this character.

The resolution recites that the claim is for services and money spent in recruiting troops and organizing the Fourteenth Michigan

Infantry. No law of this State ever authorized the payment of money for such service. Every authority to recruit and enlist men was given by Governor Austin Blair, and it was always with the distinct understanding that the person authorized to enlist men should have a commission as his compensation, and that he should have no further claim on the State.

Many patriotic citizens spent time and money in filling the quotas under the several calls for troops, and nearly very commissioned officer of our thirty regiments recruited companies or parts of companies. If this claim is a just one, they would all have equally good claims against the State. There is no effort to show a legal basis for this claim. There is no agreement, no data, no contract, no law. There is simply the statement of the claimant, honest, no doubt, that time and money were spent for the purpose stated. The claimant himself informs me that he cannot tell how much, if any, is justly his due. To consider this claim as equitable would invite a flood of similar claims whose allowance would bankrupt the riches state treasury for the benefit of those who held commissions in the army.

Respectfully,
EDWIN B. WINANS

June 27, 1891

From *Journal of the House of Representatives,* pp. 2189-2190
GENTLEMEN OF THE HOUSE OF REPRESENTATIVES:

I respectfully return herewith for reconsideration a bill entitled "An act to amend section 15 of article 4 of Act No. 198, session laws of 1873, entitled "An act to revise the laws providing for the incorporation of railroad companies and to regulate the running and management, and fix the duties and liabilities of all railroads and other corporations owning or operating any railroad in this State, and the several acts amendatory thereof," being compiler's section 3377 of Howell's annotated statutes, as amended by act No. 234, public acts of 1858, approved June 10, 188, and as amended by act No. 261, of public acts of 1887, approved June 27, 1887, and acts 26 and 165 of the session laws of 1889."

This bill proposes to amend the law which requires railroad companies to construct farm crossings across the tracks and right of way. The present law provides that in case of disagreement between a railroad company and the owner of land lying on both sides of the track the commissioner of railroads shall determine as to the necessity for such crossing. The necessity for the crossing being determined, the law requires the company to construct a convenient crossing and to place gates or bars in the right of way fences. This bill proposes to require the railroad companies to build fences on each side of the crossing from the right of way fence to the track, and to put in cattle-guards where the track divides the fences.

To construct these fences and cattle-guards would cost about $50 at each crossing, and when it is remembered that in the populous parts of the State almost every mile of railroad has a number of these crossings, it will be seen that the cost to every railroad would be many thousands of dollars, which ought not to be required of them without good reason.

While theses fences and cattle-guards might be a convenience to the farm owner in some instances, there are thousands of such crossings where they are not needed or asked for, and there is no disposition on the part of farm owners to put railroads to needless expense, or subject them to unreasonable requirements.

The traveling public also have a direct interest in this matter. Every cattle-guard, bridge, or other break in the bed of a railroad increases the dangers of travel, and from the standpoint of the traveler the less cattle-guards there are the greater his security against accident. A large proportion of the railroad accidents is due to the existence of culverts and cattle-guards, and it is certainly unwise to increase this source of danger at the many farm crossings where it is not required. If any citizen has just cause of complaint against a railroad corporation, we have a railroad commissioner whose duty it is to investigate the matter in dispute, and who has authority to enforce his decisions. I believe the present law is quite satisfactory to farm owners generally, and that the proposed change is unnecessary and unwise.

Respectfully,
EDWIN B. WINANS

1892

August 5, 1892

From *Journal of the Senate,* pp. 23-24

GENTLEMEN OF THE SENATE AND
HOUSE OF REPRESENTATIVES:

The Supreme Court of the State has declared unconstitutional and void the acts passed by this legislature and the legislature of 1885, for the apportionment of Senators and Representatives in the State legislature and has directed that the coming elections be held in accordance with the apportionment acts of 1881, unless you shall enact new measures.

The acts of 1881, while they were not passed upon by the court are subject to the same constitutional objections which were raised against the acts of 1885 and 1891, and, considered in connection with our present population, are wholly inadequate to secure a proper representation of the different sections of the State. An election under the acts of 1881 would now involve far more inequality of representation than would be possible under the acts of 1891.

Moreover, since 1881 several new counties have been organized, and in the larger cities ward boundaries have been so changed that it is more than doubtful if elections could be held in some of the districts.

I have therefore deemed it my duty to convene the legislature in special session for the purpose of considering the situation, trusting that your wisdom and your familiarity with the subject will enable you to frame apportionment acts which will conform to the requirements of the constitution and be acceptable to the Supreme Court.

That you are again compelled to legislate upon this important matter seems due to your having followed the precedents set by former legislatures, and to your having accepted the theory that the legislature is an independent, coordinate branch of the State government, whose province it is to determine the political divisions of the State.

You have just cause for congratulation in the fact that while much of your most important legislation has been contested in the Supreme Court, only two of the six hundred acts passed at your first session have been held unconstitutional.

I have confidence that your wisdom, ability, and patriotism will enable you to do well the work for which you have now assembled.

EDWIN B. WINANS

1893

Jan. 1, 1893

From *Joint Documents of the State of Michigan,* pp. 3-11

GENTLEMEN OF THE SENATE AND
HOUSE OF REPRESENTATIVES:

I am required, at the close of my official term, to submit by message to the incoming legislature information of the condition of the state, and to recommend such measures as seem to me expedient. The general condition of our people for the past two years has been prosperous, and peace and quietness have prevailed throughout our territory.

FINANCES.

The financial condition of the state is excellent. The treasurer reports a large amount of money on hand, and as we have no bonded debt to be paid, it would seem that our people should be free from excessive taxation in the future, especially as no large expenditures for public buildings are needed, and the revenue from the growth of corporate wealth should increase with coming years.

By constitutional provision specific taxes must either be applied to pay the interest on our bonded debt or be credited to the primary school interest fund. As we have no bonded debt, the entire specific tax goes to the primary schools. At the time this provision was made the amount received in specific taxes was comparatively small, but it now amounts to about a million dollars annually and will continue to increase. In many school districts the money received from the apportionment of specific taxes, together with the proceeds of the mill tax, is sufficient to maintain the schools. In other districts the money received from these sources exceeds the necessary expenditure, and results in a surplus. Every district is authorized to meet any deficiency by a district tax, and it would therefore seem that the time has arrived when some limit should be fixed to the apportionment of specific taxes among the primary schools, and all above a certain amount be applied for the reduction of direct state taxation. Any change in this policy involves an amendment to the constitution, but the disposition of the present and prospective increase in specific taxes should receive serious consideration.

STATE INSTITUTIONS.

The public institutions of the state are all in admirable condition. The buildings and grounds are well kept, the industries pursued afford good returns, and good order, discipline, and economy prevail, as may be seen by reference to the special report from each institution. No serious epidemics of disease or losses by fire or otherwise have occurred in the past two years except by the fire in the Eastern Asylum, by which no lives were lost, and no property destroyed aside from the building. The building has been restored with many improvements by the use of the surplus funds of the asylum.

PENAL AND REFORMATORY INSTITUTIONS.

Our penal and reformatory institutions were placed by the last legislature under the control of a single non-partisan board, and the wisdom of the action has been fully vindicated by the results. I ask your special attention to the reports of the State Board of Inspectors and of the several wardens and superintendents. They afford a most gratifying showing of economy in expenditures and increased earnings to the state, while the maintenance, discipline and comfort of the inmates have received careful attention. The successful management of these large interests requires businessmen and business methods, and the policy of those who would use our State institutions as a means to reward party zeal, or who view them as existing for the benefit of the towns in which they are located, should no longer be tolerated. The six institutions controlled by the State Board of Inspectors are similar in character, though varying in the age, sex and degree of criminality of the inmates. The success which attends them is largely due to the business ability and experience of the board, who can survey the whole field of operations and compare, suggest and direct for the best interests of each institution. Such general oversight is promotive of economy and efficient service and discourages time serving and favoritism. The beneficial effects of the act of consolidation will be more apparent as time is afforded for their full development, but some additional power should be given the Board of Inspectors to grade, classify and transfer inmates from one prison to another as occasion may require. The promiscuous mingling of young offenders, susceptible to both good and evil influences, with hardened and professional criminals is directly against the interests of society. Experience has shown that the courts send all classes of offenders to the same institutions, and the board should be empowered to separate them.

CHARITABLE INSTITUTIONS.

The State Public School at Coldwater, the School for the Blind and the School for the Deaf have also been placed under the supervision of a central board of control. The substitution of one board for three has resulted in a substantial saving of expense, and these institutions are in admirable condition and are model charities of their kind. The opportunities afforded a single board of using the knowledge and experience gained in one school for the advantage of prices of supplies assists in reducing expenses and promoting efficiency. The policy of uniting similar public institutions under one management will as surely be for the interest of each as the union of great private interests results in a common benefit. This policy having been adopted with good results should be continue and extended.

STATE UNIVERSITY.

Our State University is first in importance among our institutions. The high standing it has attained among the great schools of the land, and the superior advantages afforded by its faculty and courses of study, result each year in an increased number of students from all parts of the country. The attendance has increased from 1,580 in 1886 to 2,400 in 1890 and nearly 3,000 at the present time. The question presents itself, shall accommodations be provided for all who may desire to come? I believe the latter course to be the wise one, and that you cannot be too liberal in granting the appropriations asked by the board of regents. Their management has been careful and conservative in the past and I am confident that every dollar you may grant will be wisely used to promote the usefulness of the university.

AGRICULTURAL COLLEGE.

The Agricultural College at Lansing is now a school of greater value and importance than is generally known even to our own people. In its early days, struggling under many disadvantages, the impression got abroad especially among farmers, that the school was of little value to the class particularly interested in agriculture. At present no reason for such an impression exists. The college has steadily progressed and expanded until it stands at the head of this class of institutions and is one of the most practical and useful of our public schools. I commend its interests to your favorable consideration.

STATE NORMAL SCHOOL.

The State Normal School at Ypsilanti maintains its high reputation for its special work. The school is well managed and prosperous. It is among the least troublesome of the wards of the state, and no unreasonable demands upon the taxpayers will be made in its behalf.

THE MINING SCHOOL.

The Michigan Mining School at Houghton is doing good work, although, its course of study being a special one, the attendance is limited. As with all new schools time is required for its development, and a larger attendance may be expected as the advantages offered become better understood. The general public do not, perhaps, appreciate its importance as thoroughly as that of schools of general instruction, but it is one of our established institutions and should receive from the legislature a just and fair recognition.

SCHOOL FOR THE DEAF.

The School for the Deaf at Flint is one which enlists the sympathy and good wishes of every visitor. The inmates, because of their infirmity, their bright, expressive faces, their quick intelligence and cheerful dispositions, appeal to our liberality for every advantage which can be afforded them. The special training and education furnished here enable many of these unfortunates to become useful, self-supporting citizens, and lives which would otherwise be passed in solemn loneliness are rendered endurable and even cheerful. The school met with a great loss in the death of Superintendent Monroe, who had long been a faithful and beloved teacher, but his place has been supplied by one who brings the best credentials, and the management is in all respects admirable.

SCHOOL FOR THE BLIND.

The School for the Blind at Lansing is the least expensive of our charitable institutions. The unfortunate inmates, especially the young, appeal strongly for every provision by which a Christian society can lighten their misfortune. The school is under the supervision of a kind matron and an intelligent superintendent and deserves your favorable attention.

STATE PUBLIC SCHOOL.

The State Public School at Coldwater is the refuge of the neglected children and waifs of the state. They are infants and young children whose only offense is their existence, and who are there cared for by kind hands until homes can be found for them in respectable families. Humanity demands this work, and it is done at this institution as tenderly as in the homes of more fortunate boys and girls. The school is prosperous and doing good work, and I can suggest nothing better for its interests than that it be continued, together with the School for the Deaf and the School for the Blind, under the management of the central board of control.

STATE PRISON.

The most important of our penal institutions is the State Prison at Jackson. The position of warden is a very responsible one, because of the character of the inmates and the magnitude of the interests under his supervision. The state is fortunate in the present incumbent, whose administration has been a marked success. In the past two years, for the first time in its history, the prison has paid its own running expenses, and in addition has earned a handsome revenue for the state. A new cell block has been completed and occupied, new shops, new walks, and a new wall have been built, and many other improvements made. Discipline has been maintained, the inmates have been well fed and otherwise provided for, and the general condition of the prison is highly satisfactory. The report of the warden is a concise statement of what has been accomplished and contains many practical and valuable suggestions. In the management a great penitentiary it is a condition and not a theory which must be met, and it is the practical man who will succeed.

HOUSE OF CORRECTION AND REFORMATORY.

The State House of Correction and Reformatory at Ionia was found to be in need of extensive renovation and repairs. The existing contract for the output of the prison, as well as the general condition of the whole yard and plant, was unsatisfactory to the board of inspectors, but by unremitting attention on the part of the board and the warden a great improvement has been made. Extensive repairs have been made, new machinery put in operation, and the institution is now a credit to the state. The discipline and management are highly commended by the Board of Corrections and Charities and all who are interested in prison morals. All these improvements have cost money, and financially the returns to the state suffer in comparison with the state prison, but the foundation is now laid for better results in the future.

MARQUETTE PRISON.

The Branch of the State Prison at Marquette has a fine modern building, and its fittings and accommodations are of the most approved character. Considering the increased cost of supplies in the upper peninsula, the administration has, perhaps, been fairly economical, but there exists no good reason for its continuance as a prison. All its inmates could easily be accommodated at the other prisons at far less expense. There is little probability that it will be needed as a prison for years to come. It would, therefore, be wise to discontinue the maintenance of prisoners there at unnecessary expense, and to utilize the building for some other purpose.

ASYLUMS FOR THE CRIMINAL INSANE.

The new building of the Asylum for Criminal Insane at Ionia has lately been completed and is now in use. Under the very competent management of the medical superintendent and board of inspectors this institution is fulfilling its mission in a satisfactory manner. Notwithstanding the dangerous character of the inmates, order and quiet are maintained in the halls, and all is done that can be for their comfort and welfare.

REFORM SCHOOL.

The value of the Reform School at Lansing is apparent when we consider the large number and youthful character of its inmates, and the fact that ninety per cent of them are reclaimed from evil habits and tendencies and become useful citizens of the state. A visit to the school, where one can look those four hundred boys in the face, impresses one with the value and importance of this reformatory work. The late superintendent having declined to remain at the present salary, the state was fortunate in securing the present superintendent, under whose management the high efficiency of the school has been maintained at a reduced expense. I especially ask your attention to the report of the superintendent and the suggestions therein made.

INDUSTRIAL HOME FOR GIRLS.

The Industrial Home for Girls at Adrian is the counterpart of the Reform School and is doing good work in reclaiming wayward and vicious girls. The new school building is completed and in use, the buildings are ample for all the needs of the institution, and the present superintendent is admirably qualified for her position.

MICHIGAN ASYLUM FOR THE INSANE.

The Michigan Asylum for the Insane at Kalamazoo maintains its reputation and efficiency. It has an able and efficient board of trustees, devoted to their work, and a superintendent whose services are of the highest value. The inmates number a thousand, but with the completion of the new cottage all are comfortable provided for. I am impressed with the desirability of the cottage system and farm attachment for our asylums. Only a small percentage of our insane require confinement in wards. The majority are better with the freedom of cottage and farm, and the system allows classification which should be made general. I find the general conditions and management at Kalamazoo highly satisfactory and deserving of commendation.

EASTERN ASYLUM.

All that has been said in praise of the board of control, the superintendent, and the general management at Kalamazoo is equally true of the Eastern Asylum at Pontiac. The perfect order and discipline which prevail were demonstrated at the time of the fire which destroyed the north wing of the asylum building. Too much praise cannot be given the officers and attendants for their successful efforts to prevent loss of life and property. The board of trustees used the surplus funds of the asylum to restore the building, and the incident demonstrates the value of such a fund for the use in case of emergency. The appropriations which this board will ask may safely be granted.

NORTHERN MICHIGAN ASYLUM.

Of the Northern Asylum at Traverse City, I regret that I cannot speak from personal observation. No criticism of the management has reached me, which fact is the best proof that none is justified. In leaving this class of our public charities I repeat my conviction that further additions to the accommodations at the asylums should be in the direction of the cottage system, both on the score of economy and for the welfare of the inmates. Power should also be given the board of trustees to classify their population and exchange inmates from one asylum to another.

SOLDIERS' HOME.

I am glad to say the Soldiers' Home at Grand Rapids is now in a satisfactory condition, externally, internally, and financially. The board and the commandant are working harmoniously, and the inmates are well contented.

HOME FOR THE FEEBLE MINDED.

Michigan lacks one institution to complete her system of state charities, namely, a home for the feeble-minded. No special provision has been made for the care of this class of unfortunates, and they are to be found in our poorhouses, our asylums, and our state schools. The presence of feeble-minded children and epileptics among the youthful inmates of the Reform School and the Industrial Home is detrimental to the welfare of the others, and the law does not contemplate their admission, but they are sometimes received before their condition is known, and it is estimated that there are now nearly two hundred in our various institutions, and there are many others throughout the state. They are everywhere recognized as proper subjects for public charity, and the state should provide a suitable home for their reception. The need of such an institution is so manifest that its establishment could not fail to receive popular approval.

GEOLOGICAL SURVEY.

I invite special attention to the report of the State Board of Geological Survey, now laid before the Legislature for the first time in twelve years. It contains matter of public interest which cannot here be discussed in detail, but if you care to learn what has become of an annual appropriation of eight thousand dollars, continued through twenty years, from which few of our people have received any benefit, the information is there furnished. I trust the recommendations therein made will meet your approval, especially that relating to the Commission of Mineral Statistics, whose duties could better be performed by the state geologist or one of his assistants. The geology of our state is of large interest to our citizens, and the subject, as it now stands, calls for heroic treatment. The survey should either be abandoned, or provision made for its early completion.

WORLD'S COLUMBIAN EXPOSITION.

The board of World's Fair managers have drawn but $40,000 of the $100,000 appropriated. The State building is nearly completed and is in every way creditable. The work is so far advanced that the board are confident our state exhibit will be full and satisfactory, and I believe the sum appropriated is sufficient to cover the necessary expense.

GOOD ROADS.

At the late special session of the legislature, I was authorized to appoint a commission who should report a plan of legislation looking to the improvement of our highways. I submit herewith the report of the commission. In their opinion no valid legislation can be enacted under our present constitution, which will meet the requirements of modern roadmaking, and you will be asked to submit to the people at the next election an amendment to the constitution, which if adopted, will enable the legislature to put in operation a general system of road improvement. The importance of this subject is attracting attention in every part of our country. Conventions are held, societies organized, and public sentiment aroused to the necessity for better roads. It is admitted on all hands that our present system, or lack of system, involves a waste of time, labor, and money, without permanent benefit, and no other question of internal policy demands greater attention at your hands.

STATE TROOPS.

Michigan has reason to be proud of the character, discipline, and efficiency of her state militia. Their conduct in camp, their improvement in military knowledge, and their soldierly qualities insure prompt and efficient service in case of lawlessness or domestic violence. I fully concur in the recommendations of the Adjutant General, to which I invite your attention.

RAILROADS.

The Commissioner of Railroads submits an exhaustive report containing much valuable information. He points out certain defects in our legislation on this important subject and makes several practical recommendations which deserve serious consideration.

SUPREME COURT.

The necessity for some form of relief for the Supreme Court becomes more apparent each year. So many cases are heard that it is impossible to give them proper consideration without a delay which is detrimental to the interests of those whose rights are involved. Several plans for relief are suggested by the members of the court and the bar, and some early action is desirable.

LIVESTOCK SANITARY COMMISSION.

The Livestock Sanitary Commission report a healthy condition of stock throughout the state, and no serious epidemic or contagious disease has prevailed. Such diseases are always found to some extent, but by prompt attention and the slaughter of infected animals the commission have held them in check. The interest involved is large and the commission is doing good work at very small cost to the state.

BUILDING AND LOAN ASSOCIATIONS.

Within a few years a large number of building and loan associations have been organized and are operating in this state. More than one hundred Michigan associations, and many organized in other states are now doing business here, and their agents are diligently canvassing every section of the state. People of all classes are induced to subscribe for stock and make small payments from time to time under an agreement that they shall be entitled to draw out a certain sum at the expiration of a fixed period. The terms offered are so advantageous that they are accepted by thousands of people. The subscribers have no means of knowing that the associations will be able to meet their obligations when the time comes, and the business has assumed such large proportions that stockholders should be protected by having the business placed under competent state supervision, so that the financial condition of these associations may be known by those who are asked to invest in them. Associations doing legitimate business would have no use to complain of such supervision and the people should be informed as to their responsibility.

LEGISLATIVE SESSIONS.

The length of recent sessions of the legislature affords just cause for complaint, and public opinion demands a reform in this respect.

The legislatures of 1887, 1889, and 1891, were each in session about six months. Such lengthy sessions are not necessary, and it is in the power of a legislature to shorten them without diminishing the amount of work accomplished. There are two principal causes of the evil. One is the existing method of dealing with municipal charters, which consumes a large portion of every session in the consideration of separate bills. If our cities and villages were classified according to population, and a general charter enacted for each class, which all desiring to incorporate must accept, a great saving in labor and time would be accomplished.

The other principal cause of lengthy sessions is the practice by the members of accepting free passes. If they were obliged to pay their own traveling expenses most members would remain at the capitol and attend to their duties, but with free transportation experience has shown that they will vote to adjourn from Friday night to Monday night, and the result is only four working days in the week. That the points mentioned are the principal causes of our long sessions is known and admitted by all who are familiar with the subject, but, as yet no legislature has contained enough diligent and unselfish members to apply the obvious remedies. The legislature which shall enact general laws for the incorporation of cities and villages and shall do away with the evils of the free pass system, will earn the lasting gratitude of the people.

EDWIN B. WINANS

APPENDIX B

The argument made by Edwin Winans in the North American Review regarding the Miner Law:

"The change was made in the belief that the district system will enable the people of the State to give a much more definite and satisfactory expression of their choice for the Presidency. The most complete expression possible would be obtained by allowing the people to vote directly for the candidates of their choice, without the interposition of Presidential electors. This method was fully discussed in the constitutional convention of 1787 but was not then considered expedient. One of the arguments advanced was, that to submit the election of a President to direct vote of the people is to take this important power out of the hands of those best fitted for its exercise and bestow it upon those least capable of using it wisely. The system finally adopted was chosen as the best of the many plans proposed for the choice of a President by delegates chosen by the people. The object in view was the selection of a limited number of men, chosen from among their fellow citizens because of special fitness, who were to meet for deliberation upon the merits of public men, and, after careful consideration, exercise their own judgment in voting for a President.

Nominating conventions were then unknown, and the Presidential electors were not pledged to vote for particular candidates but were left free to use their own discretion or to reflect the preference of the section they represented. Appeals to this discretion were often made after the electors were chosen. It was not contemplated, when the Constitution was adopted, that all the electoral votes of each State should necessarily be cast for the same candidate, and in the earlier elections it was common for different candidates to receive electoral votes from the same State. As late as 1824 the New York electors divided their votes among four candidates for President and two for Vice-President. Moreover, had it been the design of the framers of the Constitution that each State should cast its entire electoral vote as a unit, there would have been no occasion for the appointment of electors. The whole matter could have been arranged by allowing each State so many votes for President, instead of so many Presidential electors. The Presidential votes of a State could then have been cast by one officer as well as by twenty or could have been certified to the President of the Senate by the executive officers of the State. The fact that each electoral vote was to be cast by an individual is proof that individual and independent action by the electors was contemplated. But the original intention has been so far lost sight of that in our day the electors have no discretion whatever. They simply meet and vote for the candidates previously nominated by their party conventions. The only essential qualification of a modern Presidential elector is fidelity to his party. He is merely the mouthpiece of the party who choose him, and any exercise of his individual judgment, contrary to the sentiment of his party, would be considered a crime. Our people can no longer be regarded as incompetent to exercise their own judgment, and if they were now incompetent, the electoral system would be no safeguard, for, in point of fact, it is the discretion of the people and not that of the electors to which effect is given.

While the electoral system seems destined to continue for a time, it is within the power of each State legislature to give every section of its State a fair representation in the Electoral College. The most unsatisfactory result of choosing the electors by general ticket is that it practically compels the selection in each State of electors who are all pledged to one candidate and nullifies the influence of large portions of the State where that candidate is unpopular. In any State there may be a large section, a congressional district, or several of them, in which a heavy majority of the voters are strongly opposed to the election of a particular candidate, yet, against their will, their influence is practically cast in favor of that candidate because a different sentiment prevails in the remainder of the State.

In many of the States parties are evenly divided, but by choosing the electors on a general ticket the principle of the odious unit rule is applied, which permits the majority of a delegation to dictate the votes of the minority, and which is no longer tolerated even in nominating conventions. Thus, the entire electoral vote of a State may be cast for a candidate who is opposed by forty-nine per cent of the voters. Wisconsin will have twelve votes in the next Electoral College. The political complexion of the State is fairly doubtful, and the vote will probably be a close one, yet one party or the other in that State will have absolutely no representation in the Electoral College. If the electors were to be chosen by districts, can it be doubted that the result in any State would be a more exact expression of the preferences of her people?

Objection has been made to the district system on the ground that it will divide the electoral vote of a State and thus lessen her influence in the selection of a President. I answer, that if popular sentiment in a State is divided, her electoral vote ought to be divided, be the result what it may. The political minority help to make up the basis of population upon which the electors are apportioned to the States, and common fairness demands that they be given their proportionate share of the electors. In every State the people of limited districts decide who shall represent their interests in the National House of Representatives. There is no express provision in the Constitution that members of Congress shall be chosen by districts. They are to be chosen every second year "by the people of the several States," and the people of the States, through their legislatures, divide the States into congressional districts. That this method is fair and just and secures to the people of the State a proper representation, is not denied even by those who insist upon choice of electors by general ticket. A proposition to elect by general ticket the congressional delegation of any State would be instantly resented in every district, yet the people of those districts are forced to turn over to the State at large the expression of their Presidential preferences. Surely the election of a President is as important an exercise of power and should as fairly reflect the wishes of the voters, as a congressional election. The sacred principle of majority rule would be as faithfully applied in the districts as in the State, and the application would be far less vexatious and arbitrary. The people of each district would speak for themselves, and the result would be a far more accurate and detailed showing of preferences. Most of the districts would be doubtful and every voter would feel that his influence would have its weight in the selection of a chief magistrate.

The enactment of the Michigan statute has developed, among advocates of the general ticket, a theory that a choice of electors by districts is a violation of the Constitution, which directs that "Each State shall appoint" the electors. It is claimed that a State legislature has no authority to refer the choice to the people of sub-divisions of the State. But it seems idle to discuss a question which was settled by early practice and by the acquiescence of the men who framed the Constitution. It has been shown that by direction of different State legislatures the district system was in use for many years after the adoption of the Constitution. Is it to be assumed that the men who framed that instrument permitted a misconstruction of its language in so important a particular to pass unchallenged for more than forty years? President Madison, in a letter to George Hay, dated August 1823, said: "The district mode was mostly, if not exclusively, in view when the Constitution was framed and adopted, and was changed for the general ticket and legislative election as the only expedient for baffling the policy of particular States which had set the example." Here we have the explanation of the gradual change of method. As the people divided into parties, the majorities in certain States, having control of the legislatures, decided to shut the mouths of their opponents. Hence the adoption of the general ticket. Virginia ratified the Constitution in June 1788, and in November her legislature directed, "That for the purpose of choosing twelve electors on behalf of this State to vote for a President in conformity to the Constitution of government for the United States, the several counties in this commonwealth shall be allotted into twelve districts, in manner following." One hundred and three years later it is announced that this action was unconstitutional. Judge Story, after reciting that the general ticket, the district method, and the legislative election had each been employed, remarks, "No question has ever arisen as to the constitutionality of either mode, except that of a direct choice by the legislature." Even President

Harrison, who has strongly expressed his disapprobation of the Michigan law, and who may be presumed to have fully stated the arguments against it, does not contend that it is a violation of the Constitution.

An advantage of the highest importance would be gained through the district system by destroying the commanding importance of pivotal States. A bare plurality of the popular vote in two States has decided several Presidential elections. As a general election approaches every man interested in the result can name the States in which the result is considered assured, and interest is practically withdrawn from this States and centered upon the few doubtful ones. In these, intense excitement is aroused, and the fight is waged with a bitterness and determination born of the conviction of their special importance. Indiana becomes a "bloody angle" and New York a "battlefield." Business comes to a standstill, menace crazed for the time by the intensity of their excitement, and general demoralization prevails. These decisive States must be carried at any cost, and enormous corruption funds are raised and poured into them from every quarter. Thousands of votes are bought and sold, and corruption and debauchery are openly carried on, because the perpetrators can rely upon party spirit to shield them from punishment. And when it is all over, one wonders what the result would have been in those States had the people been left in peace to vote their own preferences. If the electors were chosen by districts, this concentration of unhealthy effort in particular States would cease. The contest would be confined to the individual districts, and so many of these would be in doubt that political managers could not ascertain, as they now can, just what must be done to carry the day.

President Harrison in his last annual message to Congress used the following language: "The recent Michigan legislation provides for choosing what are popularly known as the congressional electors for President by congressional districts, and the two senatorial electors by districts created for that purpose. This legislation was, of course, accompanied by a new congressional apportionment, and the two statutes bring the electoral vote of the State under the influence of the gerrymander."

Without stopping to discuss the propriety of this aspersion coming from one who is himself a probable candidate for the electoral votes of

Michigan, let us inquire what is the chief evil of the gerrymander. The term is used to designate the practice of so dividing a State as to give one party an unfair advantage in a majority of the districts. The practice is an undoubted wrong and has at times been indulged in by each of the great parties, but it is a practice which immediately affects the voters of every district, and experience has shown that public sentiment is quick to condemn its arbitrary use. Its injustice lies in the fact that it lessens the representation to which the political minority, by reason of their numbers, are justly entitled. But if we condemn the gerrymander because it lessens the representation of the minority, what is to be said of a system which excludes the minority from any representation whatever? Yet this is the exact result attained by choosing Presidential electors on a general ticket.

In a recent article a distinguished ex-Senator of the United States discusses the gerrymander, and, referring to the apportionment of Alabama, says: "The district of smallest population has only 151,757 inhabitants, and another contiguous district has 253,891, a difference of upwards of 100,000 citizens." He adds: "Suggestion as to the motive for such geographical and numerical arrangement is quite superfluous."

At the last congressional election, the first district of Michigan had a population of 257,114, and another contiguous district, the second, had 153,655, a greater disparity than that shown in Alabama. Is comment here superfluous? Since 1880 the difference between the most populous and least populous congressional districts of Michigan has been as follows: In 1880, 64,951; in 1884, 50,607; in 1890, 103,459, and under the new apportionment of 1891, 44,253. Three of the new districts, the first, second and seventh, may be considered safely Democratic. Three others, the third, fourth and twelfth, are as safely Republican. The remainder are fairly doubtful districts, with the chances in favor of the Republicans in at least two of them, and it may safely be asserted that Michigan was never more fairly apportioned.

Equally unwarranted with the claim that Michigan is gerrymandered is the assumption that the district system was adopted for a temporary party advantage. In the last State campaign, the tariff issue was fully discussed, and although local considerations caused two of the Democratic candidates to run ahead of their ticket, the rest were elected by an average plurality of about 3,000. In the Congressional elections, upon national issues, the total Democratic vote for Congressmen exceeded the total Republican vote by 9,628. With these facts in view, there was strong reason for the belief that, without a change in the method of choosing electors, the entire electoral vote of Michigan would be cast for the Democratic candidate of 1892.

We divide our States into districts for the election of State Representatives, and into other districts for the choice of State Senators, in order that the people of all sections may be represented. We choose our Members of Congress from districts within the States, that the different views of our people may be represented in the national legislature. Every section of the State is heard in the selection of United States Senators. Only in the choice of Presidential electors is the local representation denied.

The legislature of Michigan, in the exercise of its constitutional power, and in the hope that all the States will join her in returning to the methods of the Constitution, has given the voters of every section of the State an opportunity to express their choice for the Presidency. Edwin B. Winans

NOTES:
THE EXTRAORDINARY LIFE OF EDWIN BARUCH WINANS: FROM THE STAMPEDE FOR GOLD IN CALIFORNIA TO THE CAPITOL OF MICHIGAN

Notes: The Overland Trail

1. Crossing the isthmus became easier each year. Competition among the native people to provide goods and services to increasing numbers of travelers meant better places to stay and eat. Availability of train travel beginning in 1855 made it a five-hour trip, but due to a shortage of sailors there was still a wait for a ship to take them the rest of the way to California. San Francisco Bay was full of empty ships whose sailors deserted to join the rush for gold.

2. Transportation in Michigan History Sesquicentennial Series 1987, accessed July 11, 2021, https://www.michigan.gov/documents/mdot/RR668ADMIN_8_539527_7.pdf
   "The most famous Indian trail in Michigan was the Great Sauk trail, which ran from Detroit to Chicago. Now US-12, this route was in use centuries before the discovery of America.

3. Mattes, Merrill J. *The Great Platte River Road*. University of Nebraska Press. 1992. Page 123

4. Ibid. Page 126

5. Ibid. Page 124

6. Ibid. Page 127

7. Ibid. Page 127

8. Ibid. Page 120

9. Ibid. Page 119

10. Delano, Alonzo. *On The Trail To The California Gold Rush*. University of Nebraska Press. 2005. Page 95.

11. Trimble, Marshall. "Frontier Odometers" True West Magazine. https://truewestmagazine.com/frontier-odometers/

12. Unruh, John D. Jr. *The Plains Across: The Overland Emigrants and the Trans-Mississippi West, 1840-60. University of Illinois Press. 1993. Page 270.*

13. *Stephens, L. Dow. Life sketches of a jayhawker of '49.* http://www. loc.gov/resource/calbk.148 *Library of Congress Online Catalog (1,180,859) General Collections (158,408)*

14. Evans, James. *Journal of a Trip to California.* https://home.nps.gov/ciro/learn/historyculture/upload/Journal-List.pdf California Trail Journals - National Park Service

15. National Park Service. *The Overland Migrations. Division of Publications*

16. Delano, Alonzo. *On The Trail To The California Gold Rush.* University of Nebraska Press. 2005. Pages 69-70.

17. Buck, Rinker. *The Oregon Trail: A New American Journey.* Simon & Schuster Paperbacks, New York. Page 229-230.

18. McLynn, Frank. *Wagons West: The Epic Story of America's Overland Trails.* Grove Press. New York.
According to Lloyd Coffman, in *Blazing a Wagon Trail to Oregon,* Hiram Scott became ill at a rendezvous on the Green River. The pack train leader left two men with him to take care of him. They were to meet up with the train at the bluffs. Even though Scott regained some strength for a time, the three men lost all of their supplies including guns and were subsisting on what they could scavenge. The two protectors decided to leave Scott and move on because it was obvious he was beyond help, and they would also die if they did not leave him. When they returned to civilization, they told everyone Scott had died and they buried him. When the train returned to rendezvous the following year, they found Scott's body scatted miles from where the two reported to have

buried him. The poor man had crawled for miles before he died. Obviously, they had lied. The spot has ever since been called Scott's Bluffs.

19. Abbey, James. *California: A Trip Across the Plains, in the Spring of 1850.* Kindle Edition.

20. Humboldt River named for Alexander von Humboldt. Born in Berlin in 1769, he was a scientist, a geographer, a botanist, and an artist among other things. There are many things on the planet named for him: universities, plants, animals, an ocean current, and a crater on the moon.
Schelby, Erika. *Looking for Humboldt & Searching for German Footprints in New Mexico and Beyond.* Lava Gate Press. 2017.
McCullough, David. *Brave Companions, Portraits in History.* Simon & Schuster Paperbacks. 1992.

21. Landon, Michael. *Chasing a Golden Dream: The Story of the California Trail.* www.overlandtrails.lib.byu.edu>essay_ctrail.php

22. Delano, Alonzo. *On The Trail To The California Gold Rush.* University of Nebraska Press. 2005. Page 137.

23. Abbey, James. *California: A Trip Across the Plains, in the Spring of 1850. Kindle Edition.*

24. Langworthy, Franklin. *Scenery, or The Plains, Mountains and Mines, or A Diary Kept Upon The Overland Route to California, By Way of The Great Salt Lake.* J.C. Sprague, Book Seller. 1855. Page 165.

Notes: The Gold Rush

1. Sutter, Gen. John A. The Discovery of Gold in California www.sfmuseum.org/hist2/gold.html

2. Marryat, Frank. *Mountains and Molehills.* Skyhorse Publishing 2014. Kindle.

3. Canfield, Chauncey. *The Diary of a Forty-Niner.* Lume Books 2016. Kindle.

4. California Native Plant Society. Calscape. Soap Plant. https://calscape.org/chlorogalum-pomeridianum-()

5. Buffum, E. Gould. *Six Months in the Gold Mines.* Journal page 27-28.

6. Brands, H. W. *The Age of Gold: The California Gold Rush and The New American Dream.* Page 200. Anchor Books A Division of Random House, Inc. New York. 2003.

7. Bolles, Albert, 1879, compiled and edited by Kathy Weiser/Legends of America, updated December 2019. https://www.legendsofamerica.com/we-mininggold/2/

8. Canfield, Chauncey. *The Diary of a Forty-Niner.* Lume Books 2016. Kindle.

9. Ibid.

10. Bean's History and Directory of Nevada County, California/Rough and Ready Township page 357.

11. Canfield, Chauncey. *The Diary of a Forty-Niner.* Lume Books 2016. Kindle.

12. Bean's History and Directory of Nevada County, California/Rough and Ready Township.

13. Ibid

14. Secession Days in Rough and Ready, California www.seecalifornia.com

15. Bean's History and Directory of Nevada County, California/Rough and Ready Township.

16. Canfield, Chauncey. *The Diary of a Forty-Niner.* Lume Books 2016. Kindle.

17. Vankin, Jonathan. California Local. Nevada County Water Explained: From Rough and Ready Ditch to Seven Hydroelectic Plants https://californialocal.com/localnews/nevada/ca/article/show/875-nevada-county-water-explainer/

18. Canfield, Chauncey. *The Diary of a Forty-Niner.* Lume Books 2016. Kindle.

19. California Department of Transportation and JRP Historical Consulting Service. Water Conveyance Systems in California December 2000 www.cawaterlibrary.net

20. Vankin, Jonathan. Nevada County Water Explained: From Rough and Ready Ditch to Seven Hydroelectric Plants, California Local. October 30, 2021. https://californialocal.com

21. Hamburg History Blue Library Binder July 2005 Author Unknown

22. Searls Library, Nevada City, California. Pat Chestnut, Director. https://nevadacountyhistory.com
23. Britannica. Uncle Tom's Cabin. https://www.britannica.com/topic/Uncle-Toms-Cabin and Britannica. Crimean War. https://www.britannica.com/event/Crimean-War.
24. Dunbar, Fay. Nevada County Historical Society. Volume 30 No. 4 October 1976. Rough and Ready. Parts One and Two.

Notes: The Isthmus of Panama

1. The Panama Railroad. www.panamarailroad.org
2. Borthwick, John David. *Gold Rush: Three Years in California.* Originally published in London 1857. Edited by Linda Pendleton. Create Space. Scotts Valley, California. Kindle edition.
3. Ibid.
4. Ibid.
5. Ibid.
6. Jones, James P. and Rogers, William W. *Across the Isthmus in 1850: The Journey of Daniel A. Horn.* Source: *The Hispanic American Historical Review,* Nov. 1961, Vol.41, No. 4 (Nov. 1961), pp. 533-554. Duke University Press https://www.jstor.org/stable/2509938
7. Ibid.
8. Ibid.
9. Ibid.
10. Ibid.
11. Ibid.
12. Ibid.
13. Ibid.
14. History of the Panama Railroad. www.panamarailroad.org
15. Ibid.
16. Isthmus Crossing. www.bruceruiz.net/PanamaHistory/isthmus_crossing.htm and Friar, Willie K. *Gold Rush Days on the Isthmus* http://czbrats.com/Builders/goldrush.htm
17. History of the Panama Railroad. www.panamarailroad.org

18. Panama Railroad: A Popular Account of the Railroad. http://pana-ma.lindahall.org/panama-railroad/

19. The Panama Railroad: History http://www.trainweb.org/panama/historyold-org.html) and The Panama Railroad: History of the Panama Railroad Part II https://www.panamarailroad.org/history1b.html

20. White, Stewart Edward, 1873-1946. *The Forty-niners; a Chronicle of the California Trail and El Dorado.* (Historical document - in the public domain.)

21. Marryat, Frank. *Mountains and Molehills.* Endeavour Press Ltd. Kindle edition.

22. Marryat, Frank. *Mountains and Molehills.* Endeavour Press Ltd. Kindle edition.

23. White, Stewart Edward, 1873 - 1946. *The Forty-niners; a Chronicle of the California Trail and El Dorado.*

24. White, Stewart Edward, 1873 - 1946. *The Forty-niners; a Chronicle of the California Trail and El Dorado.*

25. Britannica: History and Society. Franklin Pierce: President of the United States. https://www.britannica.com/biography/Franklin-Pierce

26. Friar, Willie K. *Gold Rush Days on the Isthmus.* The Panama Canal Review 1971. https://czbrats.com/Builders/goldrush.htm

Notes: Rough and Ready

1. Dunbar, Fay. *Rough and Ready.* Nevada County Historical Society. Part Two of Two. Vol. 31 No.2 April 1977. www.roughandready-chamber.com

2. Dunbar, Fay. *Rough and Ready.* Nevada County Historical Society. Parts One and Two. Volume 30 No.4 October 1976. www.roughandreadychamber.com

3. Bean's History and Directory of Nevada County, California. Roberts, E. W. *Historical Sketch of Rough and Ready Township.*

4. Florin, Lambert. *Ghost Towns of the West.* Superior Publishing Company. New York, N.Y. 1970, 1971.

5. Bean's History and Directory of Nevada County, California. Roberts, E. W. *Historical Sketch of Rough and Ready Township.*

6. Ibid.

7. Ibid.

8. Dunbar, Fay. *Rough and Ready.* Nevada County Historical Society. Parts One and Two. Volume 30 October 1976. www.roughandreadychamber.com

9. Ibid.

10. Ibid.

11. Ibid.

12. Charlotte (Lotta) Crabtree grew up in California. She met Lola Montez at a mining camp in Grass Valley who taught her how to dance. Lotta's dancing was received well by miners and that encouraged her to increase her skills in dancing and singing. She was soon a popular entertainer in both the United States and abroad. "For thirty-five years, Lotta was the perennial little pet of the Western theater, and when she retired at the age of forty-four, she still wore her red curls. When Lotta died in 1924, she left behind a fortune of four million dollars that went to charity." https://truewestmagazine.com/article/lotta-crabtree/

13. Trimble, Marshall. True West Magazine. July 12, 2012, True West Blog. Lotta Crabtree. https://truewestmagazine.com/article/lotta-crabtree/

14. Kelly, Martin. Thought Co. April 15, 2019, American History Timeline 1851-1860. https://www.thoughtco.com/american-history-timeline-1851-1860-104306

15. Dunbar, Fay. *Rough and Ready.* Nevada County Historical Society. Part Two of Two. Vol. 31 No.2 April 1977. www.roughandreadychamber.com

16. Ibid.

17. Ibid.

18. Ibid.

19. Ibid.

20. Ibid.

21. Searls Library Nevada City, California https://nevadacountyhistory.org and & Dallison's Directory of Nevada County 1856.
22. Placer Herald, Volume 4, Number 9, November 10, 1855, Page 3 Advertisements Column 6
23. Wells, Harry Laurenz, 1854-1940; Thompson & West. History of Nevada County, California.
24. Hamburg Historical Society, Blue Binder. July 1005 Author Unknown

Notes: Hamburg

1. Livingston County Republican Press. Wednesday July 1, 1936. Newspapers.com
2. Edwin B. Winans. Hamburg History. Blue Library Binder. Author Unknown. Recorded July 2005.
3. Bellis, Mary. American Farm Machinery and Technology Changes from 1776-1990. Thought Co. https://www.thoughtco.com/american-farm-tech-development-4083328
4. 1860 US Census, Livingston County, Michigan, Hamburg Village, page number 60, lines 5 - 9, Edwin B. Winans.
5. Livingston County Republican Press. Wednesday July 1, 1936. Newspapers.com
6. Ibid
7. History Of Livingston County, Michigan - At the meeting of the Livingston County Pioneer Society, held June 18, 1879, the following facts relating to the history of the township of Hamburg were given by Hon. Edwin B. Winans.
8. Ibid.
9. ancestry.com
10. History Of Livingston County, Michigan - At the meeting of the Livingston County Pioneer Society, held June 18, 1879, the following facts relating to the history of the township of Hamburg were given by Hon. Edwin B. Winans.
11. Ibid.
12. Terry, Joyce DeWolf. *Memories: Hamburg Settlement Days - 150 Years Hamburg Historical Society.*

13. History Of Livingston County, Michigan - At the meeting of the Livingston County Pioneer Society, held June 18, 1879, the following facts relating to the history of the township of Hamburg were given by Hon. Edwin B. Winans.
14. Ibid.
15. Ibid.
16. Ibid.
17. Ibid.
18. Terry, Joyce DeWolf. *Memories: Hamburg Settlement Days - 150 Years Hamburg Historical Society.*
19. Brighton Area Historical Society - Edwin B. Winans: Settler and Governor www.brightonareahistorical.com/index.php?option=com_content&view=article&id=236:edwinbwinans-settler-and-governor

Notes: The Michigan Legislature and the Civil War

1. Brighton Area Historical Society - Edwin B. Winans: Settler and Governor www.brightonareahistorical.com/index.php?option=com_content&view=article&id=236:edwinbwinans-settler-and-governor
2. A Brief History of Michigan www.legislature.mi.gov
3. Ibid.
4. Company K of the 1st Michigan Sharpshooters www.battlefields.org
5. President Lincoln suspends the writ of habeas corpus during the Civil War https://www.history.com/this-day-in-history/president-lincoln-suspends-the-writ-of-habeas-corpus-during-the-civil-war February 22, 2023 Access Date Publisher A&E Television Networks
6. The History Chanel. https://www.history.com/topics/american-civil-war/emancipation-proclamation and National Archives. The Emancipation Proclamation. https://www.archives.gov/exhibits/featured-documets/emancipation-proclamation
7. Ibid.
8. History Society of Pennsylvania https://hsp.org

9. Encyclopedia Britannica 20 April 2022 https://www.britannica.comhttps://www.britannica.com/topic/Copperhead-American-policical-faction

10. Infogalactic. Ross Winans. https://infogalactic.com/w/index.php?title=Ross_Winans&oldid=2958795

11. The Winans Cigar Ships https://www.vernianera.com/CigarBoats.html

12. Library of Congress. Abraham Lincoln papers: Series 1 General Correspondence. 1833-1916: John E. Wool to Edwin M. Stanton, Friday, March 14, 1862 (Telegram regarding military affairs) https://www.loc.gov/item/mal1506300/#

13. Battle of the Monitor and Merrimack https://www.britannica.com-https://www.britannica.com/event/Battle-of-the-Monitor-and-the-Merrimack

14. Infogalactic. Ross Winans.

15. Emancipation and Reconstruction https://www.history.com/topics/american-civil-war/reconstruction

16. John Wilkes Booth https://www.britannica.com/biography/John-Wilkes-Booth

17. A Brief History of Michigan www.legislature.mi.gov

18. Ibid.

19. Ibid.

20. Jonkhoff, Peg and Hoisington, Fred. *Perry Hannah's Gifts: Then and Now.* Bay Breeze Media, LLC. November 2013

21. A Brief History of Michigan www.legislature.mi.gov

22. Detroit Historical Society. Vernor, James. https://detroithistorical.org/learn/encyclopedia-of-detroit/vernor-james

23. Michigan Constitutional Convention http://bentley.umich.edu/legacy-support/politics/conventions.php

24. Results Michigan Constitutional Convention (https://www.legislature.mi.gov/documents/publications/MichiganManual/2009-2010/09-10-MM_II_pp_01-02_Intro.pdf

25. American Biographical History of Eminent and Self-made men. Michigan Volume 2 http://quod.lib.umich.edu/m/micounty/

26. Edwin B. Winans. Hamburg History. Blue Library Binder. Author Unknown. Recorded July 2005.
27. 1880 US Census, Livingston County, Michigan, Village of Howell, page 18, line 15.
28. Edwin B. Winans. Hamburg History. Blue Library Binder. Author Unknown. Recorded July 2005.

Notes: The Congress of the United States

1. Edwin Winans. Hamburg History. Blue Library Binder. Author Unknown.
2. Ibid.
3. 1883 Congressional Directory Hathi Trust https://babel.hathi-trust.org/cgi/pt?id=nyp.33433081796736&seq=9
4. Little, Becky. History. *Why Isn't Washington, D. C. A state?* https://www.history.com/news/washington-dc-statehood-reconstruction
5. Fogle, Jeanne Mason. *Washington, D.C.* encyclopedia Britannica, February 20, 2023, https://www.britannica.com/place/Washington-D.C. Accessed February 23, 2023.
6. Fletcher, Kenneth. Smithsonian Magazine. *A Brief History of Pierre L'Enfant and Washington, D.C.* https://www.smithsonianmag.com/arts-cultur/a-brief-history-of-piere-lenfant-and-washington-dc-39487784
7. DeFerrari, John. *Lost Washington, D.C.* The History Press. Charleston, S.C. 2011
8. Ibid.
9. Lewis, Tom. *Washington: A History of Our National City.* Basic Books. New York. 1942
10. Smithsonian Institution Archives. Smithsonian Institution Building, The Castle https://siarchives.si.edu/history/smithsonian-institution-building-castle
11. Washington DC. The Smithsonian Castle: Gateway to Museums and History https://washington.org/dc-guide-to/smithsonian-institution-building-castle

12. Barger, Jennifer. National Geographic. *Why the Washington Monument was once a national embarrassment.* https://www.nationalgeographic.com/travel/article/washington-monument-construction-know-nothings-elevator
13. Ibid.
14. Ibid.
15. Ibid.
16. National Park Service. *Washington Monument* https://www.nps.gov/wamo/learn/historyculture/index.htm
17. National Park Service. Washington Monument: A History. https://www.nps.gov/parkhistory/online_books/wamo/history/chap6.htm
18. Ibid.
19. DeFerrari, John. *Lost Washington, D.C.* The History Press. Charleston, S.C. 2011
20. National Park Service. DuPont Circle. National Mall and Memorial Parks. https://www.nps.gov/places/dupont-circle.htm Dupont Circle
21. Ibid
22. The White House Historical Association. The Historic Decatur House. https://www.whitehousehistory.org/the-historic-decatur-house
23. DeFerrari, John. *Lost Washington, D.C.* The History Press. Charleston, S.C. 2011
24. The White House Historical Association. The Willard Hotel. https://www.whitehousehistory.org/the-willard-hotel
25. DeFerrari, John. *Lost Washington, D.C.* The History Press. Charleston, S.C. 2011
26. Ibid.
27. National Park Service. Ford's Theatre History. https://www.nps.gov/foth/learn/ford-s-theatre-history.htm
28. Ibid.
29. DeFerrari, John. *Lost Washington, D.C.* The History Press. Charleston, S.C. 2011
30. Ibid.

31. Britannica, The Editors of Encyclopedia. "Free Silver Movement". Encyclopedia Britannica, 9 Apr. 2019, https://www.britannica.com/event/Free-Silver-Movement. Accessed 3 February 2024.
32. Detroit Free Press August 13, 1886. Newspapers.com
33. Detroit Free Press September 2, 1882. Newspapers.com
34. Detroit Free Press October 26, 1884. Newspapers.com
35. Arlington National Cemetery. History of Arlington National Cemetery. https://www.arlingtoncemetery.mil/Explore/History-of-Arlington-National-Cemetery
36. Longfellow
37. Mark Twain
38. Detroit Free Press. November 3, 1884. Newspapers.com
39. Detroit Free Press. *Points From the Press.* September 26, 1884. Newspapers.com
40. Detroit Free Press. *Prominent Public Men.* October 4, 1884.
41. Roos, Dave. *Why Was the Electoral College Created?* https://www.history.com/news/electoral-college-founding-fathers-constitutional-convention
42. Shaw, Byron Thomas, Ekstrom, George F. , Campbell, John R. , Palmer, Ralph Anthony , Preuschen, Gerhardt and Curtis, Stanley Evan. "agricultural sciences". Encyclopedia Britannica, 16 Nov. 2023, https://www.britannica.com/science/agricultural-sciences. Accessed 3 February 2024.
43. Proctor, Emily. *What are land-grant universities?* Michigan State University Extension. December 28, 2015. https://www.canr.msu.edu/news/what_are_land_grant_universities
44. Bethany. *Following Grand River Avenue Through History.* MSU Campus Archaeology Program. June 12, 2014, http://campusarch.msu.edu/?p=3076

Notes: The Nomination and the Campaign

1. Detroit Free Press, October 15, 1890, Page 4. newspapers.com

2. McCracken, Lawrence. Detroit Free Press, August 14, 1938. *Gov. Winans, Rejected by Girl, Proposed to Sister, Who Accepted in Five Minutes.* newspapers.com
3. Detroit Free Press, September 11, 1980, newspapers.com
4. Ibid.
5. Hamburg Historical Society, Blue Library Binder, Author Unknown.
6. Telegram-Herald, September 26, 1890, newspapers.com
7. Detroit Free Press, October 21, 1890, newspapers.com
8. Hansen, Alicia. *Tax Foundation. Tax History Lesson: The McKinley Tariff.* https://taxfoundation.org/tax-history-lesson-mckinley-tariff
9. Encyclopedia Britannica, April 9, 2019, Free Silver Movement https://www.britannica.com/event/Free-Silver-Movement.
10. The State Republican, September 12, 1890, Library of Michigan
11. Ibid.
12. The New York Times, *Ballot Reform in Michigan: The New System Adopted By Both Houses,* July 1, 1891.
13. Detroit Free Press. *Favors Judge Winans for Governor.* March 8, 1890. newspapers.com
14. Detroit Free Press, Detroit, Michigan. *It's A Small World.* August 14, 1938.
15. Detroit Free Press. *Winans A War Democrat.* October 29, 1890. newspapers.com
16. Detroit Free Press. *Judge Winans and the Soldier Voting Law.* November 1, 1890, newspapers.com
17. Michigan House of Representatives. February 13, 1863, pages 488,489, and 490 of the house journals.
18. Detroit Free Press. *Mr. Winans Loyalty.* November 1, 1890. newspapers.com
19. The State Republican. October 14, 1890. Library of Michigan
20. Detroit Free Press. STORMED. November 6, 1890. newspapers.com
21. Interstate News-Record of Ironwood, Michigan. November 22, 1890. newspapers.com
22. Detroit Free Press, *The Celebration,* November 8, 1890. newspapers.com
23. Detroit Free Press, *Jubilee at Flint.* November 10, 1890. newspapers.com

24. The Parsons Daily Sun, December 14, 1890. newspapers.com

Notes: The Governor

25. Former Governors of Michigan https://www.michigan.gov/former-governors/list-of-all-former-governors and Governors of Michigan https://ballotpedia.org/Governor_of_Michigan

26. Minutes, Annual Meeting 1891, Historical Collections, Michigan Pioneer and Historical Society Vol. XVIII, reprint, 1911; pgs. 7 and 10. June 1891

27. The State Republican, The Big Jubilee, An Immense Crowd Attending the Jollification. January 7, 1891.

28. Michigan Department of State, Bureau of History. *Michigan Dresses Up, Costumes of Celebration. 1989.*

29. The Livingston County Daily Press and Argus - Fighting Indians: Big Foot's Band Start a Massacre In the Bad Lands. January 8, 1891. newspapers.com

30. Detroit Free Press. *Gathering at Lansing.* January 3, 1891. newspapers.com

31. Encyclopedia. American Politics: Reforming The Spoils System. https://www.encyclopedia.com/history/news-wires-white-papers-and-books/american-politics-reforming-spoils-system

32. Detroit Free Press. *Gathering at Lansing.* January 3, 1891. newspapers.com

33. Schultz, Jim. Department of History, Arts and Libraries. Library of Michigan, 1869 - 1893: Approaching the Twentieth Century. https://www.michigan.gov/libraryofmichigan/about/history/history-articles/library-of-michigan-1869-1893-approaching-the-twentieth-century

34. Hovey, Howard. *Personal Memoirs of Gov. Edwin B. Winans Recounted.* Livingston County Republican Press. July 1, 1936. newspapers.com

35. Detroit Free Press. *Gathering at Lansing.* January 3, 1891. newspapers.com Note: Lt. Luther Baker and his commander built The Lansing House Hotel in 1865-1867 with reward money from

capturing President Lincoln's assassin, John Wilkes Booth. A fire in 1876 badly damaged the hotel, and then it was purchased by Henry Downey in 1887. The Hotel Downey was an exclusive and costly hotel during the Winans administration. It is currently the location of the Knapp's building. https://www.lansingstatejournal.com/story/life/2014/11/01/archives-soapys-mansion/18283553/

36. The State Republican March 28, 1891. Library of Michigan
37. The Lansing Tri-Weekly Republican. June 5, 1883. Library of Michigan
38. Smith, Thomas A. *1883 - 1983 One Hundred Years of the Civil Service Act. Vol IV, Number 3 Spring 1984.* Hayes Historical Journal: 1883 - 1983 Civil Service Act. Rutherford B. Hayes Presidential Library https://www.rbhayes.org/research/hayes-historical-journal-1883-1983-civil-service-act/
39. The Record-Union of Sacramento, California. February 1, 1891. newspapers.com
40. State of Michigan. Michigan State Capitol Collection https://www.michigan.gov/som/government/state-capitol.
41. Marvin, Valerie R., Historian and Curator, Capitol of Michigan. *Interview.* capitol.michigan.gov
42. Detroit Free Press. *Governor's Levee.* February 11, 1891, Page 1. newspapers.com
43. Detroit Free Press. *The Governor's Levee.* January 18, 1891, Page 14. newspapers.com
44. Detroit Free Press. *The Ladies Costumes.* February 11, 1891, Page 6. newspapers.com
45. The Marshall Statesman. *The Governor Is Very Ill Has the Hiccoughs: Michigan's Governor Very Ill and 'Tis Thought He Will Die.* March 13, 1891. newspapers.com
46. Dr. Nao. Nao Medical. *The Surprising Link Between Hiccups and Heart Disease.* https://naomedical.com/blog/hiccups-and-heart-disease-naomedical/
47. The State Republican. *The Marine Band Concert: An Evening of Grand Musical Delight - Gov. Winans Serenaded.* April 14, 1891.

48. The Marine Band. John Philip Sousa. https://www.marineband.marines.mil/Abour/Our-History/John-Philip-Sousa/
49. The State Republican. July 21, 1891. Library of Michigan
50. Niles Daily Star, Niles, Michigan. *Governors' Views: Messages of the Executives of Illinois and Michigan.* January 9, 1891. Newspapers.com
51. The New York Times. *Ballot Reform in Michigan.* July 2, 1891
52. The News Palladium of Benton Harbor. Michigan. July 7, 1866. newspapers.com
53. Weekly Expositor - Brockway Centre, Michigan. December 9, 1892. newspapers.com
54. Niles Daily Star. Niles, Michigan. *Governors' Views: Messages of the Executives of Illinois and Michigan.* January 9, 1891.
55. Detroit Free Press. *Headline: Equalization.* August 21, 1891.
56. Detroit Free Press. *The Governor's Vetoes.* May14, 1891. newspapers.com
57. Harrisburg Telegraph. Harrisburg, Pennsylvania. May 28, 1891. newspapers.com
58. Ibid.
59. Detroit Free Press. August 31, 1891. newspapers.com
60. Detroit Free Press. *He Is Dead.* July 5, 1894. newspapers.com
61. Messages of the Governors of Michigan Vol.3 Joint Documents of the State of Michigan pp. 3-11 January 1, 1893.
62. Ibid.
63. Ibid.
64. Ibid.
65. The State Republican. *Falling Chandelier.* June 22, 1891.
66. The State Republican. *Annual Report of Board of State Auditors for the Year 1892 Lighting: Chandelier.* August 10, 1891.
67. State of Michigan Archives. Records of the Executive Office 1810 - 1910. Box 246 World's Fair Managers. Note: On February 8, 1951, there was a fire at the Lewis Cass Building in Lansing, Michigan which housed the Library of Michigan. Many documents were destroyed. The State of Michigan Archives now store the unbound documents salvaged from the 1951 fire.
68. The Times. Owosso, Michigan. September 16, 1892. newspapers.com

69. The Times. Owosso, Michigan. *History of Company G.* December 2, 1892. newspapers.com Note: In 1862, Governor Blair of Michigan formed the 24th Michigan Infantry Unit. This all-volunteer military unit and other organized militias, including the 21st Michigan Volunteer Infantry and the 4th Michigan Cavalry, fought bravely during the Civil War. George Armstrong Custer was the Michigan Cavalry Brigade commander at the Battle of Gettysburg, and the 4th Michigan Cavalry captured Jefferson Davis. These militias continued as organized units and evolved into the Michigan National Guard. https://www.motherjones.com/politics/2016/10/timeline-history-militias-america/ and https://ss.sites.mtu.edu/mhugl/2020/09/23/the-activated-michigan-militia-1805-1976/

70. PBS: American Experience. World's Columbian Exposition of 1893 https://pbs.org/wgbh/americanexperience/features/chicago-worlds-columbian-exposition-1893/

71. Ibid.

72. Britannica, The Editors of Encyclopedia. "World's Columbian Exposition". Encyclopedia Britannica, 1 Feb. 2024, https://www.britannica.com/event/Worlds-Columbian-Exposition. Accessed 3 February 2024.

73. Maranzani, Barbara. History: *Chicago Was Home to a Serial Killer During the 1893 World's Fair.* https://www.history.com/news/7-things-you-may-not-know-about-the-1893-chicago-worlds-fair

74.

75. Detroit Free Press. *Michigan At The Fair.* February 12, 1892, page 3.

76. Picturesque World's Fair: An Elaborate Collection Of Colored Views. The Michigan Building page 81 https://worldsfairchicago1893.com/2019/07/06/picturesque-worlds-fair-the-michigan-building-p-81/

77. Shaw, Marian. *World's Fair Notes: A Woman Journalist Views Chicago's 1893 Columbian Exposition.* Pogo Press, Inc. 1992.

78. Simmons, Ernest J. *Leo Tolstoy: The Later Years.* The Atlantic Monthly. https://cdn.theatlantic.com/media/archives/1946/08/178-2/132324584.pdf

79. Detroit Free Press. *The Starving Peasants.* February 23, 1892. newspapers.com

80. Ketchum, Dan. *Russian Famine of 1891.* Sciencing. https://sciencing.com/russian-famine-1891-11151.html

81. The Democrat and Chronicle of Rochester, New York. February 24, 1892. newspapers.com

82. The State Republican. June 16, 1891 Library of Michigan

83. Marvin, Valerie R., Historian and Curator, Capitol of Michigan capitol.michigan.gov

84. Detroit Free Press. December 29, 1891. newspapers.com

85. The State Republican. *Winans Talks Back: He Thinks Beer Has a Salutary Effect on the State Militia. The Governor Treats Rev. Barkley's Roast as a Matter to be Expected - His Views on Beer Drinking.* July 29, 1891.

86. Detroit Free Press. *Notes from Hamburg.* October 27, 1891. newspapers.com

87. Detroit Free Press. *Headline: Gov. Winans at Yale.* October 27, 1892 newspapers.com **Note:** Pole raising consisted of cutting and trimming a tall hickory tree and setting it upright in a hole. Some had streamers on the top with candidates' names. A hickory tree was used to honor "Old Hickory" Democrats such as Andrew Jackson or Franklin Pierce. The mention of the hickory pole affirms that Edwin Winans's message to the Yale crowd was political. Turner, George A. Pole Raising: A Campaign Activity. https://colcohist-gensoc.org/wp-content/uploads/pole_raising.pdf

88. The Times. Philadelphia, Pennsylvania. *Farmers To The Front.* July 18, 1891. newspapers.com

89. The State Republican. *Edwin Winans, He Will Not Attend the State Convention.* August 16, 1892.

90. The State Republican. *Out of It: Gov. Winans Throws a Bomb Into the Grand Rapids Convention In the Shape of a Letter of Withdrawal.* August 17, 1892.

91. Ibid.

92. Dickinson County: A Brief History of Dickinson County. http://hometownchronicles.com/mitttp/dickinson/cohist.htm

93. Nick, *The 1892 Election: The Battle Over Free Silver.* December 21, 2022. https://recmovement.com/the-1892-election-the-battle-over-free-silver/

Notes: Farm and Family

1. Weddon, Willah. *First Ladies of Michigan.* NOG Press. Lansing, Michigan. 1977.
2. Detroit Free Press. *Politicians In Town: Ex-Gov. Winans Says He's Farming Now for all it's Worth.* April 26, 1893.
3. Weddon, Willah. *First Ladies of Michigan.* NOG Press. Lansing, Michigan. 1977.
4. Portrait & Biographical Album of Washtenaw County: Governors of Michigan. Edwin B. Winans 1891. Hamburg Historical Society.
5. Livingston County Daily Press. *A Life's Work Well Done.* February 3, 1926.
6. The Michigan Churchman Vol. XXI No. 3 March 1926 Whole No. 399. In Memoriam: Julia Galloway / Elizabeth Galloway Winans.
7. Year: 1880; Census Place: Howell, Livingston, Michigan; Roll: 592; Page:155B; Enumeration District: 191
8. Detroit Free Press. *A Fatal Fire.* October 6, 1892.
9. Ibid.
10. Detroit Free Press. *Gathering At Lansing.* January 3, 1891. Page 4.
11. The Daily Inter Lake. *Funerals: George G. Winans.* November 29, 1933. Pg 3.
12. Livingston County Republican Press August 27, 1885.
13. Year: 1870; Census Place: Hamburg, Livingston, Michigan; Roll: M593_687; Page: 99A.
14. Michigan Military Academy Database https://www.gwbhs.org/research/michigan-military-academy-database/
15. Find A Grave. https://www.findagrave.com/memorial/126444782/edwin-baruch-winans
16. Huachuca Illustrated, Vol. 2. 1996: Roll Call: Major General Edwin B. Winans https://net.lib.byu.edu/estu/wwi/comment/huachuca/HI2-16.htm

17. Infogalactic. Edwin B. Winans https://infogalactic.com/info/Edwin_B._Winans_(general)
18. The Monroe News-Star, Monroe Louisiana. December 28, 1927.
19. Livingston County Republican Press July 1, 1936.
20. Ibid.
21. Detroit Free Press. *Gathering At Lansing.* January 3, 1891.
22. Michigan Military Academy Database. https://www.gwbhs.org/research/michigan-military-academy-database/
23. Memmott, Jim. *Remembering a Rochester man's ill-fated journey to the Arctic.* Democrat Chronicle. August 1, 2018. https://www.democratandchronicle.com/story/news/local/columnists/memmott/2018/08/01/remembering-rochester-mans-ill-fated-journey-arctic/871024002/
24. State of Michigan Archives Records of the Executive Office Box 267 Note: On February 8, 1951, there was a fire at the Lewis Cass Building in Lansing, Michigan which housed the Library of Michigan. Many documents were destroyed. The State of Michigan Archives now store the unbound documents salvaged from the 1951 fire.
25. Weddon, Willah. *First Ladies of Michigan.* NOG Press. Lansing, Michigan. 1977.
26. Fort Worth Daily Gazette, Fort Worth, Texas, *Governor's Romantic Story.* June 21, 1891.
27. Indian-Pioneer History Project for Oklahoma. Milton Wellington Reynolds. Pages 1-3.
28. Year: 1900; Census Place: Hamburg, Livingston, Michigan; Roll:726; Page: 5; Enumeration District: 0068; FHL microfilm: 1240726.
29. Year: 1920; Census Place: Hamburg, Livingston, Michigan; Roll: T625_780; Page: 2A; Enumeration District: 145
30. Livingston County Daily Press and Argus. January 23, 1924.

Notes: Praise for the Governor

1. Detroit Free Press. *Ex-Gov. Winans: A Portrait of Him to be Presented the State by His Friends.* August 11, 1893.
2. Detroit Free Press. *He Is Dead: Ex-Gov. E.B. Winans Received a Sudden Call.* July 5, 1894.
3. The Democratic Expounder. Marshall, Michigan. *Passed From Earth: Ex-Governor Winans of Hamburg is Dead.* July 5, 1894.
4. The Democratic Expounder. Marshall, Michigan. July 6, 1894. Page 1.
5. Detroit Free Press. *He Is Dead: Ex-Gov. E.B. Winans Received a Sudden Call.* July 5, 1894.
6. Detroit Free Press. *Heard With Sorrow: News of the Sudden Death of Ex-Gov. Winans.* July 6, 1894, Page 7.
7. Detroit Free Press. *Without Ostentation: The Late Ex-Gov. Winans Laid at Rest.* July 7, 1894.
8. Ibid.
9. Ibid.
10. Ibid.
11. Detroit Free Press. *He Is Dead: Ex-Gov. E.B. Winans Received a Sudden Call.* July 5, 1894.
12. The Crawford Avalanche. Grayling, Michigan. July 12, 1894.
13. The Lima News. Lima, Ohio. July 5, 1894.

ILLUSTRATION CREDITS

- **Overland Trail to California**
  National Park Service. California Gold Fever! https://www.nps.gov/
  cali/index.htm
  https://www.nps.gov/nr/travel/american_latino_heritage/photos/
  CaliforniaTrail_1.jpg
- **Entrance to Kanesville or Council Bluffs, Iowa 1847**
  Engraving by Chas. B. Hall
  Lot 3797 (item) (P&P)
  Library of Congress Prints and Photographs Division Washington,
  D.C. 20540 USA http://hdl.loc.gov/loc.pnp/pp.print
- **Old Fort Kearny, Nebraska**
  Legends of America
  Fort Kearny, Nebraska - Protecting the Oregon Trail3.
  https://www.legendsofamerica.com/wp-content/uploads/2019/11/
  FortKearnyWilliamHenryJackson-2.jpg
- **Court House and Jail Rocks**
  History Nebraska
  https://history.nebraska.gov/wp-content/uploads/2022/10/
  8f3b505740867691030e38e1967b95d9.jpg
- **Chimney Rock**
  https://www.nps.gov/scbl/learn/historyculture/images/ND-Historic-
  Photographs-Chimney-Rock-Ezra-Meeker-2.jpg
- **Independence Rock**
  Oldest: 16 Iconic Landmarks on the Oregon Trail
  https://www.oldwest.org/wp-content/uploads/independence-rock-
  oregon-trail-landmark.gif

- **A forty-niner panning for gold.**
  California National Historic Trail (U.S. National Park Service)
  https://bleachedbonevalley.files.wordpress.com/2014/08/444px-
  gullgraver_1850_california.jpg?w=1200 and https://i.pinimg.com/
  originals/22/1f/09/221f099067062d642ea94053fe837c5c.jpg
- **James Marshall at Sutter's Mill in 1850** California
  National Historic Trail. U.S. Park Service. https://www.
  americanhistorycentral.com/wp-content/uploads/2023/08/
  Sutters-Mill-James-Marshall-1850-LOC.webp
- **The Sluice by Henry Sandham** https://i0.wp.com/www.
  theresahuppauthor.com/wp-content/uploads/2015/03/the-
  sluice-by-henry-sandham.jpg?w=753&ssl=1
- **Map of Isthmus** https://external-content.duckduckgo.com/iu/
  ?u=https://etc.usf.edu/maps/pages/000/23/23.gif&f=1&nofb=
  1&ipt=19643f5cbed5b42ace5dff89c93c2ce6adb80ae8f3dced7
  beb38263fd2025899&ipo=images
- **On the Chagres River in a bongos**
  http://www.bruceruiz.net/PanamaHistory/Isthmus_Crossing_
  bongos.jpg
- **Ships on Dry Land.** San Francisco Chronicle *How Ships on Dry Land
  helped Gold Rush San Francisco grow.* Kamiya, Gary. https://s.
  hdnux.com/photos/71/44/24/15090948/4/ratio3x2_960.webp
- **SS Pacific Mail Ship California** Putnam, John. My Gold Rush Tales.
  Steamship service to gold rush California begins. https://mygol-
  drushtales.com/wp-content/uploads/2011/04/SS-California.jpg
- **Eliza's Marker** Family Collection, Valerie Winans
- **Edwin's Poem** Family Collection, Valerie Winans
- **St. Stephens Church** Hamburg Historical Society
- **Old Rough and Ready Hotel** Rough and Ready Chamber https://
  www.roughandreadychamber.com/images/the-old-hotel/Rough
  and Ready Hotel 1910@2x.jpg
- **Fippin's Blacksmith Shop and Slave Girl tree** Rough and Ready
  Chamber https://www.roughandreadychamber.com/images/his-
  toric-trees/SlaveGirlTree2-1@2x.jpg
- **Rough and Ready 1857** Hamburg Historical Society

- **Petty's Mill** https://archives.howelllibrary.org/items/show/7467
- **Hamburg Plat Map** Pleasant Lake – 1875 Standard Atlas of Livingston County Michigan
- **Edwin 1859 Property Purchase** Livingston County Land Records
- **Edwin Property Purchase** 400 acres from Stephen Galloway – Livingston County Land Records
- **Ross Winans** Find A Grave. https://www.findagrave.com/memorial/15013871/ross-winans
- **Cigar Boat Letter** Library of Congress www.loc.gov
- **Howell Lake** https://external-content.duckduckgo.com/iu/?u=https://tse1.mm.bing.net/th?id=OIP.Q1sE2arO-DRFlNBJNwqHZ9wHaEq&pid=Api&h=160&f=1&ipt=f1bb63d22357760aac9ffc1f7a602871a2bcbb-ba46e2880e85826d061eac025e&ipo=images
- **The Tailors Float in the 1876 Centennial Parade in Howell** https://archives.howelllibrary.org/files/original/92d4a87638f01fbd-d7e5d331bb246566.jpg
- **Map of Hamburg Township** Winans Lake – 1905 Livingston County Land Records.
- **U.S. Capitol Building** U.S. History Images us-capitol-building.shtm
- **Map of Washington, D.C.** map-of-washington-dc-usa.html
- **Unfinished Washington Monument** D.C. Curbed http://dc.curbed.com/2015/3/4/9984920/photos-of-what-the-washington-monument-was-and-could-have-been
- **Dupont Circle** http://thenandnowpics.com/?attachment_id=1989
- http://thenandnowpics.com/wp-content/uploads/2016/03/Dupont_Circle_1900.png
- **The Willard Hotel** https://www.whitehousehistory.org/photos/willards-during-the-civil-war
- **Rhodes Tavern Painting** by Anne Marguerite Hyde de Neuville http://gardens671.rssing.com/chan-14035108/all_p2.html
- **Old Stone House** National Park Service https://www.nps.gov/common/uploads/place/nri/20150921/20150921/6D1A1776-C1C6-1BA0-ADAA36888199C1B7/6D1A1776-C1C6-1BA0-ADAA36888199C1B7.jpg

- **Freedman's Village** National Park Service https://www.nps.gov/arho/learn/historyculture/images/FRVI-18-Freedman-s-Village-001-NO-SOURCE_1.jpg?maxwidth=650&autorotate=false&quality=78&format=webp
- **48th Congressional Directory** – 1883 Congressional Directory HathiTrust https://babel.hathitrust.org/cgi/pt?id=nyp.33433081796736&seq=9
- **East Seating Assignment – Winans #84** 1883 Congressional Directory HathiTrust https://babel.hathitrust.org/cgi/pt?id=nyp.33433081796736&seq=9
- **Seat Numbers for the 48th Congress East Side** – 1883 Congressional Directory HathiTrust https://babel.hathitrust.org/cgi/pt?id=nyp.33433081796736&seq=9
- **Sketch of Edwin Winans** University of Michigan. Bentley Library https://quod.lib.umich.edu/b/bhl/x-bl006563/bl006563
- **Elizabeth Winans' Cloak** – Lansing State Journal March 8, 1989
- **Elizabeth's Cloak** – State of Michigan - Michigan History Museum
- **Downey Hotel** Lansing State Journal *From the Archives: Hotels from back in the day.* September 23, 2016. https://www.lansingstatejournal.com/gcdn/-mm-/dd48d819d15b29bc0f0a0746cfa0d0b-f4b2316ad/c=0-272-5754-3523/local/-/media/2016/09/22/MIGroup/Lansing/636101590772545490-Old-Downey-CADL.jpg?width=1320&height=746&format=pjpg&auto=webp
- **Head of the walking stick** – Family Collection – Valerie Winans
- **Walking Stick** – Family Collection – Valerie Winans
- **Howell Courthouse photo** of Edwin Winans– Family Collection – L. Winans Plamondon
- **First Capitol Building in Detroit** - Capitol History – Michigan Senate https://senate.michigan.gov/history/images/capitolunionschool.jpg
- **Second State Capitol Building** – Capitol History – Michigan Senate https://senate.michigan.gov/history/images/oldcapitolbldg.jpg
- **Michigan State Capitol Building 1890** Michigan Capitol Collection
- **Governor Edwin Baruch Winans** – Michigan State Capitol Collection
- **Governor's Office** – Michigan State Capitol Collection

- **Postcard Photo of Churches from the Governor's Window** – Michigan Capitol Collection
- **Contribution to Russian famine relief** -Archives Howell Library
- **Michigan Building at the World's Fair 1893** https://commons. wikimedia.org/wiki/File:Michigan_State_Building.jpg The Field Museum Library, Public domain, via Wikimedia Commons

- **Governor Winans with Michigan National Guard 1891** – Detroit Public Library. Burton Historical Collection. https:// digitalcollections.detroitpubliclibrary.org/islandora/object/ islandora%3A147599
- **On the porch of the governor's mansion:** Left to Right – Julie Galloway, Elizabeth Winans, and Mrs. Bode. *First Ladies* by Willah Weddon
- **The Howell House** – Family Collection – L. Winans Plamondon
- **Edwin Winans, Jr.** at Orchard Lake Academy Military Database - https:// www.gwbhs.org/research/michigan-military-academy-database/
- **Harry Kislingbury** at Orchard Lake Academy Military Database - https:// www.gwbhs.org/research/michigan-military-academy-database/
- **General Edwin B. Winans, Jr.** Ancestry: https://www.ancestry.com/mediaui-viewer/collection/1030/tree/181859296/ person/382365564266/media/cdd2da2d-a5ab-4b44-a648-5971dab1bcad?_phsrc=Zxi6&usePUBJs=true&galleryindex= 7&albums=pg&showGalleryAlbums=true&tab=0&p id=382365564266
- **Memorial Plaque at Site of Governor's Mansion** – Family Collection – Valerie Winans
- **Winans Marker at Hamburg Cemetery** – Family Collection – Valerie Winans
- **Winans School** Waverly Community Schools. Winans Elementary School https://www.waverlycommunityschools.net/our-schools/ winans-elementary-school/
- **Winans Lake School** Hamburg Historical Society.

INDEX

A

Abbey, James 251
Act of 1887 115
Agricultural Experimentation 115
Arlington Estate 111
Ash Hollow 27

B

Barbacoas 56, 57
Bear River 32
Benton Harbor 142, 265
Big-Foot-Mniconjou 134
Borthwick, John David 253
buffalo 21, 27

C

Chagres, Panama 20, 52
Chagres River 20, 52, 56, 57, 272
Cherokee Trail 31
Chicago Road 20
Chimney Rock 27, 28, 36, 271
cholera 24, 25, 29, 58, 61
Columbian Exposition 146, 150, 170, 213, 266, 267
Copperhead 91, 127, 258
Courthouse Rock 27, 28
cradle 41, 42, 50
Cruces 53, 63

D

Devil's Gate 30
Donner 31
Dos Hermanos 52
Downey Hotel 136, 274

E

E. Bishop & Son, Wagon Makers 83
Electoral Count Act of 1887 115
Evans, James 250

F

Ford's Theatre 93, 108, 260
Fort Bridger 31
Fort Hall 31
Fort Kearny 20, 21, 25, 26, 35, 271
Fort Laramie 27, 29, 69
Freedman's Village 112, 119, 274
Fremont's Peak 30

G

Galloway, Elizabeth 182, 275
Gatun 56
Gorgona 20, 53, 63
Grand Army of the Republic 111, 144, 217

H

habeas corpus 90, 91, 128, 257
Hamburg House 82

Index